# Tradition and Belief

T0338096

# MEDIEVAL CULTURES

**SERIES EDITORS**
Rita Copeland
Barbara A. Hanawalt
David Wallace

*Sponsored by the Center for Medieval Studies*
*at the University of Minnesota*

Volumes in the series study the diversity of medieval cultural histories and practices, including such interrelated issues as gender, class, and social hierarchies; race and ethnicity; geographical relations; definitions of political space; discourses of authority and dissent; educational institutions; canonical and noncanonical literatures; and technologies of textual and visual literacies.

*For other books in the series, see p. vi.*

# Tradition and Belief
## Religious Writing
## in Late Anglo-Saxon England

Clare A. Lees

Medieval Cultures
Volume 19

University of Minnesota Press
Minneapolis
London

Copyright 1999 by the Regents of the University of Minnesota

All rights reserved. No part of this publication may be reproduced, stored in a retrieval system, or transmitted, in any form or by any means, electronic, mechanical, photocopying, recording, or otherwise, without the prior written permission of the publisher.

Published by the University of Minnesota Press
111 Third Avenue South, Suite 290
Minneapolis, MN 55401-2520
http://www.upress.umn.edu

**Library of Congress Cataloging-in-Publication Data**
Lees, Clare A.
    Tradition and belief : religious writing in late Anglo-Saxon England / Clare A. Lees.
        p.    cm. — (Medieval cultures ; v. 19)
    Includes bibliographical references and index.
    ISBN 0-8166-3002-X (alk. paper). — ISBN 0-8166-3003-8 (pbk : alk. paper)
        1. Christian literature, English (Old)—History and criticism.
    2. English prose literature—Old English, ca. 450–1100—History and criticism.    3. Christianity and literature—England—History—To 1500.    4. Great Britain—History—Anglo-Saxon period, 449–1066.
    5. Preaching—England—History—Middle Ages, 600–1500.    6. Sermons, English (Old)—History and criticism.    7. Belief and doubt in literature.    8. Anglo-Saxons—Religion.    9. Christian hagiography.
    I. Title.    II. Series.
    PR226.L44    1999
    829'.8—dc21                                                        99-38778

Printed in the United States of America on acid-free paper

The University of Minnesota is an equal-opportunity educator and employer.

11  10  09  08  07  06  05  04  03  02  01  00  99        10  9  8  7  6  5  4  3  2  1

# Contents

✛

# MEDIEVAL CULTURES

# Preface

For those who study early Western cultures, thinking about the past is sometimes described as an exercise in nostalgia or melancholy — a way of dealing with a lost object.[1] Faced with the daunting project of thinking through the relation between culture, society, and literature, Raymond Williams (1977, 128) argues, however, that "[i]n most description and analysis, culture and society are expressed in an habitual past tense. The strongest barrier to the recognition of human cultural activity is this immediate and regular conversion of experience into finished products." The conversion of cultural activity — of subjects — into the pastness of finished products — of objects — is inevitably a great barrier to the analysis of human experience from the distant past. It is only too easy to forget that history is a process, an engagement with the past by those in the present. Williams continues, "Perhaps the dead can be reduced to fixed forms, though their surviving records are against it" (129). Right in his argument that the difficulties of studying historical cultural processes are considerable, Williams is also right that they are not insuperable. *Tradition and Belief: Religious Writing in Late Anglo-Saxon England* is written in the same spirit.

*Tradition and Belief* takes as its object of study English vernacular religious prose — sermons, homilies, and saints' lives in Old English — from the tenth and eleventh centuries, preeminent among which are the works of Ælfric of Eynsham.[2] These institutional, ecclesiastical genres are the main evidence for the preaching mission of the later Anglo-Saxon church and thus for how it was both constructed and received. I view this mission as evidence for a specific cultural process in which the traditional structures of the early medieval church — its institutional knowledge, its genres, and its beliefs — combine to produce a new Anglo-Saxon formation: preaching in English. This formation presents guidelines for practical belief — for the practice of belief — intended for the overlapping ecclesiastical and secular worlds of late Anglo-Saxon England. English preaching thus offers evidence for an idea of a Christian society that, however much it is developed within the monastery, minster, or cathedral, extends beyond those walls.

In writing this book, I have three interrelated theoretical concerns. First, by recontextualizing preaching texts as evidence for cultural work, I analyze preaching in Anglo-Saxon England as a powerful rhetorical, social, and epistemological process. Most obviously, preaching draws on the religious and theological traditions of its age as the source of its knowledge. Preaching is also active; it is directed toward an audience or congregation and employs a distinctive aesthetic to achieve this goal. Indeed, preaching texts are specific about their intended audience or congregation, however idealized are their representations of it. Preaching thus participates in the constitution of, while also being constituted by, historical sociocultural concerns specific to late Anglo-Saxon England.

Second, by concentrating on Anglo-Saxon preaching, I restore to the mission of cultural studies two aspects of culture often neglected: the analysis of traditional formations and the analysis of religious belief. The social power of tradition in general—of traditional forms of knowledge and behavior—like that of traditions of religious belief in particular, is underestimated not only by theorists of culture but also by literary critics, with whom critics of cultural processes share many concerns. My third and more general aim therefore is to direct the focus of cultural studies toward the analysis of historical cultural processes, and thereby to complement its more dominant interest in popular and contemporary cultural phenomena. Viewed as a case study of one such cultural phenomenon from the past, *Tradition and Belief* contributes to debates about the evolving meaning of cultural studies by concentrating on the theoretically problematic areas of history, religious belief, and aesthetics.

*Tradition and Belief* is not just an exercise in the theoretical and analytical problems of culture, however. Why should students of late-twentieth-century Western culture take note of religious writing in late Anglo-Saxon England? Because it is part of the cultural history of religion in the West. Important in itself as an index of early medieval religious culture, this history is crucial to the formation and understanding of modern Western societies, and thereby non-Western societies, as well. Belief and its various intellectual and ethical traditions are highly contested, as indicated by contemporary debates about, for example, creationism, abortion, the family, welfare, censorship, and identity.[3] These debates are evidence that the relation between forms of knowledge, social and cultural practice, and ethical behavior is as high a priority in late-twentieth-century society as it was in the medieval period. Those interested in the existing, emergent, and archaic forms of religious belief in the West now have much to learn from the structures of belief in earlier Western societies, which were equally—though differently—instrumental in transforming and modeling whole areas of social, cultural, and political experience.

## Looking Ahead

For most English medievalists, the first and often last introduction to Anglo-Saxon religious prose is in introductory language classes in Old English: it is well known that the prose is easier to translate than the poetry. Beyond that, the work of distinguished scholars in this field has rarely reached a wider audience. *Tradition and Belief* is aimed at just such a wider audience. This book is not a detailed analysis of the entire corpus of vernacular sermons, homilies, and saints' lives in Anglo-Saxon England, nor is it an in-depth study of the individual, uniquely named authors of works within it, Ælfric and Wulfstan.[4] It builds upon the major work in the editing and transmission of the prose as well as in its theological, liturgical, and intellectual analysis by such scholars as Peter Clemoes, James E. Cross, Max Förster, Malcolm Godden, Joyce Hill, Michael Lapidge, Milton McC. Gatch, John C. Pope, D. G. Scragg, and Jonathan Wilcox, but takes it in the direction of cultural analysis. Nor does it concentrate on the important relation of the vernacular prose to that of Anglo-Latin, a field of increasing importance within Anglo-Saxon studies. English religious writing is emphasized over its Anglo-Latin relative, the audience for which was more restricted.[5]

Given that the best-established and largest corpora of religious writing are those by Ælfric and Wulfstan, it is inevitable that *Tradition and Belief* rests heavily on their work, especially that of Ælfric. Nevertheless, I have also drawn on anonymous works circulating in the same period in order to tease out the cultural implications of these better-known writers. In general, I have deliberately selected lesser-known texts whose significance has yet to be appreciated, whether authored by named or anonymous writers. I also include, however, discussion of those prose works well known to Anglo-Saxonists, such as Wulfstan's *Sermo Lupi*. I give precedence to content and context rather than source or pre-text in my analysis, not only because these works have rarely been read in these terms, but also because I am interested in their practical and constitutive functions as well as the means by which they derive (or fail to derive) theological authority. Anglo-Saxon sermons do contribute to theological debate, of course, although this is never their only function.

One further caveat. *Tradition and Belief* is a study of late religious prose. Many of my conclusions about its aesthetic and didactic purposes, however, could be usefully extended to the poetry. I think especially of those shorter religious poems assembled in volume 6 of ASPR. The division of Anglo-Saxon writing into poetry and prose is to some extent an artifact of our methods of study, which does not necessarily reproduce accurately the historical circumstances of its production and reception (Lees, 1991, 1994b). I concentrate on the prose here for the simple reason that, with the exception of Gatch (1977), there is no full-length study of it. Nonetheless, aspects of my analysis also concern the poetry, knowledge of which is to a greater or lesser extent essential to my argument in several sections of the book. I return to the implications of my analysis of the prose for the poetry in the conclusion.

The introduction, by exploring the ways in which religious literature is crucial to any cultural analysis of the medieval period, prompts cul-

tural studies in general to reinvestigate both religious belief and historical formations. Chapter 1, "Tradition, Literature, History," focuses more
specifically on the theoretical problems inherent in studying traditionality and belief within the disciplines of literature and history. In current historiographic and literary-historical discourses, that which is traditional or popular or both (the two terms are not necessarily synonymous)
is often stigmatized in favor of that which is new or original. The twofold
concept of tradition — as a description of certain kinds of long-lasting
sociohistorical formations and as a description of certain kinds of persistent cultural genres — is rarely the subject of critical analysis. Without a firm analytic purchase on either the concepts of the traditional or
of the popular, both are used in contradictory and competing senses. This
is particularly the case in the English medieval period, although it is by
no means true of other medieval disciplines, which often prize traditional
and popular works. Periodization suggests that, in comparison with subsequent periods, that of the English Middle Ages is one of slow historical change, and hence traditional. This view, however, has obscured the
complex and conflicted nature of medieval society. Literary history privileges the unique and the new, the emergent over the archaic and dominant, and assigns little value to those genres that are both popular and
persistent. Tradition is thus a descriptive term rather than an instrument of analysis in the cases of both historiography and literary history.
In Anglo-Saxon studies, tradition is used in similar ways but with contradictory results. Anglo-Saxon poetry is often described as having a traditional, orally derived, poetic form, which literary historians celebrate
and which is the subject of considerable literary critical analysis. Religious prose is also held to be traditional — because of its dependence on
Christian Latin forms — but does not merit the same literary-historical
attention.

Chapter 1 argues that cultural theories of tradition as dynamic and
changing historical processes informed by specific ideologies clarify what
is meant by the term *tradition*. At the heart of these processes are the
ways in which tradition maintains its dominance in both literary and
social spheres by incorporating change within it, *according to tradition-
dependent rules*. This powerful ideology represents itself as universal,
but is in fact highly selective. The process of tradition-formation is vital to
an understanding of performative genres like preaching, whose purpose is
to intervene in the world in specific ways and whose vehicle of intervention is a specific form of language. Sermons, homilies, and saints' lives are
thus amenable to sociocultural and to literary analysis, and must be analyzed in terms of their traditionality in both spheres. It is, in fact, traditional works and not new, original, often canonical works that challenge
the assumptions of conventional historiography and literary history.

Chapter 2, "Aesthetics and Belief: Ælfric's False Gods," faces squarely
the criticism that religious prose is not primarily a literary genre by re-

examining the aesthetics of the prose and its relation to homiletic conventions encoding belief in salvation and transcendence. Creation, Fall, and Redemption are articles of faith, tenets of the Creed, which are direct consequences of a belief in the trinitarian God. Use of, and references to, these beliefs are so commonplace within religious writing that they have merited little attention. Yet it is precisely their commonplace nature that interests me. Constant repetition of such central tenets of the faith indicates that belief can never be taken for granted: it is evidence that belief is essentially performative and constructed by means of a process of continual reiteration. This process is known as worship.

Reiteration takes many different forms. A good example is Ælfric's lengthy tract on the false gods, *De falsis diis* (Pope, 1968, XXI). This narrative euhemerizes false idols in a sequence that begins with a eulogy on the Trinity and the creation of Adam, moves swiftly to accounts of scriptural and postscriptural idols, and includes a well-known discussion of Danish idolatry in the Anglo-Saxon period. The text asserts straightforwardly enough that there is only one God, and one faith, whose power is immanent throughout time. What is not so well appreciated is that this work is also stylistically a tour de force. Comparison of *De falsis diis* with other works by Ælfric indicates that he is working with a number of favorite topics—most notably those of the sacred significance of the Trinity and of the power of the Creator—to which he returns time and again. In this regard, *De falsis diis* is remarkable though not unique in the Ælfrician corpus. Stylistic analysis suggests, moreover, that Ælfric found such material not only theologically important but aesthetically satisfying. Ælfric's belief, in short, generates a conscious aesthetics of salvation. This is not an aesthetics appreciated by all. In Wulfstan's rewriting of the same text, as in later critical accounts of both versions, we see how Ælfric's aesthetics have been the subject of a number of significant misreadings. Via processes of iteration, fundamental beliefs become foundational—hence commonplace, traditional, and natural—but the form that iteration assumes is equally crucial. My study of Ælfric's and Wulfstan's versions of *De falsis diis* indicates that genres that express communal beliefs can also be vehicles for recovering individual patterns of worship and faith.

Essential to the concept of tradition is its construction of time in relation to Christian truth as unchanging and universal. Chapter 3, "Conventions of Time in the Old English Homiletic Corpus," explores the representation of specific historical events in such an ideology. Christianity incorporates the local and the specific into its general model of salvation history, from which the temporal gains its meaning. Anglo-Saxon homilies take liturgical scriptural readings, or lections, as their subjects for exposition and analysis. Grounded in the continuous present of the liturgy, the homilies seem barely concerned with the historical events of their own time, nor is it possible to reconstruct actual historical audiences for the works. Attention to this conceptualization of time within Christianity and to its rhetorical representation modifies our readings of even those texts known to refer to specific historical events, such as Wulfstan's *Sermo Lupi*. At the same time, however, this feature of the traditionality of Anglo-Saxon homilies must be seen in relation to the circumstances of their production—the period of the Benedictine reform. Chapter 2 therefore examines the relation between the cultural phenomenon of the reform and its representation in reform and postreform homilies and sermons. The traditionality of late Anglo-Saxon homilies is not a universal Christian phenomenon, it turns out, but a product of specific historical circumstances that express that universality.

Belief in salvation takes the form of a body of knowledge and a history, one of the purposes of which is to distinguish the true from the false, the local from the transcendent. This process of selection is an aspect of a much larger educative process central to medieval Christianity in general. Belief is not just a mental category, an inner conviction, or a matter of experience, but a specific knowledge, formulated as the attainment of wisdom, which can be transmitted and which forms the basis for other knowledge, such as social relations or politics (as demonstrated in chapter 3). This knowledge is fundamentally moral and, in practical discourses such as preaching, provides the guidelines for Christian behavior. It is for these reasons that medieval Christianity emphasizes the correct acquisition of its knowledge, and hence also the importance of its teaching and teachers. As the main vehicle of instruction of the laity by the clergy throughout the period, vernacular religious genres like homilies, sermons, and saints' lives are worthless unless they are didactic. The nature of that didacticism, however, is poorly understood.

Chapter 4, "Didacticism and the Christian Community," argues that didactic genres aim for a deliberate transformation of the auditor or reader through an educative process whereby desire for God is constructed as a desire for knowledge. This knowledge, confirmed by the application of Christian reason, distinguishes the sacred from the profane, virtue from vice, truth from falsehood. Such knowledge does not rationalize the ineffability or mystery of faith at the heart of Christianity, which all Anglo-Saxon religious writers celebrate, but heightens it. The great theme of didactic works is the continual renewal of faith via a process of moral instruction. Responsibility for teaching, which binds the teacher and the taught in a series of hierarchical though dialectical relations, rests firmly with the ecclesiast; and that for learning, with his congregation. The connection between these two groups is fidelity, or obedience, to the law of Christianity. It is this process that modern readers so quickly detect and so often find distasteful.

Modern critical distaste is perhaps due to the transparency with which homiletic writers set about pursuing the imperative of Christian education. Not only is didacticism transparent (indeed, this is what the genre aims for), but, worse still, it is celebrated. As chapter 2 illustrates, didactic instruction makes ample use of aesthetic pleasure in fostering desire for knowledge. While we cannot evaluate the efficacy of this process from the historical record, the homilies, sermons, and saints' lives discussed in chapter 4 provide ample internal evidence of how both teacher and taught are viewed in principle. Ælfric's prose, for example, constructs precise models of the ideal Christian teacher or author (and the extent to which these are synonymous), his intended readers or auditors, and the process of instruction that binds these two together.

Through the didactic process, the Christian finds his or her place in the Christian community; in consequence, instruction frequently centers on the Christian meanings of family, marriage, identity, and body, arranged in a series of hierarchies. In Anglo-Saxon society, identity is derived from a similar matrix, which explains why the ideal Christian in the homilies is less a universal Christian ideal than an Anglo-Saxon one. Moreover, Anglo-Saxon culture in general offers little sense of a unique, private, interior self. There is a language for the interior self—that of the soul—but that language, equally idealized, is in theory shared by all. Traditional belief offers, in other words, a powerful model of identification and incorporation.

"When the system of thought called monotheism confers identity," argues Regina M. Schwartz (1995, 121), "it is typically an identity that carefully establishes boundaries, drawing lines to distinguish and separate one group from another." The process of incorporation that is fostered by traditional belief is indeed highly selective. While chapter 4 concentrates on the boundaries that divide the Christian from the non-Christian, chapter 5, "Chastity and Charity: Ælfric, Women, and the Female Saints," concentrates on Ælfric's discourse of chastity to examine some of the boundaries that maintain and order Christian identity from within. Ælfric's views on chastity from his homilies provide evidence by which to assess the construction of gendered identity within homiletic ideals of Christian society and within what appears to be the most marked genre for the study of gender in the religious literature—the lives of the female saints. The narrative movement of the female life from social to spiritual rewards is analogous to the ways in which chastity is figured as an offering, or gift, by Ælfric. Chapter 5 therefore considers the dynamics of chastity as an exchange system and its implications for our understanding of gender more generally in Anglo-Saxon England.

These five chapters of *Tradition and Belief* argue that aspects of tradition formation—the construction of specific views of time, salvation, aesthetics, didacticism, and Christian identity—are all central to a cultural reading of religious works. Not all of these aspects are unique to vernacular sermons and homilies, but their combination in preaching texts provides the means whereby the church constructs a belief that is intended to be operative in the world of Anglo-Saxon society. Religious belief structures understanding of the temporal world of events according to divine patterns, which are continually iterated. By means of iteration, belief in these patterns often expresses itself as worship, a performative process of continual and often aesthetic articulation within a specific teleology, the end of which is God. However, belief is not constructed through worship alone, but also through instruction in a specific body of knowledge. Didacticism and iteration aim for a continual renewal of faith. Iteration stresses the performativity of Christian worship. Didacticism stresses the acquisition of a body of knowledge through which the individual derives his or her identity from God and from the Christian community, thereby providing the basis for action. Above all, belief—the continual process of believing—is the boundary between the believer and the nonbeliever. Distinguishing the Christian from the non-Christian, it structures divisions within, creating Christian hierarchies of clergy and laity, but also, more fundamentally, hierarchies of the soul and body, sexuality, gender, and family.

Thus generalized, these features of tradition formation could belong to any body of Christian writing in the medieval period. Such is the power of ideology. Specific analysis of each feature demonstrates, however, that the Christianity constructed as universal by this religious writing is in fact thoroughly Anglo-Saxon. Thus tradition reproduces itself as a system of similarity that expels difference. Religious traditions are ideologies of incorporation into, and identification with, a morally sanctioned and universal world that derives its power from the specific institutional practices of the Anglo-Saxon church.

In my final pages, I return to the more theoretical premises explored in chapter 1 and consider how literary and cultural history may be modified by the case study of Anglo-Saxon religious writing. If the map of medieval religious culture is now being redrawn, that map must include Anglo-Saxon religious writing. If the study of culture is committed to the study of popular forms and genres, it must include analysis of past historical formations, including those known as traditional. Only by so doing can culture examine its relation to belief.

# Acknowledgments

❖

Thelma Fenster and Jim Craddock gave me the gift of time and space by loaning me their barn with its study, in which I started writing this book. A research fellowship from the Oregon Humanities Center at the University of Oregon in the winter of 1996 helped me during the final stages. Lisa Freeman and the University of Minnesota Press have continued their exemplary support of my work, as have the series editors, Rita Copeland, Barbara A. Hanawalt, and David Wallace. The anonymous readers of the manuscript were scrupulous and insightful in their comments; they have helped me define the direction of the book. Roland Greene offered advice and support at moments when I needed it most. Ian Duncan and Sarah Beckwith both paid me the compliment of treating me as a fellow author at times when I least felt like one. David Aers was overwhelmingly generous with his time, knowledge, and intellect in his rigorous reading of several chapters. Meredith Webb provided much-needed bibliographical support at the end of the project. Gillian R. Overing continues to be my closest friend, mentor, and colleague in Anglo-Saxon studies; she knows how much I owe her. I regret that *The Intellectual Foundations of the English Benedictine Reform,* by Mechthild Gretsch (Cambridge, U.K.: Cambridge University Press, 1999), was published too late for me to give it the consideration it deserved. Happy to give the support that only parents can during the time-consuming project of writing a book, Pauline and Jack Lees can rest happier now that I've done. This book is for Julian Weiss.

# Abbreviations

❖

ASE    *Anglo-Saxon England*
ASPR   Anglo-Saxon Poetic Records (ed. George Philip Krapp and
       Elliott Van Kirk Dobbie [New York: Columbia University
       Press, 1932–53])
EEMF  Early English Manuscripts in Facsimile
EETS   Early English Text Society
EHR    *English Historical Review*
ES      *English Studies*
JEGP   *Journal of English and Germanic Philology*
JMEMS *Journal of Medieval and Early Modern Studies*
Ker     *Catalogue of Manuscripts containing Anglo-Saxon* (N. R. Ker
       [Oxford: Clarendon, 1957])
PL      *Patrologia Cursus Completus . . . Series Latina* (ed. J. P. Migne
       [Paris, 1841–79])

# Culture and Belief

## The Politics of Belief

Nu wille we þæt eal folc to gemænelicre dædbote þrig dagas be hlafe ꝺ wirtum ꝺ wætere, þæt is on Monandæg ꝺ on Tiwesdæg ꝺ on Wodnesdæg ær Michaeles mæssan.

[Now it is our will that all the nation [shall fast] as a general penance for three days on bread and herbs and water, namely on the Monday, Tuesday and Wednesday before Michaelmas.][1]

The three-day general penance enjoined on the English people in 1009 seems one of the more improbable responses to yet another threat of a Danish invasion. Issued during the politically turbulent years toward the end of Æthelred II's reign, VII Æthelred ("ða se micele here com to lande"),[2] is extant in both Latin and Old English versions. The code was drafted by Wulfstan (bishop of London from 996 to 1002, bishop of Worcester and archbishop of York from 1002 until his death in 1023), premier legislator of his age and one of the two best-known religious writers of Anglo-Saxon England. Extracts from the code were also incorporated into two late Old English homilies (Napier, 1883, XXXV and XXXVI).[3]

As the prologue to VII Æthelred clearly states, the spiritual labor of penance is intended to elicit God's mercy and assistance against the enemies of the English:

Ealle we beþurfan þæt we geornlice earnian þæt we Godes miltse ꝺ his mildheortnesse habban moton ꝺ þæt we þurh his fultum magon feondum wiðstandan.

[All of us have need eagerly to labor that we may obtain God's mercy and his compassion and that we may through his help withstand our enemies.] (Whitelock, Brett, and Brooke, 1981, 379)

This penitential practice is not unique in the early medieval period, nor is moral reformation unusual as a response to political disarray in England.[4] Alfred the Great's program of moral education in the late ninth century was promulgated between earlier waves of Viking incursions. In

1

the efforts of Alfred, Æthelred II, and Wulfstan, we see Christian knowledge and its ethics guiding English society in eras of turbulent change. Wulfstan's homily *Sermo Lupi* (Whitelock, 1976) will use similar techniques at an even more critical juncture of English history in 1014. As these examples suggest, to understand early medieval belief is also to understand political process. Like the later *Sermo Lupi*, VII Æthelred is aimed at the entire Christian people in England. In a pointed contrast to Alfred's more politically efficacious audience of the ruling classes of ecclesiasts and aristocrats in the ninth century, VII Æthelred stands out as one of the most dramatic expressions of the labor of penance enacted as civil and ecclesiastical law in Anglo-Saxon England.

Wulfstan offers precise guidelines for this general penance, which is enjoined upon all ranks of society—lord and slave, layman and ecclesiast alike—with specific financial penalties for nonobservance. Confession, processions barefoot on each of the three days, communal recitation of the psalter, almsgiving, charity, tithing, and the singing of specific masses against the "heathens" and for the king and his people (Whitelock, Brett, and Brooke, 1981, 379–82) are a web of religious practices connecting the individual to the church, the community to society, and the king to his people at a specific moment in time and place. However idealized or improbable to twentieth-century eyes, VII Æthelred enlists an image of a people united under one king and one faith in a penitential act intended to stem the tide of Danish invasions.

History proved Æthelred and Wulfstan wrong. Within the space of a decade Cnut was king of the English and Wulfstan his archbishop and legislator. No longer an enemy, Cnut rapidly established himself as more Christian and English than the English.[5] By 1018, in an early draft of Cnut's laws, the English and Danes had agreed to "ofer ealle oþre þingc ænne God æfre wurðodon ⁊ ænne Cristendom anrædlice healdan" (above all things honour one God and steadfastly hold one Christian faith) and "Cnut cyngc lufian mid rihtan ⁊ mid trywðan ⁊ Eadgares lagan geornlice folgian" (love King Cnut rightly, loyally, and zealously observe Edgar's laws).[6] In this draft and its insistence on traditions of belief and rule, we hear an echo of Wulfstan's homiletic legislation for Æthelred II that reverberates all the way back to Edgar's reign in the mid–tenth century (Whitelock, Brett, and Brooke, 1981, 431–33, 468–71). Political change in these crucial decades of the eleventh century is eased not merely by a strengthened concept of Christian kingship, independent of the person of the king, but by a coherent idea of a Christian society, which acts as the king's partner. These ideologies of right rule are the bequest of the tenth century and derive from the application of traditional forms of Christian knowledge and law, reinforced by the performance of Christian ritual maintained in English churches and monasteries in the late Anglo-Saxon period.[7]

Like the early draft of Cnut's laws, VII Æthelred is a challenge for all students of religious culture and history. It witnesses the very material vitality of the interrelations of concepts of Anglo-Saxon rule, social struc-ture, religious thought and practice, and historical change. To point to Wulfstan as the compiler of the code and to celebrate his contributions in the late Anglo-Saxon political arena is to miss part of its significance, however. Wulfstan does nothing new; rather, he recombines selectively those elements of traditional Christian knowledge already circulating in Anglo-Saxon England, which are now analyzed as the discrete fields of law, religion, and ethical behavior. In late Anglo-Saxon sociey, polity and so-ciety are coconstituted by belief. This move, which characterizes much of Wulfstan's work, builds on several decades of lawmaking in England.

The cultural meaning of VII Æthelred, moreover, only makes greater sense when seen in relation to the upsurge in vernacular religious writ-ing during this same period, most of it in the form of homilies, sermons, and saints' lives. The religious culture of the English from roughly 970 to 1020 promoted by the clerics of the late Anglo-Saxon church finds sys-tematic expression in these genres, which pave the way for Wulfstan's more dramatic invocation of a penitential people united under one God and king. Preaching and hagiography of this period map out the practice of Christian belief to the extent that Wulfstan's idea of communal spiri-tual action against the Danes becomes not merely probable but plausi-ble. Put another way, Anglo-Saxon Christian belief has a place in the history of Anglo-Saxon culture. That place is synonymous neither with the history of kingship and lawmaking in England nor with the history of the English church, its theology, canons, penances, tithes, or taxes. Homilies, saints' lives, and sermons are themselves forms of social prac-tice, which interact with these other discourses in late Anglo-Saxon sec-ular and ecclesiastical society.

## Anglo-Saxon Studies and Religious Culture

The important relationship between a culture and its beliefs is funda-mental to Anglo-Saxon studies. It is, after all, the Anglo-Saxon period that witnesses the conversion of the English to Christianity. Faced with the problem of defining cultural practices—of defining what is English about Anglo-Saxon England—the conversion and its consequences are naturally the source of one of Anglo-Saxonists' favorite questions: how pagan, Germanic, and non-Christian is Christian Anglo-Saxon society? That "odd couple" (Frank, 1992), Sutton Hoo and *Beowulf*, will always haunt Anglo-Saxon studies, and for good reason. Indeed, Anglo-Saxon-ists have often seemed more comfortable with the "search for Anglo-Saxon paganism," as E. G. Stanley (1975) puts it, than with the search for its Christianity.[8]

In the same way, the crucial relationship between a culture's beliefs and its production of aesthetic works has long preoccupied Anglo-Saxonists. Whether *Beowulf* is non-Christian or Christian and whether the Old English elegies offer Christian consolation are equally familiar critical questions. Perhaps too familiar. Recent criticism has moved away from issues of belief and aesthetics, partly in response to some justifiable dissatisfaction with the ways these topics have been explored in the past and partly in response to the reluctance of postmodern critical and cultural theory to explore religious aesthetics. In this regard, as in many others, Anglo-Saxon studies has not remained aloof from the impact of recent critical trends in the academies, as Allen J. Frantzen (1990) reminds us.

Yet questions of the relation of belief to culture persist. Anglo-Saxon studies has always explored these general issues more consistently in relation to the poetry than to the prose; hence the endless project of identifying the precise blend of Christian and Germanic cultures offered in a poem like *Beowulf*.[9] While this project ensures the prestige of Anglo-Saxon heroic poetry (which it is in no danger of losing), it does little to advance our general knowledge of Anglo-Saxon religious culture. The period of the conversion has already amply furnished such knowledge (most recently by Sims-Williams, 1990; Hollis, 1992; and, more generally, Russell, 1994), although its study is hampered by the paucity of sources generally and of vernacular material in particular, especially when measured against the recent growth in our understanding of Anglo-Latin culture of this same period. By contrast, the tenth and the eleventh centuries, which are already well known as the period in which all Anglo-Saxon poetry was produced in manuscript form, witness a huge upsurge in religious prose writing, both in Latin and in the vernacular. These centuries in fact offer the largest and earliest corpus of vernacular sermons, homilies, and saints' lives in early medieval Europe. Their importance, however, remains largely undetected and unexplored by scholars interested more generally in the cultural significance of medieval religious writing.

Study of Anglo-Saxon religious prose most often follows long established conventions of scholarly analysis that concentrate on the identification of sources or on the critical interpretation of individual texts. There are only a handful of full-length studies of the genre, mostly directed at other specialists interested in the prose, its sources, its theology, and its manipulation of homiletic or hagiographic convention.[10] The theoretical underpinning of these studies derives from a self-evident and therefore rarely examined premise: that of the traditionality or conventionality of preaching texts. This premise is an artifact of the two main methods of scholarly interpretation: patristic source analysis and stylistic analysis. Source analysis interprets Anglo-Saxon religious prose primarily as translations of patristic Latin works.[11] It confirms the English homilists' dependence on conventional, long-lasting methods of composition that are in turn dependent on conventional, long-lasting sources of Christian knowledge.

4

   The use of patristic Latin sources to elucidate vernacular religious writing is a methodology derived in large measure from the study of Latin culture in the Middle Ages initiated in the philological climate of the nineteenth century and later elaborated by scholars such as Ernst Robert Curtius (1953). Source analysis presents Anglo-Saxon religious writing as a product of Latin Western civilization. Anglo-Saxon religious prose derives a modicum of cultural prestige from this methodology, but also a considerable anxiety about its status as a vernacular cousin of this better-known, more widespread, longer-lasting, and more politically dominant Latin culture. The uneasy tensions that this model of culture generates are exemplified in studies of homiletic style, which is the second method of critical analysis dominant in conventional study of these works. Anglo-Saxon prose writers, especially the known writers, Ælfric, abbot of Eynsham, and Wulfstan, are praised for their stylistic achievement; yet these achievements are simultaneously dependent on and independent from their Latin precursors. The study of Anglo-Saxon religious writing, assimilated to that of Christianity more generally in the early Latin West, is thus a means of measuring the extent of European Latin civilization. As a result, the meaning of this vernacular writing as a cultural practice in England has not been fully assessed. Our understanding of this genre as evidence for Anglo-Saxon religious culture, along with the importance of such writers as Ælfric within it, rather than for an elite transnational culture needs to be more nuanced. Two areas of concern stand out. We need a greater understanding of the nature of the authority of vernacular religious texts—their use of Christian traditions in England. We also need a fuller understanding of the audience of these texts—their deployment in and by English social structures.

   *Tradition and Belief* moves beyond the conventional definitions of culture as civilization advanced by Curtius and others to argue that late Anglo-Saxon vernacular religious writing—with its two main subcategories of homilies or sermons and saints' lives—is evidence for a cultural practice that constitutes itself as traditional and is constitutive of social practice. The works of Ælfric are central to this process. Yet as VII Æthelred reminds us, the moral health of the entire English people is also an index of and response to political events. Vernacular religious writing is produced within a well-defined historical period that has a specific religious and cultural importance; it is roughly coterminous with the Benedictine reform, as well as with the strengthening of the idea of Christian kingship by the dynasty of the West Saxons and with the renewed external threat of Viking raids.[12] In each of these events, the clergy of the English church play major roles, formulating policy and promulgating a Christian advice literature through sermons and saints' lives. Judging from the many manuscript witnesses, homilies and hagiography enjoyed a considerable circulation that is in sharp contrast with the current critical emphasis on Latin writing and on the vernacular poetry. Moreover, Anglo-Saxon religious prose is often distinguished by a self-conscious awareness of aesthetic form, evidenced most notably by the rhythmical prose of the late-tenth, early-eleventh-century writers Ælfric and Wulfstan. History, aesthetics, and belief therefore combine as components of a cultural analysis of a genre that also invites meditation on the nature of its popularity and of its traditionality.

Composed by a literate clerical elite, vernacular homilies, sermons, and saints' lives participate in the predominantly monastic Latin culture of the early medieval period. In this sense, they offer evidence for the traditions of the English church as it interprets those of the Roman, especially when viewed via the lens of continental monastic reforms.[13] At the same time, these texts are written in English, not Latin, and they reach out to a Christian audience beyond that of the cloister or cathedral. In this sense, preaching texts are constructed as popular works, ultimately for the people, if not by them, even when presented as preaching resources, manuals for priests.[14] This twofold aspect of religious writing—its traditionality and its popularity—is crucial. The problem is how to bring these two aspects into critical relation. Religious prose is traditional with regard to its knowledge and to its methods of composition and popular with regard to its manuscript witnesses and to its intended audience, conceived ideologically as the English people. Ælfric and Wulfstan write homilies specifically addressed to the people ("ad populum"; e.g., Pope, 1967, XI; Bethurum, 1957, VIIa, XIII; *Sermo Lupi*, ed. Whitelock, 1976), as do some anonymous homilies (e.g., Napier, 1883, XXV), while the Englishness of Ælfric's homilies is loudly proclaimed by incipits to some of his major manuscripts (e.g., Ker 15, art. 3; 257, art. 1; 310, art. 6). The circumstances of the performance of Anglo-Saxon preaching is, however, both unknown and unknowable, as Gatch (1989) points out in the case of the Blickling Homilies. There is very little evidence indeed for specific Anglo-Saxon audiences or congregations who heard these works: accordingly, the nature of their popularity and their ideological use seems beyond analytical reach.

Karen Jolly (1996) reframes this problem by proposing a model of popular religion in England that subsumes what she calls the formal religion of the church. Her emphasis on the Anglo-Saxon charms as evidence for popular Christianity charts a narrative of religious acculturation accommodating both sermons and charms—Christian and folk beliefs. Existing at the interface of the formal and the popular, the work of the homilists elucidates the striking syncretism of the charms, which employ both Christian and non-Christian forms of knowledge to exert power over the world. Jolly's work is an important, though sometimes speculative, step forward in our understanding of the relation of religion to Anglo-Saxon society both within and without the court and the cathedral. At the same time, however, the vernacular work of the homilists remains background evidence for popular religion. The problem of understanding the specific nature of the popularity and traditionality of the sermons themselves, as well as the nature of their contestation of other forms of belief, remains.

Jolly is right, however, to indicate that cultural theory offers a way out of this impasse (1996, 6–34). In order to complement the emphasis on textuality provided by source study of the homilies, an emphasis on practice is required. Sermons are not simply theological musings or commentaries, writings that authorize the meaning of Christianity for the church. They are also a matter of religious practice, a set of constitutive discourses that construct, through reiteration, that meaning in the world. Religious writing as a genre bears the textual traces of its performance. Sermons, homilies, and saints' lives address implied audiences, whose presence in the text is registered by familar conventions such as "men þa leofestan" ("most beloved men" — the Anglo-Saxon equivalent, perhaps, of "Dearly Beloved"). The performative aspect of religious writing suggests a model of preaching as a practical discourse. This discourse of practices engages with the historical present in both complement to and contrast with its more conventional conceptualization as a textual genre dependent on earlier texts.

Patristic analysis concentrates on how religious writing derives its authority from the past, from its pre-texts (whether directly from the passage of Scripture it explicates or indirectly from the commentaries and sermons of the Latin Fathers associated with that passage). Preaching as practice, by contrast, explores how that authority is used as social power, backed by the institution of the church, to create and maintain belief in the world of the historic present. This latter position insists on the historical dynamism of traditional religious writing and its power in and beyond the Anglo-Saxon period — a point necessarily minimized by Jolly's emphasis on syncretism. It is no accident that the present tense characterizes Anglo-Saxon preaching. The homilists use the powerful authority of the church's knowledge, which derives from tradition, but implement it in a present social world conceived of as a series of hierarchical relations between ecclesiast and lay, between teachers and taught. The idea of popularity conveyed by the homilists is not that of an undifferentiated mass ("the people") or of a simple division between formal and popular ("the church" and "the people"); society itself is sharply structured by rank (as chapter 4 elucidates). Precisely because it is a traditional and social (that is, socializing) genre, the study of vernacular religious prose must be situated at the juncture between the disciplines of literature and history — both social and ecclesiastical — as well as between the concepts of belief and theology.

In fact, sermons, homilies, and saints' lives have often been deemed worthy of historical, though not literary, investigation. The study of hagiography, Latin hagiography in particular, has flourished. The lives of the saints — often set in a distant and idealized past — offer the Anglo-Saxon

7

church a vehicle for moral commentary on contemporary social and political life, as evidenced by analyses of the royal cults of saints, for example, or of the ways in which hagiography fosters Christian visions of social relations such as gender, the family, and marriage (Ridyard, 1988; Rollason, 1989a; Elliott, 1993). Just as the study of Latin hagiography has always merited historical analysis, Anglo-Latin writers and theologians such as Bede or Alcuin have been rightly viewed as key figures within the early medieval church. Vernacular sermons, homilies, and saints' lives, however, have not fared as well within historical discourse. Generally ignored in broad accounts of the medieval church, vernacular genres attract little more than a handful of pages in histories of the Anglo-Saxon period.[15] The historiographical emphasis on Latin religious writing makes sense if its subject is the authorizing and validating function of the Anglo-Saxon church in creating its own history (which is why everyone knows Bede's *Historia ecclesiastica*), but such a history is inevitably less interested in how the church performs its work in the larger arena of Anglo-Saxon culture. Moreover, historiography often seems more interested in the saint's life than the sermon. The distinction between vernacular preaching works and hagiography, however, is not a simple one for the Anglo-Saxon period. Different in their conventions of content and narrative yet stylistically similar, both forms often exist side by side in manuscript compilations, and both are practical discourses of the church, often directed at similar audiences.

In the sphere of literary analysis, vernacular religious works have suffered not only from the charge of dependency, in the sense of being the vernacular product of Latin patristic culture, but also that of functionality or didacticism. The critical situation is complex. Identified as primarily didactic, religious prose is justifiably viewed as a genre in which aesthetics is subordinate to ethics; at the same time, this genre is sometimes admired for its stylistic achievements, as if aesthetic form can be divorced from ethical content.[16] That such admiration is rarely analyzed in relation to the stylistic achievements of the poetry is a further symptom of the critical confusion about the nature of the prose.[17] Indeed, the use of the term *traditional* to describe Anglo-Saxon poetic techniques has a long and venerable history, whereas the traditionality of the prose has seemed so self-evident as to be spared critical attention. Given its stylistic richness, to dismiss Anglo-Saxon religious prose from analysis as didactic is lamentable enough from a formal literary perspective. Such dismissal runs the risk of misunderstanding the genre's relation to literary history. As one of the earliest examples of vernacular prose, religious writing develops specific forms of narrative, explication, and moral exhortation. But the prose cannot be dismissed from a cultural perspective either; to do so underestimates the social power of this writing. Didactic writing intends to effect change.

Literary criticism assumes that the aesthetics of vernacular religious writing differs radically from those other Anglo-Saxon genres, such as the heroic or elegiac, whose literary intent has always seemed more transparent (that is, more readily assimilable to modern conventions of literary analysis).[18] Religious works are indeed motivated by a clear, though sophisticated, didactic purpose: the fostering, maintenance, and explication of the structures of late Anglo-Saxon belief within the Christian individual and community. These structures of belief take the form of knowledge created and exercised by hierarchical rituals of discipline, whether they be the monastic disciplines of the Rule or the more secular rituals of worship—prayer, church attendance (a repeated theme in ecclesiastical and secular law), almsgiving and tithing, participation in ecclesiastical rites such as procession, listening to vernacular sermons, and veneration of the exemplary figures of the saints. Aesthetic pleasure is tapped by vernacular religious writing as an important means of securing the successful reception of these disciplines: the beauty of the word is an integral component of Christian knowledge. Style, as Ælfric puts it (and as Augustine put it before him), is a matter of *utilitas*—of ideology.[19]

Homilies and saints' lives are not primarily historical, literary, or theological documents, therefore, but cultural works—a matter of religion in the world. Their characteristics of traditionality, didacticism, and aesthetics are best explored by methods of cultural analysis that challenge the conventionally separate spheres of history, literature, and theology. Viewed as a specific cultural formation, Anglo-Saxon religious prose offers considerable insight into the nature, construction, and practice of late Anglo-Saxon belief. This evidence will substantially modify our understanding of traditional medieval religious culture in general by concentrating on a period before the twelfth century (which so often marks the beginning of detailed analysis) and by concentrating on a genre that is noncanonical, yet traditional and often popular throughout the entire period.

## Medieval Religious Culture

The study of religion has always been central to the study of the medieval period, but recent years have seen a dramatic revolution in the ways in which medievalists approach and explore this centrality. A major element of religious study continues to be the painstaking unfolding of the narrative of medieval Christian thought: the identification, editing, and analysis of religious texts, rites, and rituals; the interpretation of theological controversies and debates; and the understanding of commentaries, liturgies, sermons, and commonplace books, for example.[20] These tried and trusted methods of study are increasingly complemented, however, by an awareness that such a "master" narrative tells only one part of the story. Medieval Christianity cannot be seen as only a mono-logic, transcultural phenomenon (although to abandon this catchall de-scription would be a pedantry that minimizes Christianity's dominance), nor is the study of religion in the medieval period only the study of Chris-tianity and its theology.

As medieval studies broadens its institutional frontiers beyond the English Middle Ages, the idea of the Christian Middle Ages becomes in-creasingly nuanced. Medieval Judaism, for example, is at long last gain-ing the prominence within general accounts of Western medieval society that it merits (e.g., Elad, 1995; Stow, 1992; Cohen, 1982; Edwards, 1988; Stock, 1990, 140–58; Abulafia, 1994). Emerging, too, are studies of the influence of Islamic thought and of the relationship of Judaic and Is-lamic cultures to medieval Christian cultures, central to which are the religions of medieval Spain (Harvey, 1990; Reilly, 1993; MacKay, 1977; Mirrer, 1994). Within the study of Christianity itself, attention is increas-ingly focused on local, socioculturally specific reflexes of Christianity that interrupt, muddle, and modify attempts to provide a unified narrative of its history. Studies of orthodoxy are complemented by those of hetero-doxy and heresy upon which orthodoxy thrives (e.g., Moore, 1987; Biller and Hudson, 1994). In such analyses, concepts of periodization can be-come unwieldy constructs that elide both difference and continuity with-in those societies now known collectively as medieval. As a result, histo-rians and religious and literary scholars alike are concerned to understand the specific and often local nature of cultures within this huge period. Such realizations refocus attention on the problem of the relation be-tween culture and belief in particular historical periods. Contemporary theorists of culture would do well to take note.

These newer conversations about belief in the medieval period indi-cate that the study of religion is renegotiating its boundaries with those of the study of culture. Prominent are the remarkable achievements of scholars of women's history, who have introduced us to the worlds of the medieval female religious, thereby revealing the "master" narrative of medieval Christianity as not only a totalizing fiction, but as unwit-tingly masculine. Work by Sarah Beckwith (1993), Caroline Walker Bynum (1987, 1992), Judith Bennett (1987, 1996), Martha Howell (1986), Karma Lochrie (1991), Lynn Staley (1994), and numerous others demonstrates how putting women back into the narrative of the Christian Middle Ages complicates and enriches it.[21] Not that complication and enrichment of a single narrative is necessarily the point. Such studies have drawn on careful consideration of the social and cultural situation of women in this period, producing exciting work in both historical and literary spheres. The writing of religious history is no longer univocal nor does it mask its strategies of empowerment and disempowerment.

As the historical study of gender prompts the reformulation of notions of both culture and belief, so too are challenged the more general disciplinary boundaries between religion, literature, and history. The history of a period is not understood simply as background to, or source for, a literary work but as a dynamic component of its production and reception. David Aers (1988, 1994b), Aers and Staley (1996), Britton Harwood (1991), Allen Frantzen (1994, 1996b), and Lee Patterson (1991) have all used explicitly religious literary works to explore broadly materialist conceptions of culture, gender, literature, and history in relation to power. Religious poems such as *Piers Plowman* and *Cleanness* are currently enjoying a revival of critical attention; Langland and the Gawain poet stand comfortably side by side with the always canonical Chaucer.[22] Scholars such as Miri Rubin (1991) and Beckwith (1993) go beyond such well-known literary figures to examine the use of cultural symbols like Christ's body, thereby integrating theological debate with cultural analysis. By necessity, interdisciplinary issues such as the cultural construction of the body, space, sexuality, gender, identity, literacy, and power engage with religious thought in the period and complement the more discrete categories of conventional analysis.[23] From another perspective, heavily influenced by the Annales school and the study of *mentalités*, the work of Aron Gurevitch (1988) on popular religious culture attempts to break down the barriers between the "high" and the "low." Finally, medieval clerical understandings of conversion, for example, have much to teach us about the interrelationship of belief and culture (Morrison, 1992). As a result of such innovative studies, the map of medieval religious culture is being redrawn.

Like contemporary cultural studies more generally, moreover, these studies do not conform to one methodological or theoretical school. They are instead feminist, historical, materialist, psychoanalytic, cultural, theological, and literary. More often, they combine eclectically many of these methodologies and perspectives. In sum, the general area of culture and belief is emergent in medieval studies and is, in consequence, rich in debate and conflict.

The publication of Eamon Duffy's *The Stripping of the Altars: Traditional Religion in England, 1400–1580* (1992) has prompted one such debate. This reinterpretation of the pre- and post-Reformation periods in England argues that late medieval Catholicism was a vigorous, unified, and thriving tradition enthusiastically embraced by all levels of society. As a result, the Reformation itself is read as a radical break with the past. Duffy's position thus opposes an earlier view of this same period, one heavily influenced by Johan Huizinga's *The Waning of the Middle Ages* (1924), in which the fifteenth century, characterized by decay and exhaustion, paves the way for its dissolution and the Renaissance. David Aers (1994a) points out, however, that Duffy's own work retains another idealization—that of the medieval period as tranquilly unified by its beliefs. The crucial issue here is Duffy's use of the concept of tradition, as indicated by the phrase "traditional religion" in his title. While recognizing the vitality and persistance of that which is held to be traditional, Duffy fails to acknowledge the ideology at work in such a conceptualization. In consequence, the medieval period is reified as homogeneous, conflicts and debates within medieval Catholicism are minimized, relations within and across classes are idealized, and written cultural documents are used as uncomplicated ahistorical witnesses to historical events. We are, in short, not far from the nostalgia of D. W. Robertson for the "quiet hierarchies" of the medieval world (1962, 51). It is testimony to the vitality of work in medieval studies influenced by contemporary theories of history, culture, and interpretation that Duffy's position has not gone uncriticized.

Duffy's work illustrates that concepts of traditional religion are reemerging as central to debates about medieval religious culture. His book, however, is a contribution to the ideology of tradition and not its analysis. Debates such as these, moreover, focus on late medieval Christianity and its relation to English culture of the fourteenth and fifteenth centuries — largely, I suspect, because of the institutional preeminence of this period in English medieval studies. Within the high medieval period, lesser-known texts and events often enrich the study of religious culture, but many derive their recent prominence from studies that also examine major canonical figures such as Chaucer and Langland. The aesthetic and cultural importance of canonical works and periods remains intact, even as their significance changes according to critical fashion. The problem is twofold: other periods and other forms of cultural expression within the medieval are left unexplored, while the implications of cultural analysis in this dominant period are, as a direct consequence, partial. It is neither necessary nor realistic to suppose that the English High Middle Ages will cede its cultural capital, but a fuller understanding of the relation between culture and belief in the Middle Ages requires a broader scope.

## Cultural Studies, Cultural Materialism, and Belief

*Tradition and Belief* broadens the scope of inquiry into the relation between religion and culture by bringing the early medieval period into dialogue with the emerging critical discussion about religious culture in the later Middle Ages and by using this dialogue to resituate and redirect contemporary cultural theory. This book uses the study of a specific, historical, and traditional religious formation — that of late Anglo-Saxon preaching in general and the works of Ælfric in particular — to highlight certain strengths and weaknesses in contemporary cultural studies. The rapprochement between contemporary cultural theory and Anglo-Saxon studies, however, has yet to be fully articulated.

The need for such a rapprochement is not immediately compelling, whether viewed from the perspective of Anglo-Saxon studies or from that of cultural studies. The former is a well-established, coherent, and defined discipline, with its own methods and debates, while the latter, according to Simon During, "possesses neither a well-defined methodology nor clearly demarcated fields for investigation" (1993, 1); it nonetheless most often takes as its field of investigation contemporary cultural practices. Although this is a common enough description of cultural studies now, hindsight does offer benefits, and one of them is the contrast with the cultural practices of Raymond Williams (1958, 1961), Richard Hoggart (1957), E. P. Thompson (1963), the Birmingham Centre for Contemporary Cultural Studies, and the Open University in the United Kingdom in the late 1950s and early 1960s.[24] The study of culture then was an oppositional critical practice that grew out of the elite tradition of English letters in British universities. It concentrated on popular contemporary culture (although not to the exclusion of other cultural forms) and was motivated by a commitment to materialist thought and the politics of the Left. While there were plenty of disagreements about the shape and direction of this new practice, this earlier formation of cultural studies demonstrated that the many facets of contemporary social life were as valid an object of cultural inquiry as conventions derived from the literary study of "great" works, which had been fostered by F. R. Leavis and his followers.

Seen as the product of a specific moment of the history of British scholarship, this emphasis on contemporary social practice as an oppositional strategy makes a lot of sense. One unforeseen consequence, however, was to obscure the significance of this work for historical forms of popular culture. This legacy—an emphasis on the contemporary—remains in place in cultural studies today, and Anglo-Saxonists, like other scholars of historical disciplines, are in a prime position to challenge it. This formation of cultural studies, later to be described as cultural materialism, offers Anglo-Saxonists the challenge of thinking about the relation of texts to other material forms of society and culture. Anglo-Saxon studies, as Frantzen (1996c) reminds us, is still dominated by methods of textual analysis. What Anglo-Saxon studies offers both contemporary cultural studies and cultural materialism, however, is the analytical importance of historical formations of popular and high culture in general.

With the exception perhaps of the unique achievements of the Open University and the Birmingham school, cultural studies now exists as a subset—or related program—of English or of literary study in most universities. But it has substantially modified the premises of the study of culture within these disciplines. Although incorporated by those institutional structures that used to maintain only "high" culture, what was once known as "low" or "popular" culture is now a vital intellectual area. The price paid for the proliferation of methodologies now united under the broad umbrella of cultural studies, however, is that cultural studies is itself increasingly, and somewhat disingenuously, resistant to definition. The same can be said for other recent methodological and interdisciplinary approaches, such as critical theory, feminism, and queer theory, which also find themselves in an uneasy relation to preexisting institutional structures and disciplines. The contestation for cultural capital between these various approaches, which often substitutes for analysis of their political import, leaves little room for historically informed inquiry (Guillory, 1993, 3–82). For some, like During, this is a virtue; the domain of cultural studies is now contemporary culture. For others, heavily influenced by theories of cultural materialism and the work of Raymond Williams, this emphasis on the contemporary is indefensible.

The resistance of cultural studies to methodological definition is not necessarily a limitation, especially now that many established disciplines in the humanities are in a period of self-examination and change. Frantzen (1996c), for example, in one of the few detailed analyses of the relation of cultural studies to Anglo-Saxon studies, uses the fragmentation of contemporary cultural theory to explore the fragmented nature of Anglo-Saxon culture. Frantzen's reification of the fragment, however, contrasts with Williams's emphasis on the processual nature of sociocultural analysis. For Williams, a willingness to embrace new forms of social and cultural inquiry is integral to its Marxist dialectical stance.[25] Viewed from this perspective, debates about theory and praxis within cultural studies remain symptoms of an internal contradiction about the meanings of culture, which remain deliberately unresolved, fruitfully productive, and therefore open to historical analysis.

As Williams often points out, the problem with culture as a term is that it incorporates several oppositions. Culture can refer to high art, for example, and is associated with ideas of civilization as opposed to those of society (even if society produces that art). Curtius's map of medieval European Latin culture as an index of early Western civilization illustrates the importance of this definition of culture. But culture also refers to "whole ways of life" (Williams, 1977, 17; cf. Williams, 1976, 87–93) and thus retains some connection to notions of the social and national, as in the example of English as opposed to French or, more appropriately in the context of late Anglo-Saxon society, English Christian as opposed to Danish, non-Christian culture. Williams's investigations into culture seize on this fundamental ambiguity between "culture as art and culture as society" (Milner, 1993, 3). In the late 1970s, in order to distinguish his own work from British literary humanism, on the one hand, and British "vulgar" Marxism, on the other, Williams used the term *cultural materialism* and thereby continued his reformulation of the relation of culture to society from an increasingly materialist stance (1980, 243). He went on to argue that " 'cultural practice' and 'cultural production' (its most recognizable terms) are not simply derived from an otherwise constituted social order but are themselves major elements in its constitution.... culture [is] the *signifying system* through which neces-sarily (though among other means) a social order is communicated, re-produced, experienced and explored" (1981, 12–13).

The study of culture in this materialist sense is highly relevant to An-glo-Saxon Christian cultural production. Cultural analysis of VII Æthel-red, for example, with which this chapter opened, brings into focus its contradictions and continuities. VII Æthelred depends on two primary distinctions: that between the Christian English and the Danish enemy—a distinction later reused by the Anglo-Danish Christian Cnut—and that between work and spiritual labor. In its provisions for the slave, lord, and cleric, the code reproduces the social world of work and rank as Christian and English. By the law of Christian obedience, the code de-mands that the social be experienced collectively and individually through the performance of spiritual work such as penance and almsgiving. The code thus resituates the moral discourse of the sermons on the efficacy of Christian behavior within legal discourse. That slaves are to be re-leased from their labor on the three penitential days before Michaelmas gestures toward an image of a socially unified people that is in fact de-pendent on a highly stratified social reality. The slave remains a slave.[26] Moreover, VII Æthelred not only depends for part of its cultural coher-ence on the related discourse of the homilists, but also produces homi-lies, as the evidence of two Anglo-Saxon homilies derived from it indi-cate, both of which prescribe a general penance for any national disaster (Napier, 1883, XXXV, 171; XXXVI, 173–74).[27] VII Æthelred is a document of cultural and social work, and their mystification in several senses.

Williams's own lifelong attempt to clarify the relation of culture to society introduces plenty of other theoretical ambiguities, most notably about his relation to Marxism and to humanism, but also about the re-lation of cultural materialism to cultural studies. In the work of the best cultural theorists (e.g., Tony Bennett, 1992), the legacy of Williams's work helps maintain an openness about the meanings of culture that is an es-sential component of the dialectical process. Often, however, openness distintegrates into vagueness and results in the appropriation of other roughly analogous theoretical approaches without rigorous analysis. Ar-guments that celebrate the antiteleological stance of contemporary cul-tural studies are sometimes better seen as manifestations of a liberal plu-ralism. The relation of class to power, for example, is invoked rhetorically, by what John Guillory calls the emptiness of an identity category (1993, 11–14). In such a climate, what needs to be reemphasized is Williams's definition of culture as a constitutive social, that is, material, practice. High culture (formerly the province of Leavisites and New Critics) can-not be separated from other cultural phenomena, Williams argues, or from the study of social power. Within this arena, culture is not a shared sys-tem of meanings—a comforting unity—but a site for social opposition, conflict, and contradiction. Literature, history, culture, and society have been brought into a dynamic and demanding theoretical relation, as Williams's own work demonstrates (1977, 4–11; 1981, 9–32).

In his use of this oppositional practice committed to the redefinition of culture so as to investigate the social meanings of cultural forms, Williams tends to concentrate on popular, nonelitist formations, seeing in them a potential for radical, counterhegemonic change. This emphasis on the contemporary and the popular is only one aspect of Williams's work, however. Genres like the nineteenth-century novel and the drama remain fundamental to his thinking; the "low" does not replace the "high" but is brought into a historical and dialectical relation with it. E. P. Thompson points out in a similar vein that "generalizations as to the universals of 'popular culture' become empty unless they are firmly placed within specific historical contexts" (1993, 6). This is a simple though crucial point. Thompson's work on traditional popular culture in the eighteenth and early nineteenth centuries demonstrates that the popular or the traditional varies significantly not only within the same period, but diachronically across periods. Popular formations are not de facto radical nor are traditional formations de facto conservative. On the evidence of the English fourteenth century, some works that present themselves as within a particular tradition are in fact radical in their uses of that tradition, thereby standing in complex and conflicted relation to more ostensibly conservative aspects of it, as Aers and Staley (1996) brilliantly elucidate. Turning to the Anglo-Saxon sermons, we find radical strains within a formation that is conservative and traditional, yet presents itself as popular.[28]

In spite of Williams's and Thompson's work, however, theoretical generalizations about the meanings of culture are still explored largely with reference to contemporary popular cultures.[29] The contrast is sharpened by considering the work of cultural materialists in the early modern period and that of the New Historicists with whom cultural materialists are often affiliated.[30] In addition, medievalists such as Aers, Frantzen, and Patterson have begun the important work of reformulating the premises of the study of medieval culture, as already discussed.[31] While few proponents of cultural studies in the present engage with those interested in the past, historical materialists demonstrate how past cultural formations, popular or otherwise, alter contemporary ways of thinking about the relation of history to culture. This work continues the scope of intellectual inquiry urged by theorists such as Williams, whose commitment to Marxist and left-wing philosophies in general implies a thorough and exhaustive analysis of historical cultural formations.[32]

As the general relation between history and culture has been neglected by contemporary cultural studies, so too have specific aspects of that relation. For Anglo-Saxonists trained on a long familiarity with Christian literature, one aspect in particular stands out: that between the cultural processes of a society and its religious beliefs. The neglect of this relation in cultural studies is also in striking contrast to the recent proliferation of postmodern studies of theology and of the anthropology of religion, which are only now beginning to influence cultural and critical interpretation (e.g., Earl, 1986; Coward and Foshay, 1992; Taylor, 1984; Winquist, 1995; Asad, 1993). In fact, anthropology has always recognized that the beliefs of a society offer an important repertoire for its cultural meanings, although anthropology has conventionally taken the cultures of non-Western societies as its object of study.

Like culture, religious belief is subject to change (that is, to history) and therefore constitutive, constructing a view of the sacred that is operative in the world. That view cannot be analyzed as wholly distinct from other cultural products, such as literature, or from other formations, such as the social or the political.[33] This remains the case even in contemporary Western secular societies where belief is constructed primarily as a matter of private, individual concern, in contradistinction to, and therefore competing with, state practices and policies. Recurrent conflicts over this assumed separation of church and state in contemporary America are pointed reminders of the continual contestation of these two spheres. In Christian societies such as medieval England, moreover, belief is intimately related to social practice. Christianity organizes belief as the dominant form of knowledge in this period. It is this knowledge—Christian knowledge—that structures (though not without struggle) sociopolitical theory and praxis no less than cultural expression. The study of medieval culture without the study of belief and its formations makes little sense; contemporary theories of culture risk a similar partiality.

Neglect of the relationship between religion and culture in cultural studies may be due in part to its emphasis on contemporary secular societies in the West. But a similar neglect is evident in other varieties of critical theory, which also ignore or resist examination of religious modes of thought and expression. A good example of the critical tendency to divorce formal aesthetics from belief (and both from their historical context) is offered by Jonathan Culler in his meditation on the relation between love and literature. Taking the poetry of Gerard Manley Hopkins as his example, Culler considers "the question of poetry one knows by heart—a preeminent case of love of literature—but whose social or political implications one may deplore."[34] His analysis attempts to distinguish the aesthetic pleasure of Hopkins's language from its religious content, which leaves Culler "cold" (1994, 6).

Cold indeed. Unable to address questions such as the Resurrection—central to Hopkins's poetry—Culler dismisses them as "wishful" and hypersentimental (1994, 7, 8). I do not challenge Culler's right to find the content of religious poetry deplorable or sentimental, but distaste is not an a priori reason for ignoring either its content or its apparent sentimentality in favor of its form and aesthetic. The danger, of course, is that religious expression is left unexamined, whatever one's political views or aesthetic taste. Caroline Walker Bynum's important work on medieval belief in the resurrected body (1995) sharpens the danger by providing a compelling account of the historical trajectory of a belief that Culler cannot contemplate.[35] More generally, all medievalists are aware of the powerful relation between religion and literature. Aesthetic pleasure can be divorced from religious content and historical moment, but that divorce hardly makes for coherent critical analysis, as the best critics of Hopkins or other religious poetry such as *Paradise Lost* also know. Nor is religious poetry adequately explored by the kinds of critical practices often popular in Anglo-Saxon studies, such as the identification of the sources or origins of a particular doctrine or ritual, vital though they are to the formation of an interpretation. Poetry, aesthetics, and the Word are close relatives, and for good reason.

In spite of the strenuous efforts of Williams and more recently Terry Eagleton, the study of aesthetics (sometimes engaged by that close cousin of cultural studies, reception theory) has also failed to attract the attention it should.[36] How aesthetic form and aesthetic pleasure affect and are part of the material production of cultural phenomena requires further analysis, especially in relation to specific historical formations such as religion. As Culler's essay indicates, aesthetics is still seen as the product of conventional, nonmaterial ways of interpreting written works, especially canonical works. Anglo-Saxonists have sometimes traveled down the same path. Yet no study of culture can afford to ignore the significance of form to the production and appreciation of art, whether canonical or noncanonical, poetry or prose, religious or nonreligious.

This book argues that religious belief is not just a theology or a textual effect—a theological or readerly response to a body of sacred works—it is also a psychological, social, historical, and cultural phenomenon. If cultural studies is serious about the study of culture, then history, aesthetics, and belief are urgent, interrelated areas of inquiry. For reasons of its own cultural distinctiveness, and as a strategic intervention in the dominance of contemporary cultures within cultural studies, religious vernacular writing of the early medieval period offers a good place to take up that inquiry.

# CHAPTER 1

# Tradition, Literature, History

*Hos namque auctores in hac explanatione sumus secuti. uidelicet
Augustinum. ypponiensem. Hieronimum. Bedam. Gregorium.
Smaragdum, et aliquando Hægmonem; Horum denique auctoritas ab
omnibus catholicis. libentissime suscipitur; Nec solum euangeliorum
tractatus in isto libello exposuimus. uerum etiam sanctorum passiones
uel uitas ad utilitatem idiotarum istius gentis;*

*[For, indeed, we have followed these authors in this exposition: namely,
Augustine of Hippo, Jerome, Bede, Gregory, Smaragdus, and sometimes
Haymo, for the authority of these is most willingly acknowledged by all
the orthodox. We have not only expounded homilies on the gospels in
this book but also the passions or lives of the saints for the benefit of the
uneducated among this people.]¹*
— Ælfric, Preface to the First Series of *Catholic Homilies*

Late Anglo-Saxon sermons, homilies, and saints' lives are a genre of
religious writing best described as traditional. The very workings
of tradition in this genre have obscured its newness in England,
however. While the texts themselves regularly conform to the generic
conventions of Latin sermons and indeed depend on the works of the
Fathers for their spiritual and intellectual authority, they are written in
English. Ælfric's Latin preface to his First Series of *Catholic Homilies*,
quoted in the epigraph, neatly points out this paradox, whereby his homilies make the Latin "auctores" available for a vernacular audience. English is not the transcultural language of the church, nor are vernacular
sermons intended to participate only in this universalized elite culture.
Sermons, homilies, and saints' lives written in English in the late Anglo-
Saxon period speak primarily to the Anglo-Saxons.

If the significance of the vernacularity of these works and their dating to a specific time within the Anglo-Saxon period has been little appreciated, so too has been the force of their traditionality.² The texts themselves inhabit a tradition. For this reason, their traditionality has seemed
so self-evident as to be critically uncontentious and thus poorly understood. Only when traditions fail or are challenged does their traditionality
come into critical view. Alasdair MacIntyre reminds us, however, that
"[t]o those who inhabit a social and intellectual tradition in good working order the facts of tradition, which are the presupposition of their ac-

tivities and enquiries, may well remain just that, unarticulated presuppositions which are never themselves the objects of attention and enquiry" (MacIntyre, 1988, 7–8).[3] This is the paradox of traditional formations; their apparent universality has its own history, and is therefore a product of material history. A study of the sermons must take account of the "unarticulated presuppostions" and conventions that signify their use of a tradition "in good working order" within a specific historical and cultural formation. From the perspective of the twentieth century, English vernacular writing of the tenth century is a new development of the Christian tradition of preaching in Latin.

Similar to English sermons of the later Middle Ages in content if not form, Anglo-Saxon texts are conservative. They depend for their authority on a body of Latin Christian doctrine and exemplary writing reiterated over the centuries and transmitted into English in the form of commentaries, commonplace books, florilegia, hagiographical collections, and homiliaries. Study of this genre has concentrated therefore on the analysis of its Latin sources, commonplaces, motifs, phrases, and habitual associations of idea and doctrine. This scholarship has had far-reaching implications for the analysis of other genres. In the case of the later English Middle Ages, the study of the relation between sermons and vernacular literature initiated by G. R. Owst (1926, 1933) has profound consequences for our understanding of writers like Langland and Chaucer, as well as for genres such as the English medieval lyric (Woolf, 1968; Wenzel, 1978, 1986), notions of literacy and its uses, and understandings of the workings of orthodoxy and heterodoxy (Spencer, 1993). In the Anglo-Saxon period, study of the sermons has led to the identification of sources for and readings of canonical works like *Beowulf* (Wright, 1993, 106–36) and the *Christ* poems (Biggs, 1986; Hill, 1986; Clayton, 1990, 179–206), while the methodology of source study itself has championed new investigations into the literary culture of the Anglo-Saxons.[4] The importance of sermons for our understanding of other aspects of medieval literary culture has never been in doubt. By contrast, the importance of sermons per se as a major expression of that culture has rarely entered mainstream literary history. Few English sermons of any period within the medieval have canonical status.

We are faced with an intriguing problem of literary history: the study of sermons and other preaching works as an expression of religious culture throughout the English Middle Ages is a well-established, highly successful subfield within the discipline; at the same time, however, literary history has not served the study of religious preaching well.[5] Sermons, homilies, and saints' lives in this period are above all institutional and practical prose genres: they are not easily assimilable to the finely honed conventions of literary study that were developed for the interpretation of poetry and other "fictional" genres. Just as later medieval sermons are often marginal in the literary history of that period by virtue of their genre, so too Anglo-Saxon sermons are marginal to Anglo-Saxon literary history. But literary history has not well served the study of the Anglo-Saxon period itself, either. As an aspect of a period—Anglo-Saxon— that is often presented as tangential to the concerns of mainstream English medievalists, the genre of preaching has been doubly marginalized.

The significance of this double marginalization should not preoccupy us for long. Some of the reasons for the relative lack of attention paid to the Anglo-Saxon period are disciplinary and institutional. Their analysis has been well begun by the work of Allen J. Frantzen (1990, 1–26, 201– 26), among others, in a critical climate characterized by disciplinary and methodological reevaluation. More important, the study of religious genres like preaching has yet to participate in this reassessment. Traditional and popular genres in fact challenge the intellectual assumptions upon which English literary history still rests. Anglo-Saxon sermons offer a limit case with which to explore the implications of the rewriting of English literary history already well under way for better-known literary formations.

To study the "traditionality of tradition" (Shils, 1981, 4) in Christian preaching texts is to analyze a discourse that presents the past as a repository of normative guidelines for Christian belief and action in the Anglo-Saxon present. Preaching makes calculated use of specific institutional forms of writing—the sermon, the homily, the saint's life—to create and foster Christian belief. The analysis of such a genre intersects with that of literature in its use of particular forms and conventions, but also with those of social history and theology, since its history is connected to the institutional and cultural phenomenon of medieval Christianity in the West. From an analytical stance, the primary importance of the traditionality of Anglo-Saxon preaching is its paradoxical use of universalizing conventions and presuppositions in a specific historical period. Cultural analysis of a genre like preaching, in other words, must be interdisciplinary. The problem that such an analysis poses for the writing of a literary history that includes preaching is considerable.

It is understandable, therefore, that English literary history has regularly gestured toward a description of preaching but, at the same time, has not succeeded in fully incorporating it. Literary history for the English medieval period has had little use for the popular, the traditional, or the institutional. This is not the case for all literary histories of this period, however. Spanish literary historiography since its inception in the early nineteenth century has always privileged traditional and popular forms such as the ballad and "la lírica tradicional"—though here, too, the study of sermons has been a secondary concern. Conventional English literary history prizes the unique and the original—the new. By contrast, the Spanish "literary genius" has often been characterized as inherently popular.[6] Now that the paradigms of canon formation, periodization, and literary historiography that characterize the English medieval period are under intense scrutiny, the function of tradition in literary history and beyond it can be reassessed. This chapter examines that function first in relation to Anglo-Saxon preaching works and then considers the ways in which the evidence of their traditionality modifies the assumptions of later medieval literary history. It concludes with a brief study of how theories of tradition challenge the workings of postmodern theory. Serving as a prolegomenon to the more detailed analysis of preaching as a traditional genre in the rest of this book, this chapter is also intended to provoke general theoretical debate about the significance of the traditional. Few subjects could seem less promising in a critical climate that often emphasizes not the traditionality of the past, but its newness.

## Traditional Approaches to Old English Preaching Texts

It is an irony of literary history that its traditional emphases do not work well for traditional texts. One of the pieties of Anglo-Saxon literary history is that this period sees the production of the first and largest body of vernacular writing in Western Europe, yet, because this writing is overwhelmingly religious prose, this important insight has been difficult to develop.[7] The problem in part is one of genre. A standard of literary value that privileges poetry cannot accommodate so readily didactic prose; we all know *Beowulf*, but religious prose is for the specialists. As Anglo-Saxonists are increasingly aware, however, the binary division of Anglo-Saxon writing into poetry and prose is not always helpful when tested against the manuscript evidence.

Some of the best-known manuscripts of Anglo-Saxon poetry are not just manuscripts of Anglo-Saxon poetry. In contrast to the Junius and Exeter collections, the tenth-century Vercelli Book contains a mixture of religious poetry and homiletic prose (Sisam, 1976; Scragg, 1992). Note, too, that the *Beowulf* codex at one stage in its history contained a version of the *Life of St. Christopher,* the prose *Wonders of the East,* the *Letter of Alexander to Aristotle,* and the fragmentary *Judith* (Ker 216; Kiernan, 1981; Lucas, 1990).[8] Nor is it entirely clear from even these well-known poetic codices that there exists a rigorous cultural distinction between subjects felt to be appropriate to poetry and those more appropriate to prose; some of the items written in the Anglo-Saxon poetic style in the Exeter Book, for example, are often described with good reason as homiletic.[9]

The situation is more complex for those manuscripts conventionally regarded as prose or homiletic collections. Alfred writes both poetry and prose (in the same works); poetry is incorporated into the prose *Anglo-Saxon Chronicle;* and homilies and sermons are found in collections generally known as poetic, as already indicated.[10] Not all prose collections conform easily to the structure of homiliary, that is, according to the liturgical days of the Christian calendar—the "temporale" (masses and liturgical days distinct from the feasts of the saints) and "sanctorale" (the calendar of saints' days). Sermon collections include saints' lives; collections of saints' lives include homilies.[11] Saints' lives take both poetic and nonpoetic forms, as the poetic and prose lives of Guthlac remind us (Roberts, 1979; Scragg, 1992, XXIII), while religious prose can take on a poetic cast, as in the examples of the rhythmical styles crafted by Ælfric and Wulfstan.[12] The distinction between prose and poetry appears to collapse altogether for some late texts, where a "poetic" form is often allied with a "prosaic," religious content. Description by genre is also dubious for several religious manuscripts that include a heterogeneous mix of languages (Latin and Old English) and forms: liturgical and nonliturgical writings, grammatical treatises, letters, prayers, and prognostications, to name a few examples.[13]

Although this evidence must not be pushed too far, there are nevertheless limits to the usefulness of classification by form or genre for many Anglo-Saxon texts. This is an argument more often rehearsed for the poetry than for the prose (Bragg, 1991; Pasternack, 1995, 8–28). The problem of classification is also familiar to many later medievalists, who have long recognized that medieval poetry, for example, is used for a wider range of subjects than those deemed appropriate on the basis of post-Romantic literary assumptions. Yet the aesthetic implications of this insight have rarely been examined. Siegfried Wenzel is one of the few medievalists to explore the implications of the admixture of forms both poetic and prosaic in later medieval sermon collections such as the *Fasciculus morum*. Wenzel notes that the aesthetic upon which so much literary history is predicated "tends to neglect wide areas of poetic activity by its distinction between 'literary' and 'didactic' styles or between the 'religious' and the 'moral' lyric—distinctions which no medieval author would have thought of" (1978, 132).

Similar comments hold true for the Anglo-Saxon period; the critical evaluation of cultural products by genre sometimes obscures a slightly different emphasis in the culture itself. Generalizations based on form are contrasted by those based on a style that can traverse the generic boundaries between poetry and prose: alliteration. That all Anglo-Saxon poetry uses the alliterative line in some way or another has been emphasized at the cost of recognizing that alliteration is also an important cultural marker in the prose. In vernacular writing, alliteration often signals that which is culturally significant or memorable; this can be the case for the laws, prayers, proverbs, and homilies or saints' lives as well as the poetry, even though prose alliteration is not as rigorously metrical as poetic and does not deploy a poetic vocabulary.

Nonetheless, the conventional distinction between poetry and prose has important merits. Literary scholars must have ways of reading texts, and Anglo-Saxonists are no exception. Moreover, few Anglo-Saxonists are scholars of both poetry and prose. The study of Old English is primarily the business of departments of English; our methods of analysis therefore are unashamedly literary, literary historical, and philological. Viewed from the standpoint of the history of Anglo-Saxon studies, two trends of interpretation have evolved in response to this fundamental generic division: one—for the poetry—is more formally literary, often New Critical, and more recently textual, while the other—for the prose—is philological in its broadest sense, often exegetical, and based on the identification of sources. Literary histories for the Anglo-Saxon period maintain these two distinctions and foreground the poetry rather than the prose. Such binary divisions structure vernacular written culture hierarchically rather than dialectically. The prose is often viewed as background material or context for the poetry, while the poetry is often presented as radically other to the prose. The traffic tends to go in this one direction. Literary readings of homiletic texts have not proved particularly successful, progressing little further than the thematic studies of Marcia Dalbey on the Blickling Homilies (1973, 1978, 1980) or the richly suggestive though not widely appreciated studies of Ælfric by, for example, Peter Clemoes (e.g., 1966) and, increasingly, Malcolm Godden (e.g., 1990).

As a result, interpretations derived from the poetry are rarely assessed in relation to those from the prose, even when both genres are found in the same cultural milieu. This process makes it difficult to identify and assess connections across genres. To the example of alliteration can be added the concept of authorship. In the prose corpus, we find named writers—Alfred, Wulfstan, Byrhtferth (Baker and Lapidge, 1995), Ælfric—whereas the poetic corpus is largely anonymous or pseudonymous. That Alfred is both a named poet and writer of prose is rarely considered, as James W. Earl (1994, 87–89) points out, while Carol Braun Pasternack (1995, 12–21, 90–119) argues with conviction that the concept of an author function needs careful nuance in the case of Old English poetry. The full cultural significance of named and anonymous writing across poetry and prose has yet to be assessed.

Where the religious prose is concerned, the evidence of named writers structures its own literary history. Literary history generally presents the student of the poetry with the four major codices of Anglo-Saxon poetry; the student of the prose is offered two manuscript collections—the earlier tenth-century Vercelli and Blickling codices—and the two later-tenth-century, early-eleventh-century authored collections of Ælfric and Wulfstan. From these collections and their dates are derived the convenient subdivision of the genre into anonymous and authored texts. Anonymous homilies, of course, do occur in author-associated homiletic compilations and vice versa, and there is considerable contact between these subdivisions: anonymous homilies rewrite authored texts; Wulfstan plunders Ælfric's (cf. Lees, 1991, 162–68). Conventional literary history is well equipped to deal with concepts of authorship and associated notions of corpora, even for writers whose work is less obviously literary. As a result, Ælfric and Wulfstan are well-known figures within Anglo-Saxon

literary history, and the establishment of their oeuvres and their methods of composition is one of the major achievements of the discipline.
We are now in a position to consider whether or not concepts of authorship are in fact culturally valid for these writers, as Joyce Hill does
(1994).[14] This approach to the homiletic corpus, however, is less successful for anonymous works, which are often dispersed across a number of
manuscripts and whose stylistic features have made it difficult to identify groups of texts that may be composed by one writer (although there
have been some recent successes, for which see Wilcox, 1991, 1992, and
Cross et al., 1996).

As is the case with the generic division of Anglo-Saxon writing into
poetry and prose, the tendency to subdivide the prose corpus into anonymous and named collections results in a hierarchy of critical value, which
in this case is confirmed by dating and the methods of source study. Relatively speaking, the prose is easier to date than the poetry, since the implementation of the Benedictine reform offers a practical guideline to
homiletic production. The earlier Blickling and Vercelli collections represent the anonymous tradition of homiletic prose, most often held to
be prereform. Evidence of source study for these works indicates an emphasis on apocrypha, often featuring Insular or Irish concerns and topoi
and a generally unremarkable Latinity. The later authored collections of
Ælfric and Wulfstan represent the newer tradition of homiletic prose,
influenced by the revival of Latinity and ecclesiastical orthodoxy generated by the Benedictine reform. These works consistently demonstrate
a much higher level of Latin scholarship, a concern with accuracy and
authority, and a more consistent use of form, whether exegetical or catechetical.[15] Since it is easier to assess the works of Wulfstan and Ælfric
in relation to their sources, it is no surprise that their works are better
known.

The study of Latin and vernacular sources, which works so well for
Ælfric and Wulfstan, is the principal critical methodology for all Anglo-
Saxon preaching texts. These texts are related closely to the liturgical
year (to their feast day or to the pericope — the scriptural reading for the
day — or both), and their exegetical and hagiographical forms clearly depend on prior texts and prior authorities. Therefore, identification of
pre-texts — often Latin sources — dominates their analysis. This methodology brings the textual world of the Anglo-Saxon homily into direct relation with that of Latin Western Christendom, enabling the documen-
tation and assessment of the range of Latin texts available to English
writers in the period. Accordingly, the search for the contexts of Anglo-
Saxon preaching texts has become increasingly more specific, though only
in one direction. Reading the homilies means a particular kind of comparative textual analysis.[16]

The value of source analysis for the two major authors, Ælfric and
Wulfstan, lies in its contributions to our understanding of the develop-

ment of their careers (offering in each case evidence for a canon of texts unique in the early medieval period).[17] Source analysis of their works also provides a comparative standard for the anonymous texts of the same period—rhetorically and in terms of composition and content. Held against the standard of Latinity of Wulfstan and Ælfric, the anonymous homilies are frequently found wanting. At the same time, the homilies in general have been rightly mined for their attitudes toward such key theological and liturgical issues as eschatology, the Eucharist, Rogationtide, Marian worship, and penance, to name but a few examples (Gatch, 1965, 1977, 61–116; Grundy, 1991; Bazire and Cross, 1982; Clayton, 1990; Frantzen, 1983). The saints' lives offer instances of the development of narrative form (again via comparison of text with source wherever possible) and a body of textual material to place side by side with other evidence for the cult of saints (Woolf, 1966; Gaites, 1982; Ridyard, 1988; Rollason, 1989a).

This methodology works. The period of the late-tenth and early-eleventh centuries is, after all, that of the Benedictine reform or revival, which witnesses an increasing monastic purchase on the church and its copartner, the ruling dynasty of the West Saxons, fortified by the premises and goals of the Benedictine rule. As the term *revival* suggests, the theological, liturgical, and doctrinal content of the homilies is most often understood in terms of its relation to prior movements (most notably, the Carolingian reforms) and the prior authority of the Church Fathers. The content of the homilies, understood as theological rather than more generally religious, parallels and reinforces the study of their sources. Theological and patristic studies, furthermore, derive text-internal support from these Anglo-Saxon texts, which frequently refer to the Fathers and draw on conventional exegesis of Scripture for their authority. But the homilies are not simply the modulations of a theology honed over the centuries, any more than they are parasite versions of their Latin textual antecedents. When Anglo-Saxon writers wish to contribute to liturgical or theological debate, they write in Latin, not English; source analysis downplays the cultural significance of the language of preaching.

For all the success that the analysis of patristic sources offers the critical appreciation of Anglo-Saxon preaching texts, therefore, there are limitations. This paradigm tends to emphasize the textuality of contexts rather than the performance of texts. As a result, the homilies become a locus for tradition, yet this important insight has only been explored with reference to their textual antecedents. Homilies are indeed conservative in content, but too exclusive an emphasis on the sources of a text can evoke a tradition of intertextuality that is in fact timeless and ahistorical. MacIntyre (1988) stresses, by contrast, that traditions have their own history, however much their conventions work to obscure it.

So, too, discussion of literary value in a paradigm that emphasizes the poetry tends to deflect attention away from the cultural significance of the prose. The homilies are read as evidence for something else, something other than preaching, whether that something is a context for the poetry or material for theological analysis. This process obscures the "facts of the tradition," to recall MacIntyre (1988, 7), at work within the genre itself—its uses of conventions and presuppositions. Anglo-Saxon preaching is held to be utilitarian, nonliterary, by the critic, and is proved to be traditional by the student of patristics. Armed with a methodological apparatus that presents tradition as closed and timeless, rather than dynamic and historical, this approach has a powerful disabling effect on the interpretation of Anglo-Saxon religious prose, which appears stultified by the dead weight of the past and alien to modern taste.

Much has been and will continue to be learned from the conventional analyses of traditional genres that literary history produces. Yet in identifying their sense of timelessness, their repetitive form and content, and their uneasy relation to more apparently literary genres, Anglo-Saxon literary history fails to understand that these features are conscious functions of traditionality itself.

## The Consolation of Tradition

When traditional prose is judged by standards alien to it, such as an aesthetic derived from the poetry, or is assessed only in terms of its pre-texts, it is hard to grasp its historical and social meanings. This approach often naturalizes the complex historical processes whereby Old English writers re-present—rather than copy or translate literally—the works of the Latin Fathers. Restoring this textual tradition to history, however, modifies our understanding of homilies, sermons, and saints' lives. These texts are not simply the reworkings of the Latin Church Fathers, even when (or perhaps especially when) their content appears to point in this direction, for the simple reason that the historical and cultural conditions of the Benedictine reform are not synonymous with those of the earlier Carolingian reforms. Similarly, knowledge of the history of the production and reception of these texts within the Anglo-Saxon period needs to be central to our inquiries. The two literary-historical traditions of anonymous and named works within this genre are modified by the fact that many anonymous works circulate side by side with those of the reform period. Since this period also witnesses the production of all the major poetic manuscripts, the ground is cleared for a reassessment of the functions of both prose and poetry within the late Anglo-Saxon period. The turn to history from literary history paves the way for a study of traditionality as a cultural formation.

The perspective of culture makes the case for a reexamination of the most conventional historical sense of the traditional as the "traditum," a thing handed down from past to present. Edward Shils points out that, although a tradition has custodians, facilitates identification, and generates lines of affiliation, "[t]he decisive criterion is that, having been created through human actions, through thought and imagination, it is handed down from one generation to the next" (1981, 12). This simplest and most powerful ideological effect of tradition is vastly underestimated by literary history, which uses tradition as a term of negative aesthetic judgment rather than as an instrument in the analysis of a sociohistorical process. But, in fact, the "traditum" can be a cultural product like a sermon, which associates texts with events, writing with history and memory, the past with the present. Shils points out that anything can be a "traditum", but once accepted as a living and hence changing tradition, "it is as vivid and vital to those who accept it as any other part of their action or belief. It is the past in the present but it is as much part of the present as any recent innovation" (1981, 13). Christian texts like sermons are classic examples of "tradita"; after all, tradition is central to Christianity, where the past is connected to the present via a body of texts and via the practices of worship codified by the conventions of the liturgy within communities of believers.

The process by which a tradition is handed down from generation to generation is a selective one, however much it is formed and guided by past experiences, ideas, or artifacts that present themselves to the present as natural and universal. The selectivity of traditions is demonstrated as much by those traditions constructed by literary scholarship as those excluded from it; consider how often the canon of Anglo-Saxon literature traditionally excludes religious prose. Tradition does not mean that everything stays the same; traditions selectively reproduce the past in order to evoke an impression of sameness. This impression of continuity — however illusory — is manifestly experienced, and the powerful process whereby this illusion is maintained is best described in cultural terms, as Raymond Williams argues:

> For tradition is in practice the most evident expression of the dominant and hegemonic pressures and limits. It is always more than an inert historicized segment; indeed it is the most powerful practical means of incorporation. What we have to see is not just "a tradition" but a *selective tradition:* an intentionally selective version of a shaping past and a pre-shaped present, which is then powerfully operative in the process of social and cultural definition and identification. (1977, 115; emphasis in original)

The ideological process of tradition not only selects from the past in order to maintain an impression of continuity in the present but, at the same time, evokes identification of the individual with social *and* cultural institutions. For both Williams and Shils, this process of identification, vital for the survival of certain formations or institutions, accounts for the power of the traditional. The key to understanding the persistence of traditional institutional genres resides in cultural analysis. It is equally important to stress, however, that both Williams and Shils are outlining from different theoretical perspectives what are in fact complex historical processes.[18] Each instance of tradition must therefore be examined individually.

The first component in a cultural study of the traditionality of Anglo-Saxon sermons and saints' lives is a simple one. Fundamental to readings of the homilies has been the recognition of the conventionality of their form.[19] Anglo-Saxon homilies share a general religious subject and a didactic function, but they also share specific practices, forms, themes, and motifs. Reading across the corpus rather than within its subgroups is an exercise in familiarization with the conventions of its Christian discourse. This familiarity is a response perhaps analogous to that of the significance of the alliterative poetic line; alliteration is as important to Anglo-Saxon poetry as conventionality is to the religious prose. The obvious needs to be stated: the conventionality of homiletic and hagiographic genres is a deliberate effect and a direct product of their institutional function as didactic performative works.

Conventions of genre enable homilies, sermons, and saints' lives to present themselves as part of a much broader tradition of preaching and commentary in the early medieval church, from which they derive their ecclesiastical authority and moral impetus. The repetitive nature of form, in other words, is one product of the process by which the present is affiliated with the past. This is a feature of traditionality in general, as Shils argues. In the case of homilies and saints' lives, affiliation is not just observable in their conventionality of form, but in the conventions of their manuscript contexts. These two conventions—form and manuscript context—are, of course, interrelated.

Homiletic texts—exegetical, catechetical, and hagiographical—are most often found in manuscript collections structured around the liturgical calendar, however loosely (cf. Gatch, 1977, 27–47). Arranged in sequences that reflect the "temporale" or "sanctorale" (or both), most homilies are rubricated for the annual cycle of services and feast days that is the backbone of Christian worship. Although there are important exceptions, such as the Vercelli homilies, this general principle is useful whether or not such collections were actually intended for delivery in church (even if individual minsters and churches did not observe the same feasts and masses), in either monastic or nonmonastic contexts.[20] These prose texts, in sum, are products of the cycle of annual Christian worship, reenacted day by day, week by week. The liturgy of the church is its central enactment of traditional belief as lived, which is structured according to sacred history (discussed further in chapter 2).

What is repetitive at the level of the structure and genre of the sermon collection (that is, the ordering of collections according to liturgical or generic principles) is also repetitive at the level of the structure and genre of the individual text. Although exegesis is certainly not a method of explication unique to the homily, since it comprises the main method of interpretation of Christian texts throughout the medieval period, the exegetical interpretation of scriptural texts is a common subgenre in homily collections. Indeed, exegetical sermons or "homilia" form a specific branch of general Christian exegesis: the lection or pericope of the day (the scriptural pre-text) is announced, recited, or translated at the beginning of the text, and thereafter forms the basis for the homily itself, which concludes with a moral exhortation and doxology (a short closing formula praising God). In the Anglo-Saxon period, Ælfric is the classic exponent of exegesis, though this form is often found in the anonymous works as well.

Catechetical sermons, to adopt Gatch's terminology, allow for more flexibility of structure, but still emphasize the doctrinal, instructional value of the articles of the faith—the Ten Commandments, the Creed, the coming of the Last Judgment, for example (Gatch, 1977, 37; cf. Day, 1974). This is a form favored by Wulfstan, though it is used to great effect by Ælfric and also found in the anonymous works. Concentrating on episodic narrative rather than explication, the saint's life is also dependent on prior texts, whether it takes the form of "passio" or "vita" (and these generic distinctions between narratives of death and of life are hardly systematic). The ultimate pre-text for a saint's life is, of course, Christ's, filtered through such exemplars as the lives of Anthony and Martin. These exemplars act as retrospective reference points for the form and for the interpretation of each subsequent life, primarily through the reiteration of hagiographical motives and miracles (Woolf, 1966; Lapidge, 1991).

In each case—exegetical, catechetical, or hagiographic—the effect of similarity or conventionality of form is uppermost, and is produced by systematic methods of composition. These effects of tradition are not restricted only to specific feasts and pericopes, but extend also to themes and motifs. While it is true that apocryphal themes, such as those of the soul and body, are found only in anonymous works (including the poetry), the theological division of soul and body is everywhere explicit in Ælfric's writing. Similarly, although Ælfric does not use the signs of the Last Judgment in the form favored by the anonymous homilists, his use of the relevant scriptural passage (such as Matthew 24:29) is another indication of shared interest.[21] Cases can also be made for Descent into Hell topoi and for a general interest in visions of the Other World, even while Ælfric replaces the favored *Visio Pauli* with visions such as Drihthelm's that for him carry greater authority. All the main branches of the homiletic tradition are concerned with eschatology, as Milton McC. Gatch's studies (1965; 1977, 61–116) demonstrate. The six ages of the world, the vices and virtues, the motif of the groups at the Last Judgment, among others, are generic features common to both named and anonymous writers.[22] The iteration of these conventions produces consistency and stability, fostering recognition: the consolation of tradition. As these conventions suggest and the frequent evidence of borrowing and rewriting confirms, there is considerable flexibility and interchange between the uses of convention in homily, sermon, and life across the anonymous and named corpus (e.g., Godden, 1975; Scragg, 1977; Lees, 1986, 1988; Clayton, 1986; Wilcox, 1991). There are significant differences of attitude expressed toward such conventional knowledge—every tradition has room for necessary internal conflict—but these differences must not be pursued at the cost of obscuring general similarities. The case for Ælfric's distrust of the anonymous tradition and its taste for apocrypha is modified by the fact that he is also in debate with his contemporaries. Ælfric is not only rewriting what is now perceived as the "earlier" anonymous tradition, but is also prescribing orthodox Benedictine practice. That he does not seem to have won this debate, either, is revealed by the persistent homiletic interest in, for example, the *Visio Pauli* and the Marian apocrypha as well as by the evidence of preaching practices for Holy Week in spite of Ælfric's proscriptions (Hill, 1985; Godden, 1978; Clayton, 1990, 260–65; Wright, 1993, 228–29).

Though the purpose and function of individual collections and texts varies, the governing methods of composition remain remarkably stable. Examples of variant vernacular texts indicate a primary concern with compilation in the anonymous writing paralleled by the evidence of postreform works. The identification of the Pembroke Sermonary as a source for some of the anonymous homilies is an example of a broader phenomenon (Cross, 1987). Ælfric also draws on prior collections, such as those of Paulus Diaconus, the Cotton-Corpus Legendary, and Smaragdus, but he also compiles his own commonplace books—for both the English saints in Paris, BN lat. 5362, and for eschatological subjects in Boulogne-sur-Mer, Bibl. mun. 63 (Förster, 1894; Smetana, 1959, 1961; Zettel, 1982; Hill, 1992a; Lapidge and Winterbottom, 1991, cxlvi–cxlix; Jackson and Lapidge, 1996). This is a method of compilation also favored by Wulfstan (Bethurum, 1942; Cross, 1992). Michael Lapidge's suggestion (1988) that Ælfric learned his scholarship from Æthelwold is certainly compelling, but fails to take into account the similarities in working practices across the homiletic corpus in texts not known to be associated with the reform school. Without doubt, the standard methods of composition for the homilies are neither copying nor literal translation, but a combination of translation, interpretation, and compilation. These methods of prose composition are perhaps analogous to the repetitive use of formulae, themes, type scenes, and genres in the poetic corpus. Anglo-Saxon poetry also, though differently, makes use of traditionality. In both prose and poetry, the use of a particular convention resonates against other possibilities, offering a web of conventions that testify to an aesthetic. Overall, it remains a useful generalization that the structure of

Anglo-Saxon preaching texts is short (the length being directly related to the presumed circumstances of their delivery or performance), relatively simple, highly repetitive, seemingly static, and yet productive of a considerable variety of individual examples.[23]

Stable practices of composition at the level of genre predict the phenomenon of reusability across it. The Blickling and Vercelli Books have a number of variant texts and analogues, while variant versions of these works are also found in collections chiefly known for their Ælfrician or Wulfstanian contents (cf. Scragg, 1979, 1996). Moreover, "pure" witnesses to Ælfric's series of *Catholic Homilies* are rare by contrast with the differing recensions of his works, which reorder and rework what appears to have been his original intentions. The concept of a "pure" authorial collection is only one facet of the manuscript evidence. Ælfric's prefaces, which announce his original (though not necessarily final) intentions and authorship, have a far more restricted circulation than the texts themselves (even while they clearly carry the authority of an Ælfrician persona). Ælfric himself continued to work on and revise his collections well after their initial "publication," as did Wulfstan in the case of his *Sermo Lupi*. Reusability is as important a feature of Wulfstan's writing as it is of Ælfric's.[24]

Such use of conventions is a reminder of the primacy of a Christian discourse tacitly assumed to be natural. Naturalization, which contemporary critics register largely by comments about conservatism and repetition, is a sign that the genre has been firmly established within English religious culture. Preaching is the primary medium through which belief, by the use of conventions, is ratified and made coherent. Conventions are means of empowering the Christian community by encoding "an assumption or point of view, so that the work can be made and received," as Raymond Williams puts it (1977, 179). That English homilists are selective about their use of conventions is thus a feature of their traditionality.

## Language and Style

As an aspect of traditionality, the use of conventions affiliates preaching materials to the elite scholarly traditions of the early church. Because this affiliation is intentional, it has been hard to suggest that the homilies are a popular genre. Homiletic writing is not a cultural form generated by the people for the people, as my introduction pointed out. The evidence of the considerable numbers of these texts suggests popularity, but the popularity of an elite form — a measure therefore of the success of the church's preaching mission. The affiliation with the past traditions of the church that this genre depends upon is complemented by a process of incorporation with the present so that it can be perceived as both popular and elite: in short, traditional, timeless, and conservative. The incorporation of the past with the present is successful, as is demonstrated not only by the reusability of the form, but also by the annual cycles of worship to which these texts are affiliated in their manuscripts. This success also depends to a large extent on the efficiency with which preaching materials elicit identification with the church and its beliefs. The other factors that foster identification and contribute to the effect of popularity within traditionality are choice of language and style.

As already noted, the fundamental importance of the Anglo-Saxon homiletic corpus, in contrast with other early medieval cultures, lies in its use of the vernacular in contexts where Latin otherwise prevails. But rarely has this difference been analyzed in terms other than those of direct substitution of the vernacular for Latin contexts and domains. The homilists, in short, are seen as continuing the tradition of Latin preaching in English. This important insight ignores, however, cultural differences between source and text by concentrating instead on their evident textual similarities.

The most obvious of these cultural differences is language use (Waterhouse, 1989; cf. Lees, 1991). Writers such as Gregory of Tours, Caesarius of Arles, or the anonymous compiler of the influential Pembroke Sermonary (all of whom furnish sources for Anglo-Saxon vernacular texts) develop a new form of didactic preaching and instruction in Latin. This form is marked by its relatively simple structure and language and appears to be the precedent for vernacular preaching styles. But these newer forms of instruction in Latin do not testify easily to a decline in Latin Christian learning that might explain the replacement of the vernacular for Latin in religious domains. Gregory of Tours and Caesarius of Arles—both highly educated men—are fully conscious of the difference in audience that such style-switching implies (Gurevich, 1988, 12–21; Cross, 1987, 57–61). In continental contexts, the use of Latin for both learned and lay audiences can only be overcome by the preacher himself, who presumably translates these texts into vernacular Romance forms for preaching (McKitterick, 1977, 80–114; Wright, 1982). This situation, however, is not replicated by Anglo-Saxon homilists of the tenth and eleventh centuries, who write in English yet clearly wish to imitate their predecessors' texts in other regards.

Anglo-Saxon homilists are as alert to the relation between language choice and audience as are their continental models. Ælfric writes Latin prose of considerable sophistication as easily as he does his renowned English style, with a self-consciousness equal to that of Gregory of Tours or Bede.[25] But his language of preaching is English—a choice also made by all the vernacular homilists of Anglo-Saxon England. These homilists are responding to a radically different preaching context than that of their Latin "auctores," one heavily influenced by the achievements of Alfred and his circle in establishing the use of English for intellectual and religious inquiry.[26] This choice of English blurs distinctions between lay and learned, cleric and people, so evident in Latin works. Ælfric, for example, intends his First Series of the *Catholic Homilies* to be delivered directly to a congregation. By the time of the Second Series, however, his intentions have changed; these texts seem to offer a compendium for the preacher, who selects and sometimes edits relevant works for delivery (Godden, 1973a). The earlier Blickling Homilies, too, appear to be at least in part a collection for preachers (Gatch, 1989, 101–5). In addition, Ælfric's dedication of the *Lives of Saints* to his aristocratic lay patrons, Æthelweard and his son, Æthelmær, together with the considerable evidence for the rewriting and copying of homilies *in* the vernacular, suggests that English homilists were writing for multiple levels of intended readers, editors, and listeners.[27]

By transferring a body of theological doctrine from the Latin past to the Anglo-Saxon present, its meanings in English are newly refined, explored, and contested. Vernacular preaching incorporates elements of theological debate familiar from Latin commentaries, florilegia, and homiliaries, but since their context differs, so too does the nature of the debate. From now on in medieval culture, theological debate in Latin will run alongside that in vernacular preaching, in interrelated though separate domains.[28]

Put another way, the similarities that source analysis identifies between a vernacular text and a Latin source at the level of the word collapses differences between the same text and source at the level of discourse and culture. This may be especially true of those anonymous works so often held inferior to their Latin predecessors. Comparison between text and source has overlooked the major factors of intended reader, cleric, monk, audience, or congregation and their cultural milieu.

This is not to argue that conventional scholarship does not deal with questions of audience, but it does so within a paradigm of Latin transmission to English text that may obscure the dynamic of their reception in English and its significance. In a clerical discourse such as preaching, the choice of English is highly ideological. English fosters a sense of identification within a particular speech community across a range of audiences — clerical and lay, aristocratic and ecclesiastical — while downplaying the differences of social power between them. The use of the vernacular thereby creates a concept of an English Christian community, indicated by the frequently reiterated "we" of the homilies and sermons, which remains highly stratified (as we shall see in chapter 4).[29] English homilies are by no means democratic, nor is late Anglo-Saxon England an age of widespread vernacular literacy.

Equally important is the oral style of these highly literate texts. Sermons, homilies, and saints' lives alike are composed for oral delivery, even if this is a calculated fiction. Affiliated to the liturgy via their manuscript contexts, these works evoke an impression of immediate, contemporaneous participation in church services by using oral devices to create the illusion of a preaching voice addressing an implied audience.

Small wonder, then, that the best religious writers, Ælfric and Wulfstan, use alliteration—that most oral of styles—to enhance their style. The use of English in combination with an oral style, which is itself a prestigious cultural form in other vernacular contexts, is fundamental to the process whereby traditional genres foster and maintain identification within a specific group. In this case, the group so formed is that fostered by the idea of an English Christian community.

Precisely because the English "we" is affiliated to Latin traditions for preaching via conventions of form and context, scholars have underestimated what is radically new about Anglo-Saxon religious prose: its use of English and its use of a highly literate oral style. What is new, in short, is represented as traditional. The traditionality of this genre resides in its redeployment of Christian knowledge according to tradition-dependent rules in new contexts. Even more important, these textual features of traditionality—of form, context, language choice, and style—serve a supratextual function; preaching works are performative events. Their purpose is twofold. Preaching texts offer a forum for communal worship (the English "we"), and, at the same time, they provide instruction in the faith that offers guidelines for moral action in the world.

In preaching texts, the traditional structures of Christian worship and didactic instruction are made manifest in a natural, or perhaps naturalized, lived experience of the faith. These texts, in other words, offer evidence of living traditions (though this is not to argue that all who listened or participated actually lived them). By structuring experience via the interpretation of the Word, the homilies map out a daily, ritualized observance of the faith that is individual, communal, and institutional. The homilies assume an orientation of an individual self with a Christian one, and that self is encouraged to embrace the Christian "familia" by repeated displays of communal behavior (attending church, worship, prayer, penitence, participation in ritual, and almsgiving, to name but a few). These conventions of repeated exhortation to modify behavior attempt to ensure individual identification with social and cultural institutions, as discussed further in chapter 4.

It is a final irony of Anglo-Saxon literary history that this overwhelming evidence of the performative language of preaching is neglected or rather displaced by critical anxieties about their so-called lack of literary value. To be sure, these texts instruct; they also cajole, wheedle, and impress. They invite meditation, encourage, console, and evoke wonder, awe, and fear. In whom, if not their intended audience and readers?

## Traditional Texts and Other Medievalisms

The study of traditionality in Anglo-Saxon religious prose has implications for the study of medieval literature more generally. Precisely because conventional literary history has not served the study of traditional or popular texts well, such texts are well situated to clarify how literary history addresses its subject and what this subject excludes. Traditional texts lay bare the often implicit assumptions upon which literary history is based, exposing the artificial nature of literary chronologies and their complex relation to historical formations.

In fact, the study of the Middle Ages makes little sense without some understanding of the concept of tradition. Any medievalist will find it hard to escape the insight that, whether in literature, social history, or religion, the Middle Ages are conventionally presented as highly traditional. Though the term itself is treated with increasing distrust, there remains some value in C. S. Lewis's comment on this period's use of its past: "We are inclined to wonder how men could be at once so original that they handled no predecessor without pouring new life into him, and so unoriginal that they seldom did anything completely new" (Lewis, 1964, 209). Medievalists cannot ignore the implications for vernacular texts of Ernst Robert Curtius's great work on the Latin Middle Ages (1953). In Latin and in vernacular writing, the same topoi, motifs, genres, and representations surface time and again. Certainly each representation is differently received, and much fine critical work has attuned our ears to this sensitive interplay between individual manifestations and conventional genres. But the similarities remain, and they form one terrain over which medieval societies debate their differences and conflicts, whether those conflicts are viewed in literary or sociocultural terms. Every refinement in understanding of the English feudal society in terms of particular, culturally specific, social formations does not deny the usefulness of the term feudalism, especially in terms of its relation to precapitalist, transitional formations.[30] Every detailed nuance of the social construction of gender further emphasizes that the concept of patriarchy is essential to analysis of the Middle Ages, precisely because it is a sophisticated, and therefore changing, form of power relations. And what remains fascinating about investigation of medieval belief systems is the ways in which Catholicism (at least in Western Christendom), in all its varied and institutional forms, maintains its hegemony in part by a continual policing of its borders with heresy.

As is equally clear from these literary, cultural, and historical examples, however, the problem is how to determine what tradition means in such a culture. Curtius (1953, 3–16), for example, defined culture in relation to concepts of civilization in his classic argument about the Latin Middle Ages and its influence on vernacular literature of the same period. In his argument, literature and the literary traditions associated with it are removed from the sphere of social praxis (and conflict) and assessed instead as an index of civilization. This critical stance paves the way for certain forms of nostalgia for the past that are still pervasive in medieval studies (as noted in the preface). By taking Raymond Williams's emphasis on culture as a socially formative practice, discussed in my introduction, the social significance, and therefore power, of those elements of a society that are represented as traditional comes into clearer focus. Claims about the relevance of a term like *traditionality* in general need careful analysis in respect of their specific historical and sociocultural formations. Such an analysis must include recognition of the fact that traditions are themselves always conflicted, from within and often from without. The argument from the general always has limitations. For most medievalists, however, the concept of tradition is so familiar that it is revered, naturalized, or stigmatized, depending on point of view. The view that the Middle Ages are traditional is itself traditional; few bother to quote C. S. Lewis these days.

Instead, the literary history of the Middle Ages is dominated by a binarism of the old and the new; what is old (or traditional—and the old and the traditional are frequently associated) is deemed less significant than what is new or original. This binarism is confusingly used in medieval studies to refer to methodologies (as in the example of the New Medievalism), to concepts of periodization (where the old always makes way for the new), and even to the canon (the only Old English text traditionally given pride of place in the canon is *Beowulf*). These uses of the old and the new are rarely differentiated, and the slippage between them has profound consequences for the meanings of both traditional and nontraditional formations.

The problem of defining tradition is cast in sharpest relief when its function is assessed in relation to concepts of periodization and canon formation. Wherever the line is drawn between past and present, old and new, whether that line is called the Renaissance or early modern or even modern, what is before is Other, premodern, medieval. If the modern is new, then the medieval is traditional, old: if the medieval is new, then Anglo-Saxon is traditional. Medievalists are highly sensitive to this obvious consequence of the structures of periodization, with the strongest challenges to it coming from scholars of the high medieval period. Brian Stock, Lee Patterson, and David Aers have each addressed the ways in which this period is used as the unanalyzed, therefore idealized, Other from which are derived claims for the emerging modernity of the Renaissance.[31] Scholars of the early medieval period, however, have yet to enter this debate, with the only too familiar result that the English Middle Ages are still characterized by evidence from the twelfth century onward.

The pervasiveness of cycles of old and new in scholarship is well illustrated by the examples of New Philology and New Medievalism. These contemporary movements have highlighted the weaknesses of conventional methodologies with important and valuable results, but the strategy of contrasting the old with the new is not in itself new.[32] Earlier calls to revitalize medieval studies have been well documented, however, most notably by Frantzen (1991, 1–33, for the Anglo-Saxon period) and Patterson (1987, 3–39, for the later medieval period). Gerald Graff (1987) sug-

37

gests that cycles of the new and the old are inevitable in scholarship, but by relocating the new in the old without recognition of this dilemma, all that happens is a readjustment of the boundary between the two (Frantzen, 1991, 1–3). In consequence, the binarism of the old and the new is an artifact of literary history rather than an instrument for analyzing historical change in either literary or social formations. This is perhaps why New Philologists have been heard to deny that there is such a thing as New Philology or why, to use another example, the debate over what is New Historicism (or New Historicisms, as we are now encouraged to call it) seems unresolvable.[33]

That the concept of the old and the new is an artifact of literary history is also plainly illustrated by the Modern Language Association anthology, *Redrawing the Boundaries* (Greenblatt and Gunn, 1992). Here, roughly half of the twenty-two essays deal with conventional literary-historical periods, while the other half explore more recent methodologies that suspend, at least in their titles, notions of periodization. Anne Middleton's essay, which calls for a new literary history for the medieval period, illustrates the dilemma. Middleton mentions the one canonical Anglo-Saxon text — *Beowulf* — once, in a footnote (1992, n. 21), and mentions the Anglo-Saxon period once, too — this time in the text but in that familiar phrase, "Old and Middle English" (13). Middleton in fact restricts her often valuable insights to such canonical figures as Chaucer and Langland. Her essay suggests that the debate about literary history for the medieval period rarely addresses either traditional or early texts, but is conducted over the most canonical, most obviously literary authors, usually of the fourteenth century.

More interesting than Middleton's account of literary history in this regard is Patterson's *Chaucer and the Subject of History* (1991), which uses the concept of modernity to examine Chaucer's lifelong fascination with, and exploration of, the construction of the subject in relation to history. Patterson addresses what might be called Chaucer's self-fashioning in creating a poetic identity and a poetic corpus that is intentionally poised between the worlds of the literary past and the claims of his historical present: "the making of himself as a man at once in and out of history" (46). Interested in exploring this representation and the philosophies of the historical upon which it depends, Patterson's study mimes Chaucer himself, returning him to history but also to literary history. Chaucer is embedded both in the historical world of events and in the literary world of texts, and thus remains the Chaucer familiar to us from so many other literary histories — in his time and yet beyond it. The book therefore is a highly sophisticated version of an old argument. Claims for Chaucer's "newness" (his modernity, or what used to be called his humanism) are themselves traditional in literary history. A. C. Spearing's strenuous argument that Chaucer was the only English writer to participate in the Renaissance is Patterson's immediate predecessor, and

Dryden is his literary ancestor, as Patterson is well aware (Spearing, 1985, 1–22; cf. Patterson, 1991, 13–19). In Patterson's hands, however, Chaucer's use of the interplay between past and present furnishes us with a subtle twist to the tradition: "If we must have a label for this kind of historical consciousness, perhaps we should call it *postmodernism*" (1991, 22; emphasis added). In this formulation, Chaucer is no longer the first modern writer but the first postmodernist, and the old, it seems, really is new. This is a powerful analysis of what many medievalists sense to be one of the most important features of the literary history of the Middle Ages; the self-conscious awareness of the subject in relation to history. And there are good reasons why such an awareness should settle on Chaucer as one of its major exponents. Patterson's argument, however, now demands that literary historians move beyond this conventional concentration, which unintentionally reifies yet again the High Middle Ages and one of its most important writers.

Perhaps it is Chaucer's postmodernism that leads Middleton to claim that medieval studies was invented twenty-five years ago (1992, 12–24). This tactical statement is intended to call attention to the newness of what are often deemed conventional, long-lasting methodologies but, at the same time, it is somewhat cavalier in its treatment of the history of the discipline.[34] Whatever validity there might be in asserting the postmodernity of the medieval period by collapsing the object of study with the methodologies used to study it, it is remarkable how little has really changed. In Patterson's Chaucer as in Spearing's, or in the New Philology vision of the medieval period as in Middleton's, the map of the Middle Ages is instantly recognizable: the individual remains too often the ungendered male; the authors, canonical; the period, high medieval; the cultures, French and English. In spite of regular claims to the contrary, the disciplinary structures of medieval studies have recombined in much recent work made in the name of the new to produce an extremely selective, familiar, traditional encoding of the past. The new, it seems, really is old—it is located in fourteenth-century England. Correlatively, the old, as in the case of the Anglo-Saxon period, is another discipline.

In general, an emphasis on the new—the new canonical author, the new methodology, the new period—maintains the locus of the old and the traditional at a point further remote in time—in an earlier period. Strategies such as these contribute to the process whereby the Anglo-Saxon period—the earliest period of all English literary history—is continually placed as the new/old Other. In this case, the old is not just too old; it is originary, as Frantzen (1990) argues. This process tends to go hand in hand with the critical perception, now increasingly misplaced, that Anglo-Saxon studies employs the most conservative methodologies of all medieval disciplines.[35] These arguments about periodization and methodologies are not adequate explanations for the marginalization of the Anglo-Saxon period from medieval literary history, of course; they omit institutional factors of discipline formation. The argument from literary history, however, does have the advantage of highlighting the constructed nature of our literary chronologies and their effects.

These effects are clear: in literary history the binaries of the old and the new, tradition and modernity, enfold history into a hermeneutic process that renders sociohistorical difference and change resistant to analysis. An emphasis on the self-consciously new, as in the case of the twelfth-century renaissance or of Chaucer in the fourteenth, minimizes other formations of the subject and of history in medieval culture. Traditionality and its relation to historical and literary change in such a construct is barely worth consideration; those periods and texts that are not new, however broadly defined, are therefore often invisible. Whence the uneasy relation between literary history and traditional texts such as sermons. Only by making traditional formations more visible, in other words, can the current emphasis on the new or the innovative be rethought.

Scholarship on medieval genres is constructed along similar lines, as is evident from Curtius's work on medieval Latin literature (1953) or Paul Zumthor's structuralist analysis of the medieval lyric (1972). What appears to make a text traditional is the ease with which it conforms to the paradigm of a particular genre that persists over a considerable period of time, and the repeated use of certain topoi, motifs, themes, and even phrases identified with that genre. A traditional text is one that makes no significant break with or contribution to its genre; a traditional text is one that is not new. Literary traditions, then, imply stasis: as an evaluative term of aesthetic judgment, tradition as a concept of literary history tends to be ahistorical. Yet, as the example of the medieval lyric suggests, the genres so analyzed are themselves already literary. Traditionality of form and content is valued as a feature of the medieval lyric, whereas other genres, especially didactic ones, which also make use of conventionality and traditionality, are weighed against this categorization of the literary and found wanting. Some traditions are praised by literary history, while others—notably didactic works—are excluded from it.

This process of selection according to ideologies of what constitutes the literary is better understood than its parallel case—the selectivity in formations of the traditional (noted earlier). In "Tradition and the Individual Talent," T. S. Eliot redirected the ways in which concepts of tradition were used to value and censor certain kinds of writing by relocating the relation between tradition and the artist in a dual historical sense of "not only of the pastness of the past, but of its presence" ([1917] 1932, 4). Eliot's historical sense, however, is primarily filtered through a literary sensibility. Accordingly, the meaning of tradition splits into two: first, those literary traditions that have positive aesthetic value; second, those that do not. Critics still "dwell with satisfaction upon the poet's difference from his precedessors" (Eliot, [1917] 1932, 4), even in works from periods such as the early medieval that could hardly be said to be interested in the concept of "individual talent" at all. This is probably one of the reasons why there is so much distrust of the concept of traditional orality as an explanation of features of early medieval English poetry.[36] It is hardly surprising that many texts considered traditional—sermons, saints' lives, and proverbs, for example—are not valued for their literariness.

The binaries of the old and the new, the traditional and the modern, as used by literary history are aspects of an aesthetic judgment that risks the denial of difference, the suppression of history, and the obscuring of the connections and disconnections between past and present. The result is a stigmatization of tradition. Tradition in this sense is as ahistorical as modernity; in consequence, claims for the postmodernity of the Middle Ages—as a methodology and not a chronology—make perfect sense. Such paradigms, however, do not advance the understanding of traditional texts, but clear a space in which the new, the modern, and the aesthetically significant can emerge. The way out of this impasse lies in the direction of some better historical understanding of both traditional and nontraditional texts and genres, as those critics influenced by materialist philosophies are well aware. Literary history as currently formulated is inadequate to this task. Paradoxically, it is traditional texts that challenge paradigms of old and new rather than new texts, which such paradigms exist to confirm.

## Beyond Literary History?

As the disciplines of literature and history draw closer together, encouraged by interdisciplinary approaches and cultural studies, the issue of how to explore the alterity of the Middle Ages in ways that take account of the fact that the primary evidence is textual though not necessarily literary becomes foregrounded. Recent analyses of medieval textuality and Latin *grammatica*, though often grounded on the canonical, offer a promising way forward.[37] These approaches are conducted, however, almost exclusively at the level of theory where vernacular traditional texts are concerned.[38] More important, the emphasis on textuality does not address the conceptualization of texts-as-events, as written and used by human beings in specific historical moments. Culture thus becomes an abstraction—little more than an assembly of texts or web of intertexts— and the roles of human agency and historical change in producing culture are understated. By treating all texts as intertexts, the specificity of certain kinds of writing is downplayed: writing that appeals to the imagination, emotions, or the morality of their readers—writing, in other words, that does work in the world.[39]

In this regard, it is instructive to contrast Hans Robert Jauss's earlier work on the aesthetics of reception, more recently modulated into reader-response theory (1982b, 3–45; cf. Holub, 1984, 53–69), with Brian Stock's work on literacy, most especially his inquiries into the relationship between social change and "textual communities" (1990, 159–71). Both scholars make an invaluable contribution to the processes of historical change and difference in relation to literary history.[40] Jauss himself realized the need to move beyond literary history in order to address the historical nature of traditional or "culinary" genres.[41] Anglo-Saxon traditional prose genres have an important contribution to make to such a history of aesthetics, explored in chapter 2.

Similarly engaged with the analysis of historical change is Stock's "Tradition and Modernity: Models from the Past" (1990, 159–71), which rightly ponders medievalists' lack of theoretical engagement with traditional formations. Stock returns to and slightly enlarges upon Eliot's concept of the "pastness of the past" by insisting upon the importance of social institutions and of cultural specificity in the maintenance of traditions. The value of Stock's work is twofold: he acknowledges the value of concepts of tradition in our thinking about medieval societies, while simultaneously stressing the difficulties inherent in the examination of such an acknowledgment. In the second half of his essay, Stock offers a productive reformulation of the binarism of the new and the old: "Tradition is said to be created by the consciousness of modernity, much in the way that oral culture is set in relief by writing. But in the Middle Ages, modernity was more often than not the creation of tradition" (1990, 166). Tradition here remains bound to modernity, but Stock emphasizes the productivity of traditional formations rather than their apparent stasis. However vague Stock's conclusions and however frustrating his lack of evidence, he makes it possible to consider the formation and maintenance of traditions as worthy of analysis in their own right.

Stock's important revision of the relation of modernity to tradition, the emphasis on the historicity of aesthetics in Jauss's version of reception theory, and the role of discourses such as Latin *grammatica* in the formation of culture pave the way for an analysis of traditional forms. That a discourse such as preaching is interrelated to other medieval discourses such as rhetoric or grammar is well known. If *grammatica* is one central method for organizing the word in the Middle Ages, moreover, preaching deserves to be analyzed alongside the other products of grammar, whether or not they are now identified as literary. In addition, the insight that aesthetics is historically constructed enables us to reinterpret those features of similarity (often viewed as transcultural and atemporal) that characterize traditional texts. The repetitive form of traditional texts—their effect of familiarity or pastness, in other words—is not just bad writing (though sometimes it is, of course), but a deliberate rhetorical effect at work in certain historical formations. Both grammar and rhetoric in the light of reception help to explain the persistence of certain kinds of writing in the medieval period whose very popularity then seems alien now. As Stock realizes, however, such approaches do not adequately account for the relation of traditional written forms to paradigms of social behavior or institutional life. Textuality alone, in other words, cannot account for the dynamics of social power that produce and maintain certain textual formations.[42]

In cases like Anglo-Saxon sermons, moreover, we have little historical evidence for performance or audience (cf. Gatch, 1977, 40–59). Unlike the later medieval period, with its records of preaching and preachers, Anglo-Saxon evidence for preaching resides primarily in the sermons themselves. Yet studies of textuality alone cannot explain the numbers of preaching texts, their persistence, or their prolonged use. Where texts are directly connected to institutions and practices, study of their textuality must be complemented by study of their historicity in ways that take account of the material production of their aesthetics. In moving beyond literary history so as to rewrite it from the perspective of cultural materialism, the way forward is detailed, historical analysis of the specific and the local.

The move beyond literary history that this book charts has radical implications to which I return in the conclusion. An emphasis on traditionality in Anglo-Saxon religious prose has the unsettling effect of recontextualizing current investigation of the uses of tradition in the poetry. It also challenges the primacy of poems like *Beowulf* in the canon. From the perspective of the prose, *Beowulf*'s splendid isolation as a treasured cultural monument stands in stark relief in need of further analysis. In addition, the persistence of traditional formations across periods within the medieval turns critical attention from innovation to notions of continuity and change. The Anglo-Saxon period cannot be excluded from such a concept of periodization, but reemerges as crucial to our formulations. Its historical difference opens the way for understanding the variety of historical formations within this huge period. Medievalists who exclude the traditional will not only continue to exclude the Anglo-Saxon period, but vast areas of social and cultural experience from the high medieval period as well. Finally, the turn to history demanded by an emphasis on the traditional puts pressure on the increasing absence of historical analysis within those contemporary postmodern theoretical discourses with which many medievalists, such as Patterson and Middleton, have been recently engaged. The study of traditionality in the Middle Ages is a strong provocation to postmodernism's neglect of history.

## Tradition and Postmodernism

For many contemporary theorists, tradition is unsurprisingly associated with terms such as the *canon, great works,* or *Western Civilization,* which are viewed with considerable distrust. Given the ways that the past, coded as traditional, is and has been used in the academy, there are good reasons for this distrust. Debates over the so-called canon stress how traditions — of literary works, ideas, or inherited social formations — inevitably turn out to be massively unreliable. Tradition encodes the individual as communal; it is selective and oppressive and forces a seamless continuity on a much disrupted and discontinous past. Traditions make connections where, from another perspective, there are only disconnections: traditions, as we have already seen, are ideological; so too are canons. Both testify to the limits of historical methods when used in relation to the binary of the old and the new.

The ideologies that inform processes of tradition formation and maintenance are prime topics for theoretical meditation. The debate over the canon has succeeded in changing its emphases but not in dismantling it. Traditions are extremely tenacious when enforced by institutional and disciplinary formations; tinkering with the canon only increases the pressure to elide history, as John Guillory neatly points out (1993, 3–82). The ideological force of tradition as it functions within literary history and within contemporary critical theory in relation to history can bear greater emphasis. At present, traditionality seems little more than a convenient way to explain away, and sometimes dismiss, those works, genres, and formations that are not new or original. In consequence, neither old nor new, neither traditional nor postmodern, is rendered accountable to history.

In general, traditionality is viewed most often with distrust (cf. Shils, 1981, 2–10). Tradition is associated with the old, the static, the conservative, and the Right. These views are not necessarily misplaced, but distrust is not a good reason for avoiding analysis. Understanding tradition continues to fall outside the purview of intellectual analysis largely because of the persistence of the Enlightenment view of history as progressive change. A paradigm that associates change with progress (however problematically) tends to downplay those sociocultural formations that associate change with the past. This paradigm has had a profound influence on the shape of literary history, which is so often informed by a distinction between those traditions that are constructed by literary history as new and those that remain outside or beyond literary historiography.

As in the case of medieval literary history, tradition within literary discourse in general is the product of two interrelated and overused yet little understood binaries: tradition and modernity, the old and the new. What is new is always more vital, more exciting, more important, more radical than the other side of this binary coin: the old, the traditional, the conservative. These binary formulations, as I have already argued, conceal difference and similarity *on both sides of the binarism*. This binarism makes for good polemic, but not necessarily good theory or practice. Indeed, the most common, and least interesting, use of the term *tradition* in postmodern circles is to foster polemic.

The new is glamorous in the theory business and participates in the increasing commodification of the humanities. Those who study the past cannot escape this process; calls for the new — whether for the new text, field, formation, or methodology — bear witness to the powers of incorporation in the postmodern academy. The increasing fetishization of the new in postmodern methodologies is itself a cultural product of highly advanced capitalist societies, but makes little sense for those historical formations that are precapitalist. One undesirable consequence of this process, therefore, is the devaluing of historical study, if not the stigmatizing of the past altogether.[43] As students of a period that is in transition from feudalism to capitalism, to recall one famous debate, medievalists are in a good position to articulate the important differences of the past from the capitalistic present, thereby bringing both into sharper focus.

The careful analysis of tradition and modernity in relation to this difference is crucial to the maintenance of historical methodologies. This book offers a more modest first step, however — the analysis of the relation of history to tradition in particular formations. It begins with the aesthetic of the traditional, which is always more vulnerable to critique from those who emphasize the new and the innovative, and which is therefore one of the most vexed issues facing the student of Anglo-Saxon religious prose.

# CHAPTER 2

# Aesthetics and Belief

## Ælfric's False Gods

*AN angin is ealra þinga þæt is god ælmihtig.*

*[There is one origin of all things, that is God Almighty.]*
—Ælfric, *De initio creaturae*

The Anglo-Saxons were as interested in the origins of their culture as are Anglo-Saxonists. Contemporary investigation of Anglo-Saxon origins tends to be partial, however. Critical fascination with the beginnings of English culture most frequently takes the shape of analyses of ethnic origins and cultural affiliations.[1] We are stirred by the dramatic accounts of the migration, the invasions and settlement of the Danes, and the tenth-century poetic versions of Germanic myth. Bede's *Historia ecclesiastica*, the *Anglo-Saxon Chronicle*, and *Beowulf* offer classic scripts for thinking about Anglo-Saxon cultural identity (cf. Howe, 1989; Hill, 1995; Davis, 1992). The English Renaissance, by contrast, looked to the Anglo-Saxon period in search of a distinctively English Christianity, as Frantzen has documented (1990, 35–50). Each era has its own reasons for exploring the past; our own, intrigued by the syncretism of Germanic and Christian in Anglo-Saxon England, has yet to focus on those explicitly Christian narratives of origins that also inform this culture.

In Anglo-Saxon religious writing, questions of cultural definition find their answer in a larger transcultural narrative of origins and ends—the scriptural history of salvation. Within salvation history, specific myths of origins, whether ethnic or institutional—the story of the migration or of the "golden" ages of English monasticism—are narratives of divine Providence. Homiletic accounts of the past are structured by God's providential law, which forms the basis for spiritual understanding and worship. God's law—and Christian obedience to it—is the origin of both secular and canonical law, as exemplified by Alfred's law codes (Godden, 1991, 216). Spiritual commentary on the past, therefore, can provide a vernacular medium for political and social commentary, as chapter 3 explores. Standing outside time (though not scriptural narrative), there is only one myth of ends, which is endlessly reiterated by the homilists—that of the Last Days. Tempting though it is for modern critics to relate this phenomenon of reiteration to the pressure of the millenium—the coming of the year 1000—the homilists themselves present their interest in eschatology as a means of instituting Christian vigilance. Fear of death is transformed into readiness for it; transcendence of death is the consolation of the Christian tradition.

For the Anglo-Saxon Christian, only the psychodrama of sin and redemption can fully explain an otherwise chaotic and arbitrary existence.[2] This drama provides a template for understanding desire, both human and divine. Desire has its origins in Creation and Fall, and finds its rest in death and transcendence. Sacred narrative renders life coherent in terms of another life—Christ's—and another history—that of Scripture. Narratives from the Old Testament are witnesses to, and therefore types of, the New Testament. The life of the first man, Adam, is fulfilled by the second, Christ. The story of the individual, the community, or the institution finds resolution only after death (the persistence of this belief is underlined by Bynum, 1995). The drama of salvation, simultaneously re-presented and commemorated by the cycles of the liturgy, is transcendental. It offers a way to escape the constraints of the body (as Paul explains in, for example, 2 Corinthians 5), the limits of individual history, and the "prison" of this world.[3] Transcendence is the spiritual correlative of the many Anglo-Saxon images of exile (cf. Greenfield, 1955).

Ideologies of transcendence, however, have been severely tested by postmodern criticism. Skeptical of the power of the mystified and universalized, some forms of postmodernism invest their faith instead in narratives of the specific and the local. This belief in the power of the local is itself historical—that is, a product of postmodernism. Claims to specify and to locate have proliferated to the extent that they begin to appear uncannily transcendental (Simpson, 1995, 113–59). Transcendence haunts the academic postmodern as its unanalyzed Other. Such a position is unable to explain the historical, social, or ethical power of an ideology of transcendence. Anglo-Saxon Christianity offers a chance to explore both the cultural appeal of a transcendental belief system and its particular historical construction. Indeed, what connects the local and the specific of medieval Christian formations to the general and the universal ideology of Western medieval Christianity is this historical belief in transcendence. No account of medieval religious experience can afford to leave unexplored this central issue. "To leave a space for transcendence means to allow for the possibility that, when historical subjects assert religious belief or experience as the motive for their actions, they may at times be telling the truth," Barbara Newman points out (1995, 17). Religious prose offers the fullest evidence for the cultural interrelation of Christian origins and ideologies of transcendence in Anglo-Saxon England.

Belief in divine origins, which incorporates within it an account of human origins and their ultimate transcendence, is fundamental to religious prose and to its aesthetics. Proceeding from the more familiar—the Christian Anglo-Saxon elegies—to the less so—the homilies—this chapter argues that belief in origins is foundational for understanding the dynamic of Christian aesthetics in both poetry and prose. Ælfric's style in particular is shaped by this belief to the extent that his language can be seen as mimetic of his convictions. Conventional references to Christian origins in Ælfric's writing are indexes or signatures of his believing style. The fullest defense of the truth evident from belief in Christian history is found in one of Ælfric's least-known works, *De falsis diis* (On the false gods; Pope 1968, XXI). Read in the light of Ælfric's other works, *De falsis diis* emerges as a milestone in the maintenance of the Christian spiritual tradition in English, providing evidence of that moment when a tradition consolidates its beliefs and defines its truth. Few other religious writers of the period appear to have recognized the intellectual significance of *De falsis diis*, however. Conflict is integral to any tradition, MacIntyre reminds us (1988, 9–12), and Wulfstan's revisions to Ælfric's work in his own *De falsis deis* (Bethurum, 1957, XII) are symptomatic of the conflicting interests of these two writers in the maintenance of the religious tradition. Ælfric's work strives to understand God, and the world through God; Wulfstan's aims to understand sin and law. In Wulfstan's writing, Ælfric's emphasis on the labor of the intellect in the service of the divine is less important.

## Origins and Transcendence

The belief in transcendence encoded by originary narratives is a creative force generally in Anglo-Saxon Christian writing. Transcendence finds powerful expression in the Christian elegies, with their great theme of life as loaned ("læne"), temporal, and transitory. In part a response to Anglo-Saxon emphasis on community, itself a consequence of a highly stratified social formation that identifies the self in relation to a group, cultural exploration of life as "læne" — as a state of exile from community (from family, lord, and God) — is a defining feature of much Anglo-Saxon poetry. Inevitably, secular exile is metonymic of spiritual exile. The emphasis on exile in *The Wanderer* and *The Seafarer* is a vehicle for exploring desires for, and the cultural significance of, community and home. In these poems, as in *The Dream of the Rood*, transcendence promises security from alienation and exile in the community of the dead.[4] No longer "eðle bidæled" (deprived of homeland; Dunning and Bliss, 1969, line 20b), the believer is granted "fæstnung" (security; line 115b), as *The Wanderer* puts it, in the ultimate "eðel" of the Christian homeland (*The Dream of the Rood*, Swanton, 1970, line 156b).

While the aesthetic of Anglo-Saxon Christian poetry turns on transcendence, it is the prose writers who are masters of this general Christian theme. In his First Series homily for Shrove Sunday, *Dominica in Quinquagessima*, Ælfric characteristically takes us to the heart of the matter:

Nis þeos woruld na ure *eþel:* ac is ure wræcsið; for ði ne sceole we na besettan urne hiht on ðisum swicelum life: Ac sceolon efstan mid godum geearnungum to urum *eðele.* þær *we to gesceapene wæron.* Þæt is to heofonanrice. (Clemoes, 1997, 264/161–64; emphasis added)

[This world is not our homeland, but our journey-in-exile; therefore we must not set our hope on this deceitful life, but must hasten with good merits to our homeland, for which we were created, that is to the heavenly kingdom.]

Ælfric's vision of the world as a realm of conflict, alienation, or Augustinian unlikeness is a conventional one, derived from the traditions of Christian discourse.[5] Read in the light of the Christian elegies, however, his emphasis on exile and the idea of place or "eðel" resonates with distinctively Anglo-Saxon concerns. Yet there could be no greater contrast between the poetic style of the elegies and Ælfric's prose. Written in the famed plain style of his earlier writing, Ælfric's straightforward syntax in this Shrove Sunday homily encodes a complex thought: necessarily alienated in the postlapsarian world, Christian desire in this world must focus on earning a place ("eðel") in the next. Desire for this world is thus a misrecognition. The true object of human desire is the transcendental heavenly home; the "eðel" is the "heofonanrice," as Ælfric puts it. By using a combination of balanced and contrasting syntax, alliteration, and semantic repetition (note the contrast between the first and second uses of *eðel*), Ælfric's harmonious style here performs a belief in "the regularly patterned character of the divinely created universe" (Clemoes, 1975, 114). His style, in short, enacts belief.

Spiritual interpretation of sacred narrative yields the same belief in salvation time and again—a salutary, if obvious, reminder that interpretation is governed by traditional, consensual patterns of belief that depend on rearticulation for their vitality. Themes similar to those of the Shrove Sunday passage are amplified in Ælfric's First Series homily for the Epiphany, for example, which explicates Matthew 2:1–12 (where the wise men are warned by a divine dream not to return to Herod):[6]

sum þing miccles gebicnodon ða tungelwitegan us: mid þam ðæt hi ðurh oðerne weig to heora *earde* gecyrdon; Ure *eard* soðlice is neorcsenawang: to ðam we ne magon gecyrran þæs weges þe we comon; Se frumsceapena man. ⁊ eall his ofspring wearð adræfed of neorxenawanges myrhðe þurh ungehyrsumnysse. ⁊ for þigene þæs forbodenan bigleofan ⁊ þurh modignysse. þa ða he wolde beon betera þonne hine se ælmihtiga scyppend gesceop; Ac us is micel neod þæt we þurh oðerne weg þone swicolan deofol forbugan: þæt we moton

gesælilice to urum *eðle* becuman: *þe we to gesceapene wæron.*
(Clemoes, 1997, 239/247–240/255; emphasis added)

[The star-prophets symbolized for us one great thing when they returned to their country by another way. Our country truly is paradise, to which we cannot return by the way we came. The first-
created man and all his offspring were driven from the joy of paradise
through disobedience, and for eating the forbidden food, and through
pride, when he would be better than the almighty Creator created
him. But there is great need for us that we should move away from
the deceitful devil by another way, so that we may come blessed to
our homeland, for which we were created.]

Creation, Fall, and the promise of redemption are sketched quickly
here. The life of the Christian is a Pauline journey in exile "þe we to
gesceapene wæron" (for which we were created)—a clause that Ælfric
uses, deliberately I suspect, both here and in the earlier quotation from
the homily for Shrove Sunday. Both quotations illustrate Ælfric's incidental though insistent interest in Creation and Fall—the origins of desire—which balances his equally emphatic interest in eschatology—the
ends of desire, where desire finds its rest and place, its "eðel." Like the
Shrove Sunday homily, this excerpt from the Epiphany homily recapitulates some of Ælfric's most obvious themes, repeated so often by him
and by other English homilists that they appear conventional. Conventions are evidence for a process of reiteration that reproduces the articles of faith; as chapter 1 points out, they are integral to traditional formations. Salvation history is a given of homiletic writing; fortified by the
reiteration of conventions, it is a foundational belief whose premises are
infinitely adaptable.

When the force of reiteration is underestimated, however, homiletic
conventions seem little more than repetitions of formulaic language. Such
an approach pays no attention to the fundamental (that is, ideological)
unity of style and content (or belief) central to Anglo-Saxon preaching.
Similar aesthetic judgments have been offered on the so-called homiletic
endings of elegies like *The Wanderer* and *The Seafarer.* Moreover, recent
criticism that favors the openness or polyvocality of the Christian elegies downplays their dynamics of transcendence, by which the poem finally identifies the object of desire as divine.[7] The endings of elegies such
as *The Wanderer* and *The Seafarer* register a belief system characterized
by its reproduction no less than the homilies. Conventional utterances
of traditional beliefs are the necessary route to transcendence—necessary
because the promise of salvation is one offered to all Christians via an
appeal to the ideal, imaginary Christian community that is a vital symbolic component of all Christian writing. Conventions are constructed
differently by the genres of poetry and prose, of course (most obviously

by the demands of meter and vocabulary), but these generic differences should not be stressed at the expense of their shared referents. In homily and poem, for example, both "eðel" and "eard" are richly symbolic, associating secular with spiritual homelands. To describe the end of *The Dream of the Rood* as mere homiletic convention or to point to the sources for a particular passage in the prose displaces this symbolism into the language of precedent and derivation—foreground and background—and minimizes the force of their use of conventions. Belief is a process of finding community and place—a commonplace.

The two passages from the Shrove Sunday homily and the Epiphany homily by Ælfric register the confidence of a faith that derives in part from its traditional expression. In place of such assertions, the elegies offer unique narratives of the process by which that confidence is found, narratives of how the fictive, exiled "I" finds a place, an "eðel"—whence the use of similar conventions of transcendence in both genres. The voices of the homilist and the narrating "I" in the elegies are essentially anonymous, although each is constructed differently according to the demands of their respective genres. The homiletic voice is the authoritative and universal "we"—the pluralized voice of the preacher, who speaks on behalf of the ideal Christian community. The fragmented, experiential voices of the elegies—warrior-thane, seafarer, dreamer—find their common place and consolation only when they are subsumed into this "we." These are two sides of the same Anglo-Saxon coin: in spite of obvious generic differences between poetry and prose, Christian belief in transcendence is expressed by similar semantic and linguistic patterns with the same cultural referents—exile and "eðel," in this instance.

Christian elegy and homily thus alike testify to a dominant belief in the illusory nature of earthly existence made intelligible only by reference to the idea of a universal and transcendental salvation. History is a matter of returning to God. Transcendence acts as a powerful brake on representations of the specific historical event, as chapter 3 argues; the history of the individual or group are incidental expressions of this larger universal pattern. Belief in salvation history thus offers the Anglo-Saxons entry into Christian world history and a powerful model of incorporation. It is no accident that Alfred wanted a vernacular translation of the Orosius as well as translations of more obviously pastoral or philosophical works, nor that the Danish Cnut consolidated his authority as an English king with public expressions of his Christianity. Christian identity subsumes and resituates ethnic identity.

The conversion was one step on the path toward unifying the disparate and often conflicted interests of the early Anglo-Saxon kingdoms; so, too, later West Saxon hegemony rested heavily on its identity as a Christian culture (especially in its resistance to the Danish incursions). Ælfric's general and conventional emphasis on Christian origins is part of the same ideological move. In social terms, however, narratives of salvation history are conserving, that is politically conservative; the moral struggle for the heavenly home deflects attention away from the earthly. As chapter 4 explains, the homilists envisage social life as a series of unchanging hierarchies, each with their specific places and responsibilities. At the same time, however, this brief study of exile and transcendence reminds us that salvation history is also a source of a distinctively Anglo-Saxon Christian aesthetic in both poetry and prose.

## Christian Aesthetics

The fact that conventions of transcendence are shared by both poets and preachers is one indication that, on occasion, a religious aesthetic traverses the radically different genres of poetry and prose. The Christian content of Anglo-Saxon poetry has always proved a fertile subject for critical analysis; its relation to the prose less so. Despite persistent if periodic comment on the interrelation of poetry and prose, the nature of their shared aesthetic has proved illusive. Defining the difference between and the interrelation of these two genres is itself a critical problem. "Baffled, we suspect the worst, that nothing fundamental separates the two modes," notes Roberta Frank (1994, 87).

Frank's own contribution to this occasional debate surveys the incidence of poetic words in the prose corpus, and it is on this terrain—of semantics and prosody—that the differences and similarities between prose and poetry are most often assessed. Few have risked the overview of prose and poetry that Peter Clemoes advances in his important studies on the symbolism of Old English poetry (1986, 1995). Clemoes argues for a commonality between these two genres, best understood as a progressive continuum from poetry to prose. This continuum rests on a habitual association between thought and language at the level of Anglo-Saxon culture. The particular concreteness or materiality of Old English as a language finds its correlative in social structures, or as Clemoes puts it, in a "socially established semantic potential" that is allied to a "culturally established conformity" (1986, 10). These cultural features, which amount to a historically situated aesthetic, constitute and are constituted by the traditional art of the poetry, and are subsequently redeployed by religious writers in the service of a transcultural system of belief. In spite of the power of Christian poetry of the period, "the future inevitably lay with prose," suggests Clemoes (1986, 12). The cultural capital of Anglo-Saxon poetry is a legacy ultimately captured by the prose writers for Christianity.

Clemoes thus emphasizes the poetic formula as evidence for a powerful sociocultural symbolism rather than only for a habitual mode of poetic expression. Prose conventions, too, encode patterns of cultural symbolism, as my discussion of exile and transcendence indicates. For this reason alone, the aesthetics of Anglo-Saxon poetry may yet help to elucidate that of the prose.

One practical objection to this view is that Anglo-Saxon prose is neither formulaic nor metrical. Nor, for the most part, does it employ the vocabulary so distinctive of the poetry. Preachers, like poets, construct the fiction of an oral style, however. Homilies are written to be heard, and the voice of the preacher is an inheritor of the vatic voice of the poet. To argue that the didactic voice of the homilist is antithetical to analysis of aesthetic form and appreciation is reductive at best, and ignores the emphasis on style in the communication of Christian ideas by writers such as Augustine and Gregory.[8] Closer to home, A. P. McD. Orchard's argument (1992) that Wulfstan's prose style draws on techniques of orality better known from the poetry demands a reassessment of the cultural significance of the homiletic style in general. The alliterative noun and verb phrases so favored by the homilists of the Blickling Homilies, the occasional eruption of poetic meters (however clumsy) in the Vercelli Homilies, the rhythmical styles of both Ælfric and Wulfstan, and the metrical translations of the Creed and the Lord's Prayer, for example, all offer evidence for a cultural repertoire of rhythmical, alliterative styles found in both prose and poetry.[9]

Although homiletic styles are literate in nature, they are oral in effect. Recent work on the orality of Anglo-Saxon poetry by John Miles Foley (1991), Carol Braun Pasternack (1995), and Ursula Schaefer (1991) can therefore offer further insight into the aesthetic dynamic of the written and oral in the prose. In their work on the immanent aesthetics of what Pasternack calls "inscribed" poetry, these critics dismantle boundaries between oral and written composition by concentrating instead on their shared aesthetic. Religious poetry (which used to be a code name for literate poetry) in this argument displays an aesthetic not dissimilar to that of the heroic poetry. It therefore seems probable that, at the level of culture, this aesthetic might extend to the prose. After all, scholars of orally derived poetry are united in their agreement that the manipulation of traditional aesthetic conventions is a source of a compelling cohesion for Anglo-Saxon culture.

The concept of tradition, long the domain of the oral theorist in Anglo-Saxon studies, remains central to these more recent discussions of aesthetics. Used as a foundational term, however, *tradition* incorporates both specific and abstract referents. Traditional art, which lacks the concept of an author function, is evidenced by the linguistic phenomena of the formula, conventions of syntax, patterns of narrative such as the type scene, and the use of fictions of voice such as "I" or "we." Traditionality thus refers to the shared linguistic conventions of the poetry. At the same time, critics agree that these conventions also encode extratextual references to community and culture. It is these traditions of community and culture that remain abstract, and often idealized. In the absence of other forms of evidence, community and culture depend largely on the poetic corpus for their realization. The important clues of the Cynewulfian "signatures," for example, are read as literary fictions, which are the products of linguistic conventions. Yet the aesthetic power of Cynewulf's signatures resides not only in the assumption of a poetic identity—however fictional—but in their extrapoetic form as prayers.[10] The prayer joins Cynewulf to the believing Christian community, transforming his poetry from artifact into enactment of belief, with its own repertoire of conventions. Like the endings of the elegies, the Cynewulfian signatures draw on Christian traditions of incorporation and belief that are concrete instances of extratextual references to ideals of community and culture to a far greater extent than the conventions of heroic verse. Put another way, the polyvocal effects of "inscribed" verse—the ability of poetic conventions to be multireferential—have their limits. Christian meanings are not limitless precisely because they are governed by the transcendental sign, which is God.

Cynewulf's construction of an utterly conventional believing self points to an analogy between preacher and poet at the moment where the ethical system of traditional heroic poetry meets that of Christianity.[11] The techniques used in the prose, therefore, offer some parallels to the conventions of traditional verse. These center on a repertoire of inherited material (in this case, scriptural, hagiographic, and exegetical), the use of the ethical or preaching voice, and the construction of an implied Christian congregation or reader. These features of the prose resonate with the repertoire of poetic conventions, uses of voice, and emphasis on reception by the implied reader or audience identified in accounts of the aesthetics of "inscribed" verse. Like the poet or fictive "I" of the elegies, the preacher uses conventions that draw on an intertextual web of meanings. These conventions, however, also encode extratextual references to an ethical epistemology, which structures Anglo-Saxon cultural identity as primarily Christian rather than heroic, Germanic, or, in the loosest sense of oral theory, traditional.[12] This epistemology, better known as salvation history, defines the ideal Christian community as one synonymous with English culture, within which the implied audience or reader is embedded. In such ways, as Clemoes rightly argues, Christian prose makes use of, or rather makes over, the constructs of traditional poetry.

In place of Germanic myth, Christianity offers a comprehensive, coherent, and ordered narrative, which structures the history of the individual and the communal by means of the drama of original sin and its transcendence. The fact that this worldview is a narrative, or rather a series of interrelated narratives, reminds us of its aesthetic resources; the narrative structure of Christian origins and ends is eminently suited to the binary system of cultural expression encoded in the two-part poetic line. At the level of genre, however, this is where poetry and prose diverge. Ælfric's rhythmical prose is also often binary, though not rigorously metrical. Nevertheless, symptoms of a religious poetic aesthetic find their parallel in the religious prose, with its repertoire of narratives from Scripture and their authoritative patristic interpretation, together with the use of homiletic conventions, repetitive structure, phenomenon of reusability, and construction of preaching voice. Individual reflexes of the homiletic style can be identified within the general homiletic corpus in much the same way that we hear individual voices in the poetry, despite the general rule of anonymity in both genres. Both religious poetry and prose can thus be described as traditional, though their uses of that traditionality vary. At the level of culture, however, religious prose and poetry occupy the same aesthetic continuum; this aesthetic resides in a cultural system of belief, whose evidence is textual conventions.

All Christian narratives point in the end to God. In so doing, many such narratives return to Creation. Creation is a favorite subject of the poets and a well-worked theme for the critics. Cædmon's hymn, the so-called hymn to Creation in *Beowulf,* the *Genesis* poems, and the *Christ* poems are all narratives of origins with considerable aesthetic power that justly merit their place in the canon. The cultural intent of this aesthetic, however, is to generate both worship and understanding; an intent embraced more systematically by Ælfric than any other Anglo-Saxon writer. In pursuit of this aim, Ælfric's style becomes transcendental (Clemoes, 1966, 206). It is devoted to revealing the invisible of the divine in the visible, material world. Ælfric's writing thus offers us an opportunity to examine in greater detail the harmony between subject and form central to the construction of a believing homiletic prose style.

## Beginnings: Ælfric on Origins

As a monk, masspriest, and later abbot, who dedicated his life to God and to the care of souls, Ælfric's writing is not only structured by the originary narratives of salvation history, but is also saturated with its implications. Clemoes is one of the few critics of Ælfric to insist, however, that salvation history, which informs the content of his writing, also informs his style. Ælfric is both a scholar of origins and an original writer. His importance both in and beyond literary history resides not only in his shaping of a Christian discourse in English according to the rules of Christian traditions, but also in the creation of a prose style uniquely suited to that discourse.

Critical discussion of Ælfric's style is itself structured as a debate about origins. His style has been assessed in terms of genre (the familiar problem of whether his prose is actually poetry) and of influence (whether that of the Latin "cursus" or of earlier and contemporary vernacular forms). In the best summary of the debate so far, John C. Pope argues that Ælfric's style can indeed be explored in terms of these questions and yet, on the basis of his use of vocabulary, syntax, and meter, it remains uniquely and recognizably his own (Pope, 1967, 105–36). The frequent critical descriptions of his prose as brief (that is, to the point), useful (that is, reusable), memorable (that is, alliterative and rhythmical), and balanced (that is, ordered) all originate in Ælfric's own comments (cf. Wilcox, 1994, 60–63). Like the styles themselves (both plain and rhythmical), these comments are instantly familiar. Familiarity fosters identification with a particular tradition, as already argued. Ælfric's style, recognizably the product of his wide reading in both vernacular and Latin prose works, refines the art of the traditional to the point where we can identify his stylistic creativity. His writing elicits a thorough recognition of content — and thereby understanding — by means of a consistent relation between thought and word. Creativity is closely related to creation, as Milton also knew. Like Milton, Ælfric has an aesthetics that derives from his belief in salvation.

In Ælfric's writing, belief is a simple thing; his Christian truths are always deceptively and elegantly straightforward. Exegesis can produce remarkably complex arguments about, for example, the nature of the Eucharist, as in the Second Series homily for Easter (Godden, 1979, XV), but in stressing the mystery of the faith, Ælfric never leaves behind his pastoral mission and its equally crucial practical components — attendance at mass, the efficacy of prayer, the necessity of penitence, and the importance of spiritual understanding. Faith depends upon repeated acts and upon repeated disciplines of knowledge and behavior, as further detailed in chapter 4. Insistent repetition is a symptom of the homiletic style in general, but it would be a mistake to read repetition as narrowly didactic; that is, redundantly dogmatic. Most obviously repetitive and general are those homilies by Ælfric intended for seasons when the lay were expected to attend church — Lent, Rogationtide, Easter Day, Pentecost, and the Ember days.[13] In these texts, as in those dedicated to Ælfric's lay patrons and contacts, repetition and variation of key ideas is an index of a process of believing that is never taken for granted and, therefore, never completed. Repetition maintains dogma. This is the point of the annual cycle of the liturgy. Reiteration is a source of divine meditation and "gastlice andgit" (spiritual understanding). The confident tone we detect in Ælfric is the product of this process of believing. For Ælfric, writing is a religious act — part of the Opus Dei (cf. Leclercq, 1982).

Simplicity and repetition are not signs of simplemindedness, therefore, but of order, clarity, and precision. These features also signal Ælfric's stylistic independence from the more florid Latin hermeneutic style of the Winchester school (cf. Lapidge, 1975). The plain truth of works such as the *Catholic Homilies* cannot be read as evidence only of Ælfric's need to reach a wide and unknowing lay audience. Some of Ælfric's most memorable analogies, to which he returns time and again, are indeed straightforward, conventional metaphors of the most complex tenet of the faith, the Trinity. This is by no means unique to Ælfric. To cite only one anonymous example, from Vercelli XVI for Epiphany (Scragg, 1992, 266–77), the Trinity is compared to fire, with its threefold qualities of heat, color, and light (lines 153–65). Ælfric, however, handles similar analogies much more cleanly. In his First Series homily for the third feria of Rogationtide, *De fide Catholica* (On the Catholic faith), fire exemplifies the paradoxical relation between the Father and the Son (Clemoes, 1997, 337). As light is generated by and simultaneous (line 63, "efeneald") with fire, so too the Father and the Son are coeternal, both standing outside the natural order of paternal relations in which father precedes son (cf. Cross, 1964). An equally familiar association between the sun and the Son is used as a metaphor for the Trinity and for the omnipresence of God on several occasions throughout Ælfric's writing, including *De fide Catholica* (Clemoes, 1997, 338–39). In such conventional examples, the created world is a source of analogies for the Creator, and Ælfric's interest in natural phenomena is well known—he translated Bede's *De temporibus anni*, for example (Henel, 1942). The most complex mysteries of the faith are thus found in the most commonplace matters of daily life—a source of meditation for unlettered and lettered alike. Moreover, Ælfric's repeated use of the plain metaphor from nature is evidence of his belief in Christian paradox. Paradox explores the ability of human language to express the inexpressible: in Ælfric's writing, analogies are produced on the basis of a belief in a created world that points toward the uncreated, the Creator.[14] Whence the aptness of the metaphor ("bysne") that compares Christ's incarnation—the intermingling of the divine and the mortal in one body—to an egg with its white and yolk in his First Series homily on the Nativity (Clemoes, 1997, 196). The mysteries of the faith are communicated in these and similar examples by comparison to the already known. The plain metaphor in fact carries considerable ideological weight, since its vehicles—the egg, the family, the sun—are not ones whose meanings are restricted to a particular class or group, but are shared or rather universalized for all believing communities.[15]

The revelation of the divine in the created world requires an authoritative interpretation of a salvation history that remains consistent across time and community. Ælfric is always careful to present himself as an interpreter guided by the rules of tradition. Misinterpretation—the danger of heresy, or "gedwyld" (error)—is dealt with contemptuously and sometimes with humor, though humor is a quality rarely ascribed to Ælfric or to religious writing in general. Knowledge is guided by traditions of interpretation; a desire to step outside traditional truths is excessive, a prideful mimesis of the Fall. Whence this metaphor of the ladder in the Nativity homily from the *Lives of Saints*:[16]

Gif hwylc gedwola. oððe awoffod man. wyle furðor smeagen and þæt anginn oferstigan. mid dysilicere dyrstignesse. þonne bið he þam men gelic þe arærþ sume heage hlæddre. and stihð be þære hlæddre stapum. oðþæt he to ðæm ænde becume. and wylle þonne git stigan ufor. astihð þonne buton stapum. oð þæt he stedeleas fylþ mid mycclum wyrsan fylle swa he furðor stah. (Skeat, 1, I, 12/19–25)

[If any fool or madman wishes to consider further, and to step beyond the beginning with erroneous error, then he is like a man who raises up a high ladder and climbs the rungs of the ladder till he comes to the end. And then he wishes to climb still higher, he climbs without rungs till unsupported he falls, with much worse a fall the further he climbed.]

The Neoplatonic ascent to God is a spiritual one, guided by wisdom. It is, in the final analysis (and the analysis is itself part of the process of gaining wisdom), the assent not to know God. Ælfric's metaphor of the ladder is a reminder that the desire to know more than God is an error, breaching the law of obedience. A desire to know the origin is destined to fail. Step by step, the cumulative syntax of this metaphor leads to the top of the ladder, but without that ladder (or the support of tradition-dependent rules of belief), the thinker falls. Long before Edward Said (1975, 5–6) or Allen J. Frantzen (1990, 23–26), Christianity fully grasped the power of beginnings; one cannot know the origin to which all beginnings point.

Origins initiate the great series of the *Catholic Homilies* with the account of salvation history in *De initio creaturae* (On the beginning of creation; Clemoes, 1997, 178–89) and recur time and again, particularly (though not exclusively) in those works directly involving the laity. As the crisply alliterative opening sentence from Ælfric's First Series Rogationtide homily, *De fide Catholica*, insists (following canon law), the essential texts for the Anglo-Saxon Christian are the Creed and the Pater Noster: "Ælc cristen man sceal æfter rihte cunnan ægþer ge his pater noster ge his credan" (Every Christian must know by right his Pater Noster and his Creed; Clemoes, 1997, 335).[17] The preceding Rogationtide homily in this series, *De Dominica oratione* (On the Lord's Prayer, 325–34), is an exegesis of the Pater Noster.[18] *De fide Catholica* accordingly tackles the Creed — the confirmation of belief — via Augustine's exposition of the Trinity and begins with a powerful statement of origins: "An scyppend is ealra þinga gesewenlicra ⁊ ungesewenlicra" (There is one Creator of all things, seen and unseen; 335/7–8). Similar passages on origins, Creation, and the Trinity are also found in the item on penitence, *In XL. De penitentia*, appended to the Second Series of the *Catholic Homilies* (Thorpe, 1846, 603; cf. Godden, 1973b, 227–28); in the Nativity homily from the *Lives of Saints* (Skeat 1, I) previously discussed; in the homiletic *Letter to Wulfgeat* (Assmann, 1889, I), a version of which also appears in the late homily, *De Sancta Trinitate* (On the Holy Trinity; Pope, 1967, XIa); and in two of the three items that conclude the *Lives of Saints* in its principal manuscript witness — the *Interrogationes Sigewulfi* (MacLean, 1883–84) and *De falsis diis* (Pope, 1968, XXI). Composed at different points in Ælfric's writing career, these texts are written in both plain prose and its later rhythmical counterpart. They also appear in works of significantly different subject matter and genre: the catechetical *narratio* of *De initio creaturae* (cf. Day, 1974); explication of the Nativity and the Creed; the question-and-answer format of the *Interrogationes*; the euhemeristic *De falsis diis*; and homiletic letters. Equally important, although Ælfric is sometimes following quite closely a Latin source, more often these passages lack direct sources. On common agreement, many appear to be free composition.[19]

Or perhaps free association. Beginnings hold a strong attraction for Ælfric, though not simply because Creation offers an obvious opportunity for doctrinal instruction. Christian origins are necessarily trinitarian. These trinitarian passages on origins are also stylistically similar; they constitute a set of variations on a commonplace. While it is a simple matter to argue that economy of composition and the operation of memory — both well-known features of Ælfric's writing (cf. Cross, 1972) — lie behind these similarities, their content suggests something more: an affinity of style, conviction, and psychological character. The most obviously repetitive and conventional passages in Ælfric's writings can thus be read as signatures of his believing self in a manner reminiscent of the poetic signatures of Cynewulf. Manipulation of conventions are one indication of the style of this preacher; Wulfstan, too, reuses time and again certain distinctive formulaic phrases and vocabulary.[20] Ælfric's style, in other words, inhabits tradition.

Three short examples will help illustrate Ælfric's signatures of creation, all of which occur in the opening paragraphs of their respective texts. The first is the introduction to the first homily in the *Catholic Homilies, De initio creaturae,* which is itself an abbreviated homiletic version of salvation history:

AN angin is ealra þinga þæt is god ælmihtig. he is ordfruma ⁊ ende; He is ordfruma for ði þe he wæs æfre; he is ende butan ælcere geendunge. for ðon þe he bið æfre ungeendod; He is ealra cyninga cyning. ⁊ ealra hlaforda hlaford. (Clemoes, 1997, 178/6–9)

[There is one beginning of all things, that is Almighty God. He is origin and end: he is origin, because he ever was; he is end without any end, because he is ever unended. He is King of all kings, and of all lords Lord.]

The second is from the First Series homily for the third feria of Rogation-tide, *De fide Catholica*, the explication of the Creed, which has already been mentioned:

An scyppend is ealra þinga gesewenlicra ⁊ ungesewenlicra. ⁊ we sce-olon on hine gelyfan. for þan ðe he is soð god. ⁊ an ælmihtig. se þe næfre ne ongan ne angin næfde ac he sylf is anginn. ⁊ he eallum gesceaftum anginn ⁊ ordfruman forgeaf þæt hi beon mihton ⁊ þæt hi hæfdon agen gecynd swa swa hit ðære godcundlican fadunge geli-code; (Clemoes, 1997, 335/7–12)

[There is one Creator of all things, seen and unseen; and we must believe in him, because he is true God and the only Almighty, who never began nor had beginning; but he himself is beginning, and gave to all creation beginning and origin, that they might be, and have their own kind, as it pleased divine order.]

And the third is from the Nativity homily in the *Lives of Saints:*

Nu ge habbað gehered hu se hælend be him sylfum spræc. þæt he is ordfruma. and angin ealra þinga. mid his heofonlican fæder. and mid þam halgan gaste. Se fæder is angin. and se sunu is angin. and se halga gast is angin. ac hi ne synd na þreo anginnu. ac hi ealle þry synden an angin. and an ælmihtig god æfre unbegunnen. and ungeæn-dod. (Skeat, 1, I/11–16)

[Now you have heard how the Savior spoke about himself, that he is the origin and the beginning of all things, with his heavenly Fa-ther and with the Holy Spirit. The Father is the beginning, and the Son is the beginning, and the Holy Spirit is the beginning, but they are not three beginnings, they are all three one beginning, and one Almighty God ever unbegun and unended.]

Each of these passages is an exemplary instance of Ælfric's plain style, which might be better described as biblical, since it takes Scripture with its straightforward syntax as its model. Each uses alliteration to link clauses and to make thematic associations by affinities of sound. This is one of the defining characteristics of Anglo-Saxon poetry, but Ælfric's plain prose deliberately lacks the poetry's rigorous use of meter and vo-cabulary. Variation — another characteristic of the poetry — is achieved by a system of semantic oppositions, relations, and repetitions. Nouns are reused as verbs or participles, as in the patiently cumulative explica-tion of the Trinity in the third passage from the Nativity homily, where the trinitarian beginning or "anginn" — three in one — is transformed into an image of the unbegun and unending ("unbegunnen," "ungeæn-dod") God. Wordplay reproduces the hierarchy of creation, as in the example of human nature ("gecynd") granted freedom by divine ("godcundlican") in the second passage, from *De fide Catholica*. Elegance of syntax, variation, and alliteration combined with prosaic vocabulary are hallmarks of Ælfric's style: "AN angin is ealra þinga þæt is god ælmightig," the opening sentence of *De initio creaturae* in the first passage, is a perfectly crafted sentence.

These excerpts are examples of Ælfric's distinctive aesthetic of beginnings. Beginnings offer occasions for worship. References to origins — conventional across the homiletic corpus — anchor a homily in the beliefs of salvation history regardless of its specific contents. When read as a group, the lyricism of Ælfric's beginnings emerges in greater force. These passages offer an architectonics of sound, a shaping of language that is consciously patterned on Creation itself — though always from the obedient perspective of the believer. In such examples, even Ælfric's plain style approaches art. This claim, however, runs counter to most critical analyses of Ælfric's style as primarily utilitarian (even if this view is always offered with the caveat that the plain prose is, after all, good prose). Ælfric, by contrast, is fully aware of his Christian aesthetics and claims for it great spiritual significance. In his First Series homily for mid-Lent Sunday, which explicates the miracle of the five loaves, Ælfric offers this brief insight into the aesthetics of his prose:

> oft gehwa gesihð fægere stafas awritene. þonne herað he ðone writere
> ⁊ þa stafas ⁊ nat hwæt hi mænað; Se ðe cann þæra stafa gescead. he
> herað heora fægernysse. ⁊ ræd þa stafas. ⁊ understent hwæt hi
> gemænað; on oðre wisan we scawiað metinge. ⁊ on oðre wisan stafas.
> ne gæð na mare to metinge buton þæt ðu hit geseo. ⁊ herige; Nis na
> genoh þæt ðu stafas scawie. buton þu hi eac ræde. ⁊ þæt andgit un
> derstande; (Clemoes, 1997, 277/64–70)

> [One often sees beautiful letters written, then praises he the writer and the letters, but knows not what they mean. He who knows the reason of letters, praises their beauty, and reads the letters, and understands what they mean. In one way we look at a picture, and in another way, letters. There is nothing more to the picture save that you see and praise it: it is not enough that you look at letters, unless you can also read and understand their significance.]

This passage rehearses the traditional harmony between aesthetics, conviction or belief, and Christian knowledge (or reason) that informs Ælfric's style. A beautiful letter may be seen and praised in much the same way as a picture; only with reading and understanding, however, is the association between sight, appreciation, and spiritual meaning fulfilled. Unusual though such a comment is in the vernacular, Ælfric follows Augustine in emphasizing that signs are miraculous evidence of the divine. Most commentators on this and related passages stress either Æl fric's interest in survival of miracles in the postapostolic age, as do Malcolm Godden (1985a) and Karen Jolly (1996, 82–84), or the importance of literacy as a route to wisdom and knowledge, as does Seth Lerer (1991, 67–68). Augustine and Ælfric, however, make the case for the beauty of spiritual understanding, and therefore oppose the visual sign to the written. Beauty is synonymous with the word and its interpretation—the process of Christian exegesis—and Ælfric is a traditional exegete; small wonder that so many of his works include prayers that his writing be copied accurately (cf. Wilcox, 1994, 70–71).

Ælfric's emphasis on the spiritual beauty of beginnings is one of the most distinctive and, at the same time, most traditional features of his writing. Distinctive because passages dealing with origins occur throughout his writing in both early and late works to the extent that they suggest a habitual preoccupation. Beginnings provide the occasion for largely free composition, stylistic self-consciousness, and worship—a rehearsal of conviction. Traditional because these passages offer a glimpse of a spiritual aesthetic articulated first by the Church Fathers and applied consistently in the vernacular by Ælfric. By reiteration, Ælfric plumbs the depth of his understanding of the Trinity and of the great meditations on it by patristic writers such as Augustine and Alcuin. He invites his audience to do the same. What echoes throughout these passages is the Creed in its various versions—one of the two texts that Ælfric, following canonical law, urges every Christian to know. And the Creed, although a text, is always more than a text, since its recitation is a ritual performance of belief. In his stylistically self-conscious writings on the Trinity, we find evidence of Ælfric's habitual association between belief, aesthetics, and a universalized Christian discourse. The beauty of belief is one to be appreciated by all because, in ideal (that is to say, ideological as well as theological) terms, it is shared by all.

## True Belief: Ælfric's *De falsis diis*

Ælfric's use of beginnings is a symptom of his larger convictions about salvation history—Creation, Fall, Redemption—that structures all his writing. His references to Anglo-Saxon history are metonymous of the same process, as argued in chapter 3. One text brings together origins, style, and salvation history with particular force, however: his tract, *De falsis diis* (On the false gods).

Composed in the first instance in the same years that Ælfric was working on the *Lives of Saints,* originally forming one of the concluding items in its authoritative manuscript and displaying a stylistic interest in narrative, *De falsis diis* is one of several works that offer an apt counterpoint to the general hagiographical emphasis of the collection.[21] To the stories of the individual saints and their imitations of Christ is added a lengthy account of the history of belief—true and false—itself.

*De falsis diis* was excluded from Walter W. Skeat's edition of the *Lives of Saints* because the copy in his base manuscript is fragmentary and, as a result, has been neglected critically.[22] Although best known for its euhemeristic treatment of the Graeco-Roman and Danish gods (Pope, 1968, XXI, lines 99–209), this passage, comprising roughly a sixth of the homily, is no indication of the complete work. Until Pope's excellent edition, *De falsis diis* was known only from four unrepresentative versions, all of which include the section on the classical and Danish gods: the fragment of two hundred or so lines that concludes the authoritative manuscript of his *Lives of Saints,* BL, Cotton Julius E. vii; a similarly damaged but much later version in Oxford, Bodleian, Hatton 116; a single folio of extracts on the Danish gods from the Paris manuscript, BN lat. 7585; and Wulfstan's own reinterpretation of the same discussion (Hatton 113; cf. Bethurum, 1957, XII). The full text, best represented by the version in Cambridge, Corpus Christi College 178, is a lengthy piece of writing even for Ælfric, but most certainly for Wulfstan, whose own version runs to some ninety-five lines in Bethurum's edition. Only a reading of the entire text of *De falsis diis* reveals the extent to which critical emphasis on the classical and Danish gods passage has obscured Ælfric's own ambitions for euhemerism. In fact, Ælfric uses euhemerism throughout *De falsis diis* in this early and lengthiest English example of the genre (shorter examples are evident in Bede's *Historia* and in the Anglo-Saxon genealogies). Other Latin examples of euhemerism are much better known—those by Gregory of Tours and Saxo Grammaticus, for example—as are the later vernacular examples such as Snorri's prologue to the Prose Edda and Milton's *Paradise Lost.*[23]

Ælfric uses euhemerism to demonstrate that all gods other than the Christian are the products of human, not divine, creation. The distinction between created gods and the uncreated divinity maintains a boundary between Christianity and all other beliefs that is consistent throughout time and across cultures; it is a primary means of discerning the true from the false. Just how much Ælfric knew of Danish practices is therefore only one aspect of his own concern with Christian truths and practices. As the strongest defense of Christianity in the vernacular in this period, *De falsis diis* is evidence for a high point in the tradition of English religious writing. There comes a point in every tradition when its beliefs are consolidated and institutionalized in a particular culture. Ælfric's homilies in general offer the most systematic evidence for this consolidation in English in Anglo-Saxon England. When thus regulated, appeals to beliefs enshrined in a particular tradition are appeals to their authority as established truths, as in the case of the conventional and widespread references to the Trinity throughout the homiletic corpus. At this point in the development of a discourse, truth is tradition-dependent, although its traditional verities may be subject to challenge from within, and hence conserved, or from without, and hence realigned, at subsequent moments in the culture (MacIntyre, 1988, 354–57). That is to say, traditions are historically specific. In its concern with demonstrating the truth of the Christian God and exposing the falsity of beliefs in other gods across historical time and culture, *De falsis diis* represents one important moment in the conservation of traditional Christian truths in Anglo-Saxon England.

It is therefore historically significant that Ælfric should embark on such an enterprise in the late tenth century—a period that in retrospect represents the triumphant consolidation of Christianity in Anglo-Saxon England. Critical emphasis on the section of *De falsis diis* that addresses the Danish gods together with the textual evidence of the copying of this passage within the period points to the significance of the very real presence of the Danes in England. If this tract is one of Ælfric's responses to the Danes, however, it is a response that also speaks more generally to the late tenth-century interest in cultural origins. While Ælfric may or may not have known of a *Beowulf*, evidence of his fascination with Christian origins is ample, as already indicated. *De falsis diis* is the fullest demonstration of that interest, which is constructed within the tradition of Christian reason and dependent on its authority; the tract, in other words, is manifestly not in dialogue with competing traditions. As a result, Ælfric's discussion of Christian origins is not of the same order as discourses of ethnic origins or alternative belief systems available elsewhere in the culture, evidenced by the heroic poetry, the charms, or the Anglo-Saxon genealogies, for example. It is, instead, a mystification of them. Englishness—insofar as the concept exists for Ælfric—is a specific realization of a more universalized Christian worldview; Danishness is incidental—a contemporary illustration of the persistence of false belief rejected by that world. Fully assimilated into Christian belief, any desire for ethnic identification is necessarily defended against. For Ælfric, knowledge of Danish practices is subordinate to the question of what those practices reveal about Christian belief.

The narrative content of *De falsis diis* is indeed the false gods, therefore, but its subject is the one Christian God. Given the insistent harmony between content and form in Ælfric's writing, it is not coincidental that the work is also one of his most stylistically accomplished.

*De falsis diis* begins with a synthesis of two quotations from Scripture in both Latin and Old English (Ephesians 4:5–6; Romans 11:36), which take the form of a prayer to the one true God and establish the ironic tone of the entire work—here indicated as the gap between the text's rubrication, *De falsis diis,* and its framing subject:

An Drihten is, and an geleafa, and an fulluht; an God and Fæder ealra þinga, se ðe is ofer ealle þing, and þurh ealle þing, and on us eallum. Of þam synd ealle þing, and þurh þone synd ealle þing, and on þam synd ealle þing; sy him wuldor a to worulde, amen. (Pope, 1968, XXI, 677/7–11)

[There is one Lord, and one faith, and one baptism; one God and Father of all things, who is over all things, and through all things, and in us all. All things are of him, and through him are all things, and in him are all things; glory be to him always in the world, amen.]

In even these close translations from Scripture, we hear Ælfric's characteristic aesthetic of beginnings: the doubled and reversed syntax of the two sentences; the obsessive repetitions; and the—by now—distinctive phrase ("An god and fæder of ealra þinga"), which echoes similar phrases from *De initio creaturae, De fide Catholica,* and the Nativity homily from the *Lives of Saints,* all quoted earlier. As we might expect therefore, this passage ushers in another of Ælfric's familiar and stirring summaries of the Trinity. *De falsis diis* begins and ends with the worship of Christian origins.

In contrast with the remainder of the text, this beginning (lines 12–24) is not formally cast in rhythmical prose, however self-evident are its rhythms, but Ælfric moves quickly into a lyrical, more formally rhythmical and largely free composition on Adam's creation and fall (25–71). This section develops the theme of the Trinity by emphasizing the power of the Creator and the obligations of the created. Moving from eulogy and worship in the introduction to elegy and lament in the next section— from obedience to the Law to disobedience from it—Ælfric meditates on the loss that is humankind's lot after the Fall. Incorporating a familiar Anglo-Saxon description of prelapsarian bliss, the fall of Adam— through disobedience—initiates a reversal of power, and hence a reversal of subject and object. Adam, in falling, becomes subject to the temporal world:

Ne nan wildeor ne mihte, ne nan wurmcynn ne dorste
[derian þam menn] mid hys muðes slite.
Ne hungor ne þurst, ne hefigtyme cyle,
ne nan swiðlice hæte, ne seocnyss ne mihton
Adam geswencan on þam earde,
þa hwile þe he þæt lytle bebod mid geleafan geheold.
Eft, þa þa he agylt hæfde, and Godes bebod tobræc,
þa forleas he þa gesælþa, and on geswincum leofode,
swa þæt hine [biton lys] bealdlice and flean,
þone þe ær ne dorste se draca furþon hreppan.
(39–48)

[Nor might any wild animal or any serpent dare harm the man with a bite of its mouth. Neither hunger nor thirst, nor oppressive cold, nor excessive heat, nor sickness might afflict Adam on the earth while he kept that little commandment with faith. Yet, when he had sinned, and broke God's command, he lost the blessing, and lived in hardships, so that lice and fleas bit him boldly whom before even the serpent dare not harm.]

In examples such as this, the binary structure of Ælfric's rhythmical prose reveals its symbolic relation to the Anglo-Saxon poetic line; thought and expression find order through syntax. More important, in its use of the negative particle, "ne," this quotation neatly illustrates Ælfric's habitual rhetorical mode of expression for *De falsis diis*. The world before the Fall is defined negatively against the world after it; so too the world of false belief defines that of the true.

The introduction on the Trinity and the section on the Fall frame Ælfric's discussion of the false gods and shape its themes. *De falsis diis* is about creation, origins, and false beginnings and centers on the nature of power, divine and human. The power of the Creator to create is a subject for worship. The power of the created to create and imitate the divine, by contrast, is an illusion—a negation of divine power. The worship of illusory idols is a diminishment of the potential of the human as created by God, and takes the form of a series of falls, failings, or reversals in the chain of hierarchy. In illustration of these themes, *De falsis diis* offers a series of narrative exempla on the false gods, inspired by Martin of Braga's *De correctione rusticorum*, organized for the most part according to the sequence of sacred history and beginning with the origins of idolatry before Noah (72–98).[24] Then follows the famous classical gods/ Danish gods passage (99–209), after which Ælfric moves on to the Old Testament stories of the overthrow of Dagon by the Ark of the Covenant (210–85, cf. 1 Kings 4–7) and Daniel's triumph in the lion's den, his defeat of the false god Bel, and his defeat of the dragon (291–493, cf. Daniel 3–6, 14). The period of grace, in part derived from the histories of Rufinus and Cassiodorus, is represented by the defeat of Serapis by the command of the emperor Theodosius in Alexandria (521–71) and by Gregory the Thaumaturgist's debunking of Apollo (575–648, also from Rufinus), with which Ælfric echoes his earlier discussion of the classical gods. This historical sequence concludes with a final exordium on the eternal power of the Trinity and the doctrine of salvation (649–76). The theme of the one true God thus frames the entire work, introducing and concluding it. Beginnings are also endings:

Nis nan oðer god, ne nan oðer scyppend,
buton seo halige Þrynnyss, þe is þrymwealdend God,
se ðe ana gewylt ealra gesceafta,
and ælcum men forgylt eft be his weorcum
on þissere weorolde geendunge, and eac hwilon ær.

(664–68)

[There is no other god, nor any other creator, save the Holy Trinity, which is the omnipotent God, who alone rules all creation, and grants each man according to his works at the end of this world, and sometimes earlier.]

Such a cursory survey of the content and structure of *De falsis diis* cannot hope to do it justice. Stylistically, it is a tour de force, incorporating both plain—though highly rhetorical—and rhythmical prose narrative as well as authorial commentary. In the series of exemplary narratives that form the body of the work, Ælfric selects episodes that stretch his rhetorical skills to the utmost. It is, of course, vitally important that no single episode be identical to the next; this is the lesson of salvation history, whose providence is known only to God. Nonetheless, each episode repetitively and cumulatively ironizes the diminishment (a literal belittling) that is the consequence of false belief. At the same time, each episode stresses the revelation that there is only one true and mysterious God, who stands outside creation, at the origin. Within this cycle of turning from and returning to God, the complexity of human experience of the false gods is fully explored. Each episode represents a different historical challenge to the faith—a different god to be combated. As a result, the encounter with the struggles of Daniel against his false gods is necessarily different to the newer historical challenge of the false god, Serapis.

Of equal importance is the range of tone that Ælfric commands. This is a performance that moves from ritualized worship of the Trinity to elegiac lament over the loss of Eden to wry, ironized, and sometimes downright hilarious narratives on the follies of the false gods. In the hands of Ælfric, Saturn is a man living on Crete (104–5); the god Dagon is mysteriously found prostrate in front of the Ark of the Covenant and, when resurrected by his Philistine believers, is subsequently discovered decapitated by the door the next morning (221–35). To select another example, the distinction between the true God and the falsely alive gods is humorously demystified by Daniel, who exposes Bel's need for food as a human trick (400–420). The feeding of Bel is neatly paralleled by Daniel's feeding of the dragon, who promptly bursts apart; we hear Ælfric's own view echoed in Daniel's dry comment at line 450: "Nu ge magon geseon hwæne ge swa wurðodan" (Now you can see what you so worshiped). Similarly, Ælfric's emphasis on the ornate building of the fabulous shrine for Serapis is humorously contrasted with the execution of this false god, whose hollow body is full of mice:

Hine mann sloh þa swiðe mid scearpre æxe,
ac he hit ne gefredde, for þam þe he wæs treowen,
ne he nan word ne cwæð, for þam þe he cucu næs,
ne seo heofon ne feoll, ne seo eorðe ne tobærst;
ac man cearf ardlice him of þæt heafod.

(546–50)

[He was cut down firmly with a sharp ax but he felt it not, for he was wooden; he spoke no word, for he was not alive, nor did the heavens fall in, nor the earth burst apart: but his head was quickly carved off.]

It is hard not to hear the relish in Ælfric's voice in such carefully composed examples, nor can we miss the ironic inversion of the Crucifixion (no dying speech, no earthquake) in this particular case.

Time and again, Ælfric ironizes the capacity of the created to worship what they themselves create:

Smiðas hi worhtan sm[e]alice mid cræfte,
and oft gesealdon þa sylfrenan godas,
sumne to maran *wurðe*, be þam þe he gemacod wæs,
sumne eac waclicor, be þam þe his *wurð* wæs.
And swa lange swa he sloh þone samworhtan god,
and mid his græfseaxe holode hetelice þa eagan,
ne stod him nan ege for þære anlicnysse;
ac þonne heo geworht wæs, he *wurðode* hi for god.
                          (202–9; emphasis added)

[Smiths worked subtly with skill, and often gave the silvered gods a worth, to one a greater, as he was made, to another a lesser, as was his worth. And as long as he carved the half-made god, and hollowed out the eyes fiercely with his carving-knife, he stood in no fear of the image; but when it was made, he honored it as god.]

These artifacts are the idols of the created. Their value (*wurð*) is judged according to the skill of their craftsmen. That the craftsman stands in awe of his finished product is a subject for more humor, emphasized by the details of the process by which the idol is made. As in the passage on Adam's fall, subject and object are reversed: the object of human making becomes the subject of human worship. Creation here is a matter of making and working ("worhtan," "macode") in a process that is known, rather than mysterious; once made, the idol is worthy of worship. From this circular economy of creation and worth, the divinity is explicitly excluded. And yet, since the noun *wurð* and related verb *wurðian* carry both their literal meanings as material value and their spiritual senses of honor and worship, even the idea that the false gods are created by men alone is exposed as a fallacy. The mystery of the true God and the true Creation shadows the entire passage, implicit if not acknowledged in language itself.

Conspicuously absent from this passage is Ælfric's alternative lexical set for Creation: the verb *gescippan*, "to create," and the nouns *gesceaft*, "creation," and *Scyppend*, "Creator." These are consistently used by

Ælfric to refer to the truth of divine Creation, as the following example illustrates:

Ac hi mihton tocnawan, gif hi cuðan þæt gescead,
þæt se is ana God þe hi ealle *gesceop,*
us mannum to bryce, for his micclan godnysse.
Þas *gesceafta* doð swa swa hym gedyhte heora *Scyppend,*
and ne magon naht don butan Drihtnes willan,
for þan þe nan *scyppend* nis butan se a[n] soða God,
and we hine wurðiað mid gewissum geleafan,
cweþende mid muðe and mid modes incundnysse
þæt se is ana God þe ealle þing *ges[c]eop.*
(90–98; emphasis added)

[But they might know, if they perceived the distinction, that there is one God who created them all, for men's use, because of his great goodness. These creations do as their Creator directed them, and are not able to do anything without the Lord's will, for there is no creator save the one true God, and we worship him with certain faith, saying with our mouths and with inward mind that there is one God who created all things.]

The ability of human reason to make distinctions ("gescead") in obedience with God's desire ("willa") reveals that there is only one Creator or "Scyppend," who created all things, including the false gods. Ælfric's reasoning here is conventional and recognizably Augustinian. Faith is prior to understanding, which reason justifies retrospectively; belief in God fortified by rational understanding is the only subject worthy of worship, prayer, and meditation for all Christians (hence the use of "we" at the end of the passage). In their emphatic restatement of the truth of creation, these lines echo the opening lines of *De falsis diis,* as well as its conclusion, quoted earlier.

Each episode concerning the false gods concludes with similar authorial comments (lines 66–71, 286–91, 494–520, 649–75). These are textual moments where Ælfric seems most free of his sources and, as we might expect by now, are assertions of faith—hymns to the Creator, to the Trinity, and to the mysteries of divine Creation. With each reiteration, moreover, retrospective understanding of these beliefs deepens by continually directing the intellect toward the faith. Forming the perfect contrast to the lengthy narratives of the false gods, these brief passages are persuasive demonstrations of the importance of spiritual understanding of the history of the faith. In apprehending the false, the intellect is redirected to the true.

Such confidence in using a plain, resolutely nonpoetic yet highly symbolic language suggests a text carefully and self-consciously polished. In other words, Ælfric found his material satisfying theologically and aesthetically. This is borne out at least in part by the codicological evidence for Ælfric's revisions of the text. Ælfric issued one version of *De falsis diis* around the time of the composition of the *Lives of Saints*, but then revised it a few years later (Pope, 1968, XXI, 673–74). In addition, Ælfric's use of his sources—both scriptural and nonscriptural—indicates a certain degree of deliberate independence. But the best evidence of Ælfric's harmonious accord between style and belief is offered by the text's repetitive yet progressive structure of a turning from and a return to God.

*De falsis diis* is indeed a narrative of return and repetition for Ælfric, though not simply because this is the structure of the text nor because he revised it—a habit familiar to us from much of his writing. The tract has points of contact with other compositions, whose dates span Ælfric's career—from those roughly contemporary with it, such as the *Interrogationes Sigewulfi*, to those written earlier, such as the *Catholic Homilies*. His equation of the Danish gods with the classical gods, for example, echoes his *Life of Martin* from the *Lives of Saints* (lines 143–44, cf. Skeat 2, XXXI, 264/713–17); longer versions of the story of Azarius and the Prayer of the Three Children (lines 292–99) occur in the Second Series Christmas homily and more briefly in his *Life of Clement* in the First Series of the *Catholic Homilies* (Godden, 1979, I, 9–10; Clemoes, 1997, 503); the identification of the origins of idolatry with the building of Babel and the worship of giants, "entas," was already in Ælfric's mind when composing his First Series homily, *De initio creaturae* (lines 99–103; cf. Clemoes, 1997, 185–86) and is also implied in a discussion of the tongues of fire in *In die Sancto Pentecosten* from the same series (358). Other points of contact are with the *Interrogationes Sigewulfi* (lines 181–86; cf. MacLean, 1884, lines 114–35) and the *Hexameron*, with which the account of the fall of Adam is closely related (lines 33–55; cf. Crawford, 1921, lines 460–64). To these intertextual references can be added the group of texts that are evidence for Ælfric's habitual concern with aesthetics, salvation history, and origins, such as *De initio creaturae, De fide Catholica*, and the Nativity homily from the *Lives of Saints*. Such points of contact suggest that Ælfric is dealing with a topic close to his heart. It is, in other words, no accident that *De falsis diis* begins and concludes with a eulogy on the Trinity or that the text is one of Ælfric's most stylistically accomplished works: both signal that we are in the presence of a strongly felt belief.

The manuscript evidence bears out the argument that *De falsis diis* represents a significant composition in relation to his other, better known works, but only in part. Its eight manuscript recensions (excluding the Old Norse version) divide roughly into two groups on the basis of Ælfric's revisions of lines 141–49, as Pope first suggested (673–74). But two of these versions are extracts, whose direct connections to the full text are difficult to assess: one (Paris, BN lat. 7585) comprises a single folio; the other (BL, Cotton Vespasian D. XIV) appends the Daniel episode (lines

300–493) to one of Ælfric's Second Series homilies (for the twelfth Sunday after Pentecost) and reminds us that at least one compiler of Ælfric's work was less interested in the classical gods/Danish gods section than was Wulfstan or, indeed, many twentieth-century commentators. However, the text survives in full and relatively reliable form only in Cambridge, Corpus Christi College MS 178; other copies are damaged (Oxford, Bodleian Library, Hatton 116—missing a quire), fragmentary (BL, Cotton Julius E. vii, and Cambridge University Library Ii. I. 33) and/or very late in date (Cambridge, Corpus Christi College 303, Hatton 116, and Cambridge University Library Ii. I. 33). This problematic evidence is itself a salutary reminder of the difficulties of codicological interpretation of the reception of the prose or Ælfric's own intentions.

Viewed from the standpoint of the other contents of these manuscripts, however, our understanding of such important subjects as the genres of religious writing comes into sharper focus. It is immediately apparent, for example, that the critical and editorial preference for what is thought of as Ælfric's major genres—the homily and the saint's life—obscures some of the manuscript evidence. In terms of their contents, the manuscripts associated with this particular group of texts divide into roughly two groups of chiefly passionals and "quando uolueris" collections, which more or less confirm Pope's grouping on internal textual evidence. *De falsis diis* circulates regularly in the company of a number of other texts, such as the First Series *De initio creaturae*; the *Interrogationes Sigewulfi*; the *Hexameron*, with which *De falsis diis* shares textual affinities; or the First Series *Dominica oratione*, the *Duodecim abusivis saeculi*, and extracts from the *Passio Machabeorum* (Skeat, 2, XXV), for example, with which *De falsis diis* shares an interest in Old Testament history. These texts or extracts of texts are often described as miscellaneous or "obiter dicta"; clearly, they conform neither to our generic expectations for exegetical homily or saint's life. Perhaps this is why we have yet to see an edition of the *Lives of Saints* that includes *De falsis diis* as one of the works that actually concludes this collection, at least according to the manuscript evidence. More important, however, the codicological evidence demands that all these miscellaneous texts be reassessed. What these texts offer is evidence for a body of writing or subgenre that Ælfric returned to regularly throughout his career and that was recognized by later compilers of his work.[25] This subgenre has a form fluid enough to be accommodated in either passional or homiliary, and has a content—that of the fundamentals of the faith—that Ælfric lovingly repeated and explored.

## Productive Misreading: Wulfstan's *De falsis deis*

What did the tradition of religious writing in Anglo-Saxon England make of Ælfric's *De falsis diis*? Its anomalous status as neither homily for a specified occasion nor saint's life, together with its length and intellectual ambition, marks it as firmly within the monastic milieu, albeit intended for the vernacular sphere (as the preface to the *Lives of Saints* might suggest, Skeat, 1, 1–7, cf. Wilcox, 1994, 119–21). Within the context of Ælfric's writings, the text performs the necessary work of maintaining traditional Christian verities to an extent unparalleled elsewhere in the culture. Its very success, however, points to its failure when judged from the standpoint of Wulfstan's revisions to the Ælfrician text in his *De falsis deis* (Bethurum, 1957, XII).

Using the standard homiletic methods of abbreviation and compilation, Wulfstan's own version amounts to a significant misreading of Ælfric's *De falsis diis*, whether or not Wulfstan actually saw the original version in its entirety. Wulfstan's own misreading interestingly parallels modern critical reception of the Ælfrician *De falsis diis* as a text of primary interest for its information about Danish practices. Even Pope, with the full text in front of him, talks of Ælfric's "academic distance" (1968, 669) from his subject of the Danes, thus failing to notice its energetic commitment to the maintenance of Christian truth. If anyone is guilty of "academic distance" or of writing a "cool and unimpassioned" tract, as Dorothy Bethurum suggests (1957, 334), it is not Ælfric but Wulfstan. In misunderstanding Ælfric's text, Wulfstan offers insight into the eventual fate of Ælfric's writing and a measure of the extent to which Ælfric is unique in his understanding of the importance of tradition maintenance.

The most obvious evidence for Wulfstan's dramatic reinterpretation of *De falsis diis* is its length. Wulfstan only uses lines 71–161 of the original version, which was probably known to him from Ælfric's own second rewriting (Bethurum, 1957, 333; Pope, 1968, 673). His introduction and conclusion also reveal an indebtedness to Ælfric, however, indicating that he may have seen Ælfric's full text rather than an extract. Whether or not this is in fact the case, in reusing only the classical gods/Danish gods section of the Ælfrician version, Wulfstan makes it thoroughly his own and fashions a new work from that of his predecessor. Ælfric's own context for the false gods—the discussion of origins, the Trinity, and Creation—is almost completely absent, as are all the narrative exempla. The resultant text conforms neatly with Wulfstan's concern to contest Danish beliefs, best known to us from his *Sermo Lupi* (Whitelock, 1976), but his *De falsis deis* lacks the urgent call to the faith so characteristic of that sermon, or indeed the rest of his writing. Put another way, Wulfstan removes from Ælfric's text its structure of salvation history and its revelation of the true by knowledge of the false.

Changing the emphasis of Ælfric's themes—a practice found elsewhere in Wulfstan's revision of Ælfric's work—Wulfstan's radically excised text takes idolatry and paganism as its subjects, rather than God.[26] The first sentence of *De falsis deis* firmly announces this departure from the Ælfrician text in its use of Wulfstan's own rhythmical style, and also firmly suppresses the inspired account of the Trinity from which Ælfric's text derives meaning:

> Eala, gefyrn is þæt ðurh deofol fela þinga misfor, ⁊ þæt mancynn to swyðe Gode mishyrde, ⁊ þæt hæðenscype ealles to wide swyðe gederede ⁊ gyt dereð wide. (Bethurum, 1957, XII, 3–5)

> [Alas, long ago it is that many things went wrong because of the devil, and mankind disobeyed God so readily, and paganism did great harm all too widely, and still harms widely.]

In contrast to Ælfric's introduction, with its insistence on God as the origin of all things and the lyricism of its worship of the Trinity, Wulfstan's sternly negative tone stands in some relief. For Wulfstan, in consequence, Ælfric's use of irony makes less sense. The relation between idolatry, paganism, and the devil is uppermost in Wulfstan's mind, and his characteristic theme of disobedience to the Law finds little counterpart in the revelation of its truth and the rewards of obedience to it, so characteristic of Ælfric. Wulfstan's modifications to the passages from Ælfric used in the conclusion similarly emphasize this theme of the Law and sever Ælfric's complementary balance of God's love. Ælfric puts it this way:

> Se syrwienda deofol, þe swicað embe mancyn
> gebrohte þa hæþenan on þæt healice gedwyld,
> þæt hi swa fule menn him fundon to godum,
> þe þa leahtras lufodan, þe liciað þam deofle,
> þæt eac heora biggengan heora bysmor lufodan,
> and ælfremede wurdan from þam ælmihtigan Gode,
> se ðe leahtras onscunað, and lufað þa *clænnysse*.
>    (Pope, 1968, XXI, lines 159–65; emphasis added)

> [The deceiving devil, who deceives mankind, brought the heathens into that shameful error, so that they who loved vices found foul men as gods, which pleases the devil; so, too, their worshipers loved their shame and were estranged from Almighty God, who shuns vices and loves chastity.]

Ælfric begins with the deceptive power of the devil, but ends by spelling out plainly the consequences of worshiping the false gods: estrangement from God's love. Wulfstan, by contrast, emphasizes human agency in choosing to worship the false and amplifies the rule of false law. Obedience to a self-created law is obeying the desire for sin ("unclænnesse"), not love ("clænnysse"):

And se syrwiende deofol þe a swicað embe mancyn gebrohte þa hæðenan men on þam healicon gedwylde þæt hi swa fule to godum gecuran þe heora fulan lust heom to lage sylfum gesettan ⁊ on *unclænnesse* heora lif eal lyfedan þa hwile ðe hi wæran. (Bethurum, 1957, XII, 85–89, emphasis added)

[And the deceiving devil who always deceives mankind brought the heathen people into such shameful error that they chose as gods the foul whom their own foul lust established as their law and lived in uncleanness their whole life while they were alive.]

What is missing from Wulfstan's passage is Ælfric's sense of balance, whereby the heathen's love of vice is contrasted with God's love of the pure. Wulfstan stresses instead the love of vice that creates false law and colors faithfulness to it. The intent of the two passages is thus quite different: Ælfric's enhances understanding of God's love; Wulfstan's is directed toward understanding the connection between humanly created laws and sin. Wulfstan's conclusion, which follows directly on from this passage, does move into Ælfrician territory, however, with its emphasis on true love and true Creation:

Ac se bið gesælig þe eal swylc oferhogað ⁊ ðone soðan Godd lufað ⁊ weorðað þe ealle þing gescop ⁊ geworhte. An is ælmihtig God on þrym hadum, þæt is fæder ⁊ suna ⁊ halig gast. Ealle þa ðry naman befehð an godcund miht ⁊ is an ece God, waldend ⁊ wyrhta ealra gesceafta. Him symle sy lof ⁊ weorðmynt in ealra worulda woruld a butan ende, amen. (89–95)

[But he is blessed who despises all such things and loves and honors the true God who made and created all things. Almighty God is one in three forms, that is Father, Son, and Holy Ghost. One divine power encompasses all three names and is one eternal God, ruler and maker of all creation. Praise be to him and glory always in the world of all worlds forever without end, amen.]

Yet for Ælfric, as we have seen, this is where the problem of the false gods both begins and ends. Wulfstan's conclusion, lacking a firm connection to his prior discussion of the law of the devil, seems redundant. As a conventional homiletic ending, it inspires worship, but necessarily cannot develop the relation of worship to spiritual understanding of God so carefully articulated by Ælfric. Wulfstan has here taken over the spirit of Ælfric's discussion of the Trinity, but in his own words.[27]

Wulfstan's emphasis on the devil and his false law in the introduction and conclusion to *De falsis deis*, therefore, cannot be thoroughly integrated with his appropriation of Ælfric's discussion of the classical and Danish gods that forms its body. In consequence, it is his *De falsis deis* and not Ælfric's that emerges as something of a disinterested treatise, and it is Wulfstan, not Ælfric, who puts the labor of understanding truth before us. The comparison with the *Sermo Lupi*, with its passionate engagement with the law and the Danes, could not be greater. The effect of *De falsis deis* is one of distance, of Wulfstan's distance from his subject, which suggests a consonant failure to engage his intended audience. These effects are enhanced by Wulfstan's cluttering up of Ælfric's carefully pared and often chiastic style, which far more consistently and effectively ironizes the fallen gods and their worshipers than do Wulfstan's modifications. One quick but illustrative example will suffice. A blurring of Ælfric's focus is achieved by quite literally glossing over his deliberate description of the sexual perversions (in the Miltonic sense of the word) of the classical gods. Of Venus, Ælfric writes:

> Sum wif hatte Uen[us], seo wæs Ioues dohtor,
> swa fracod on galnysse þæt hire fæder hi hæfde,
> and eac hire broðor, and oðre gehwylce,
> on myltestrena wisan; ac hi wurðiað þa hæþenan
> for [halige] gydenan, swa swa heora godes dohter.
> (Pope, 1968, XXI, 150–54)

> [Jove's daughter was a woman called Venus, so indecent in her lust that her father kept her, so too her brother, and others also, in the manner of a prostitute: but the heathens worshiped her as a holy goddess, as the daughter of their god.]

Wulfstan's modifications are revealing:

> And sum wif hatte Uenus seo was Ioues dohtor, ⁊ seo wæs swa ful ⁊ swa fracod on galnysse þæt hyre agen broðor wið hy gehæmede, þæs þe man sæde, þurh deofles lare, ⁊ ða yfelan wurðiað þa hæðenan eac for healice fæmnan. (Bethurum, 1957, XII, 77–80)

> [And Jove's daughter was a woman called Venus, and she was so foul and so indecent in lust that her own brother slept with her, so the man said, through the devil's teaching, and the heathens worship this evil one as a noble lady.]

Ælfric, unlike Wulfstan, does not shy away from the sexual excesses of Venus by omitting the account of paternal incest or by assigning her agency to the devil ("þurh deofles lare"). Wulfstan's alterations here and elsewhere perhaps derive from his sensitivity to oral delivery, as Orchard has recently argued (1992). Ælfric's writerly style, by contrast, with its balanced and inverted phrasing and its symbolic use of alliteration (note the alliteration on "gydenan" and "godes," for example), is the more sophisticated as well as the more pointed. Wulfstan's revisions, with their qualified handling of some of Ælfric's ironic and certainly most cultivated prose, serve to isolate his own version even more. In spite of his emphasis on law, Wulfstan's *De falsis deis* is a text oddly distinct from the rest of his work, and one emphatically in need of a context—one that only Ælfric's text can supply. To put it another way, Ælfric's aesthetic sits uncomfortably on Wulfstan's shoulders.

Like Ælfric before him, Wulfstan writes a group of catechical sermons on the fundamentals of the Christian faith (e.g., Bethurum, 1957, VI, VIIa, Xc). He too stresses the importance of knowing the Pater Noster and the Creed (Bethurum, 1957, VII, lines 6–9; VIIa, lines 3–6), as well as the seven gifts of the Holy Spirit (IX; cf. Napier, 1883, VII) and the Ten Commandments and the vices and virtues with which they are so frequently associated (Xc; cf. Godden, 1979, XII). That these homilists share a similar attitude toward their pastoral mission is equally evident from their letters (Fehr, 1914; cf. Hill, 1992b). Nor are these general topics exclusive to these two homilists; the anonymous corpus too repeatedly writes or rewrites sermons on the faith, especially for Rogationtide and Lent (see Wilcox, 1992). Where Ælfric is unique, however, is in his sustained reiteration of the transcendental power of the Trinity and the Creator. In his general works on the Christian faith, Ælfric has his eye firmly on directing the mind toward God, which has a causal (that is, rational and intellectual) link to moral reform of behavior. Wulfstan's revisions of Ælfric's most sustained meditation on truth in *De falsis diis* reminds us, however, that this most traditional Christian desire is in fact quite radical within late Anglo-Saxon England. In the hands of Wulfstan, Ælfric's text becomes one that inspires fear of sin and the devil rather than passionate engagement with truth. Wulfstan offers important evidence, therefore, that there can exist internal divergences in the emphases of a tradition.

At the same time, Wulfstan's emphasis on paganism and the Danes is also a response to the external threat of a competing belief system, the particular historical importance of which Ælfric's conceptual framing of Christian origins must necessarily minimize. Only in Ælfric's writing do we see the work of maintaining the beliefs of Christianity that are integral to it taken to its logical intellectual conclusion—the defense of truth from the premises of the tradition. In consequence, Ælfric offers us the firmest conviction that there is only one origin, God, and one history, salvation history. In such a paradigm of belief, all other origins are myths—products of the created, not the Creator. Ælfric's accounts of origins, therefore, demand a reassessment of current critical paradigms for the period. Late Anglo-Saxon concern with ethnic origins, as indicated by, for example, the heroic poetry, must also account for Ælfric's revelation of the truth of Christian origins. Put another way, Anglo-Saxon narratives of Christian origins are in cultural contest with those narratives that explore and commemorate, however partially, ethnic origins;

*Genesis A* and *B* must be read with *De falsis diis* or *De initio creaturae,* and against *Beowulf.*

Finally, Ælfric's *De falsis diis* is one of his most accomplished and ambitious works, as well as one of the finest examples of English prose of the period. Its primary achievement is its fundamental unity of the process of spiritual inquiry, worship, and aesthetic form. Such an achievement belies our conventional understanding of didactic works as utilitarian products of the preacher as moralist. Ælfric's systematic deployment of salvation history within an aesthetics of belief paves the way for a more general reconsideration of both the historicity of Anglo-Saxon homiletic writing in chapter 3 and of didacticism in chapter 4.

# Conventions of Time in the Old English Homiletic Corpus

## "A Long Remembrance of the Past": Representing Time

Traditional genres such as wisdom literature, heroic legends, or myths construct particular notions of time. From the perspective of the present of the narrative, the past is hardly chronologically specific; that is, few clear distinctions are made between kinds of pastness (the distant or the immediate, for example). The Germanic legendary past, which spans the entire migration period, is recreated in Anglo-Saxon heroic poetry from just such a stance. *The Battle of Maldon* (ed. Scragg, 1981), which presents the defeat of Byrhtnoth and his army against the Vikings in 991 through the lens of a triumphant heroic ethos, is the late Anglo-Saxon cousin of Germanic myth. History is idealized as heroic legend. *Beowulf* and *The Battle of Maldon* say as much about Anglo-Saxon attitudes toward their legendary past as they do about that past itself.

A similar process is more systematically at work in Christian writing, where the past is rationalized according to the scheme of salvation history with its epic cycles of Fall and Redemption. Like heroic literature, Christian writing encodes specific beliefs about time. The Christian present reconstructs the past, which in turn renders that present explicable. The present unveils the past, as the past prophesies the present, and revealed in both are God's providence. Whence the common medieval notion of typology, reenacted and re-presented by the annual cycles of the liturgy. Concepts of futurity are equally achronological, even when governed by the eschatology of the Last Days, which is a belief and therefore subject to description and spiritual interpretation, though not to definitive dating. The effect of such constructions of time in traditional genres is to reorient distinctions between past, present, and future. The past is re-presented, the present is continuous, and the future is an expectation made in the present.

For Augustine, these effects are the product of the mental activities of "expectation, attention, and memory." In his meditation on how to measure time in Book 11 of *The Confessions*, Augustine argues that the mind or soul expects the future, which "passes through the present, to which it attends, into the past, which it remembers." The past is therefore a "long remembrance of the past" made in the present.[1] For Ælfric, as for Augustine, time is performative; past, present, future, and memory form the place of the extremely transitory present. Ælfric draws on Augustinian notions of the soul or mind indirectly in his homily on the Nativity in the *Lives of Saints* (Skeat, 1, 18/120–22) when he describes the tripartite soul comprised of memory, will, and understanding: "Ic undergyte. þæt ic wylle undergytan and ge-munan. and ic wylle þæt ic under-gyte and gemune. þær þær þæt gemynd bið. þær bið þæt andgyt and se wylla" (I understand that which I will understand and remember, and I will that which I understand and remember. Wherever memory is, there is understanding and will).[2] Augustine and Ælfric frame my exploration of how the past, through the faculties of memory, will, and understanding, is re-presented in Anglo-Saxon religious writing.

Proceeding chronologically from the earlier anonymous homilies through Ælfric's work to the writing of Wulfstan in the second decade of the eleventh century, three studies here examine the interplay between Christian conventions of time and the historicity of homiletic and hagiographical discourses. Each study offers a particular perspective on the view that conventions of time are genre-specific, encoding past, present, and future in terms of the moral and spiritual ethos of the Christian present, but also that these conventions are themselves a product of a specific period in English history, roughly 975–1025. First is surveyed the extremely slender evidence in the homilies for specific references to contemporary events, such as the Benedictine reforms and the Viking raids. The examples of Blickling XI and Vercelli XI establish how the eschatology of the Last Days situates present events within a moral framework that emphasizes the universal virtue of vigilance. Awareness of the eschatological future governs moral understanding of the present, as is also exemplified in Ælfric's English prefaces to the *Catholic Homilies* and his own incidental references to contemporary events in these homilies in general.

The second study demonstrates how Ælfric remembers the English past in his hagiographical collection, the *Lives of Saints*, in order to provide moral examples for the present. Ælfric locates the history of the English church and its saints so familiar to us from the pages of Bede in a much broader "sweep of Christian history" (Greenfield and Calder, 1986, 76). By emphasizing the spiritual significance of this particular history, Ælfric offers the past as a source of present meditation for his intended aristocratic audience. Within this frame of pious advice literature, incidental references to the ideal king, Edgar, evoke implicit comparison with his contemporary, Æthelred. Rather than comment explicitly on past or present, however, Ælfric is much more interested in the moral lessons generated by both.

In general, vernacular religious writers are only interested in the historic present and past insofar as it elucidates Christian salvation history and reveals the presence of divine Providence throughout time. In the writings of Ælfric, emphasis on divine rule in this world amounts to an implicit political theory. Wulfstan's *Sermo Lupi*, by contrast, uses the politics of the present to emphasize, explicitly, the necessity for divine rule. Wulfstan's *Sermo* stands out in the homiletic corpus precisely because it refers to the vexed contemporary events of 1014. The *Sermo* thus tends to be read as evidence for history rather than as homiletic discourse. The final section of this chapter argues, however, that a more modulated view of the *Sermo* is required. Wulfstan uses the conventions of time familiar to him from the homiletic and hagiographic tradition in order to reinvent that tradition. The "fit" between text and event in the case of the *Sermo* remains mediated by Christian discourse. Indeed, the response of all the vernacular religious writers to this period, which sees the Benedictine reforms, the resurgence of the Danish raids, and the problematic policies of the reign of Æthelred II (the Unready), is to emphasize the virtues of good Christian behavior in general and to idealize a past when peace and religion flourished harmoniously; these are implicit comments on the present of late Anglo-Saxon society.

Analysis of the aesthetics of religious writing in chapter 2 argued that religious writing is a distinctive and cohesive genre, similar to but separate from vernacular religious poetry. This chapter argues that vernacular religious prose as a genre formulates history according to the traditions of Christian discourse. This genre must therefore be seen as a distinctive contribution to and product of the history of the late Anglo-Saxon period.

## The Historic Present: Anglo-Saxon Homilies in History

One of the achievements of Anglo-Saxon studies this century has been the painstaking analysis of homiletic manuscripts in terms of their compilation, dating, and provenance. The homiletic corpus has in fact proved more amenable to analyses of date and genre than the poetry largely because of its size. Homiletic mansucripts are compiled throughout the late Anglo-Saxon period in a process that begins in roughly the mid–tenth century and continues well into the twelfth. Although individual texts may have been composed much earlier or later, the high point of manuscript production occurs during the years 975–1025. This period is coterminous not only with the production of poetic manuscripts and the writing careers of Ælfric and Wulfstan, but also with the resurgence of the Viking raids and the monastic reforms.

Knowledge of the Benedictine reform and, to a lesser extent, of the Viking incursions is thus essential to the formulation of dating criteria for the homiletic corpus. The two best-known anonymous collections, Blickling and Vercelli, which are both compilations of diverse origins put together over a considerable period of time, are our best witnesses to homiletic production a generation or so before Ælfric. The reform period is a convenient watershed, dividing these compilations from the later postreform works of Ælfric and Wulfstan.[3]

By a fine paradox, however, Anglo-Saxon religious writing as a genre strongly resists attempts to locate it in this historical present. One of the key features of the genre is its lack of literal reference to contemporary or near contemporary events, or indeed to specific audiences. Although the increase in production of religious prose is often related to the phenomenon of the Benedictine reform, one of the puzzles of this writing is its apparent avoidance of any sustained or literal mention of it. Avoidance of reference to the Viking raids is an even greater puzzle. The fullest evidence for the events of this period is offered instead by the *Anglo-Saxon Chronicle,* as well as by cultural documents — foundation charters, laws, and monastic documents such as the *Regularis concordia* (e.g., Keynes, 1980; Dumville, 1992). Such evidence sharpens, by contrast, awareness of the conventions of time operating in religious writing.[4] In the *Anglo-Saxon Chronicle,* chronology anchors the narrative of events; laws and charters likewise have their own dating conventions, and the *Regularis concordia* is the product of a specific moment in the reform. Homilies, saints' lives, and sermons, however, most often use conventions of liturgical time in their rubrics, incipits, and contents, and thereby define the corpus in reference to the Christian seasons. These seasons and the present they mark are characterized in performative terms. The scriptural passage, saint's life, or catechesis that forms the basis for explication offers a repository of guidelines for Christian behavior that remains consistent across time and space, regardless of any specific historic instance. Frequent reiterations to remember the content of the homily, sermon, or saint's life spur Christian action in this universalized present — to pray, to venerate, to repent, and to give alms, for example. For Milton Gatch, the historical audience of the Blickling Homilies is "unknowable" precisely because of these reiterations, whereby homiletic content appears little more than an assembly of "ancient and commonplace materials" (Gatch, 1989, 115). Gatch suggests that the project of source identification will enable the formation of more definite conclusions about the history of a collection like the Blickling Homilies, and I agree. Augustine and Ælfric remind us, however, that time in religious writing is structured according to the Christian present, via the processes of memory, will, and understanding. Repeated calls to remember and understand the past of Christian history are important indices of these processes. When examining the few text-internal references to contemporary or near contemporary events that are encoded in this genre, therefore, we must ask why these specific historic events are worthy of desire, memory, understanding, and, hence, representation.

The unique reference to the year 971 in Blickling Homily XI for Ascension Day is a good example of the need for such a methodological approach:[5]

Nis þæt þonne feor toþon þæt þæt eac geweorþan sceal; *forþon* þes middangeard nede on ðas eldo endian sceal þe nu andweard is; *forþon* fife þara syndon agangen on þisse eldo. Þonne sceal þes middangeard endian & þisse is þonne se mæsta dæl agangen, efne nigon hund wintra & lxxi. on þys geare. Ne wæron þas ealle gelice lange, ac on þyssum wæs þreo þusend wintra, on sumre læsse, on sumere eft mare. Nis *forþon* nænig mon þe þæt an wite hu lange he ure Drihten þas gedon wille, hwæþer þis þusend sceole beon scyrtre ofer þæt þe lengre. Þæt is þonne æghwylcum men swiþe uncuþ, buton urum Drihtne anum. (Morris, 1874–80, 117/34–119/7; emphasis added)

[Nor is it far from hence that this also must happen; because this earth needs must end in this age which is now present; because five of these are past in this age. Then must this world end, and of this the greatest share is passed, even nine hundred and seventy-one years, in this year. Nor were all these alike in length, but in this was three thousand years, in some less, in others yet more. There is therefore no one man who knows how long will our Lord complete it, whether this thousand must be shorter or longer than that. That is to every man wholly unknown, save to our Lord alone.]

That this reference to 971 has proved at best a frustrating guide to the dating of the Blickling Homilies in general is well known, but many still regard the collection as representative of earlier tenth-century monastic or clerical practices on the basis of that reference (e.g., Gatch, 1977, 8). Dating Anglo-Saxon manuscripts makes for cautious scholarship. The Blickling Homilies constitute an incomplete "temporale" combined with "sanctorale" of a mixed and stylistically uneven authorship that reflects the collection's diverse origins.[6] Arguments about dialect, for example, whether a ninth-century Mercian dialect is used, are at best tenuous, and Latin sources identified thus far are sufficiently early to be of little use for dating.[7] When viewed in terms of the content of the homily, however, 971 is worthy of memory and reason (note the number of times "forþon" is used) not because it locates the Christian present in a particular time or place, but because it emphasizes, by contrast, the unknowability of the future. The limits of human knowledge about the future structure the historic present according to God's time.

Couched in the familiar topoi of the six ages of the world and the coming of the Last Days, 971 in Blickling XI is a means of identifying the beginning of the end. Thus, 971 years have passed in the last age, which is the present, but when this age will end is unknown. Precisely because this is secretive ("degol"; Morris, 117/25) knowledge (for God alone), references to it elicit vigilance, or watchfulness, as Vercelli Homily III puts it (Scragg, 1992, 77–78)—a state of ever-present readiness for the Last Days. Ælfric makes a similar point in his first English preface to

82

the *Catholic Homilies,* linking the circumstances of the composition of the collection as a whole to the need for instruction in the "geendung þyssere worulde" (Clemoes, 1997, 174/58–59). For Ælfric, too, the unknowability of this end is a frequent topos.[8] That the topos of the Last Days is a commonplace in homilies associated with the earlier phase of the Benedictine reforms (in Blickling and Vercelli) as well as in postreform homilies seems to indicate a conflation of Christian eschatology with the coming of the first millenium.[9] Wulfstan's *Sermo Lupi,* of 1014, also begins "ðeos worold is on ofste, ⁊ hit nealæcð þam ende" ("this world is in haste, and it approaches the end"; Whitelock, 1976, lines 4–5). What is stressed by the homilists in these and similar references to the end of the world is its Christian significance; the millenium has little literal meaning.[10] Ælfric uses the eschaton of the Last Days in his English preface to the First Series of the *Catholic Homilies* in part to point to the moral significance of the entire collection—the constant, that is eternally present, need for vigilance that enables recognition of error, heresy, and the Antichrist (Clemoes, 1997, 174–77). It is thus no accident that this series begins with *De initio creaturae;* Christian beginnings and endings are closely related, as discussed in chapter 2. Similarly, Wulfstan's *Sermo Lupi* begins with the end in a homily that presents the particularly problematic political circumstances of the second decade of the eleventh century via the lens of Christian meanings of time. In its use of this familiar topos found across the corpus, the passage from Blickling XI quoted above serves as one reminder among many that the events of this world can only be understood in relation to God's providence, which is known fully only to God.

The need to remember and understand events in terms of eschatology and salvation history is also immanent in the section of Vercelli XI for Rogationtide, which Celia Sisam argues refers to the historical events of the late tenth century, the Viking raids, and the confusion that spread in the antimonastic backlash (1976, 36; cf. Willard, 1945). D. G. Scragg argues persuasively that the Vercelli Book, as "the earliest extant collection of homiletic texts in England," is not a homiliary but a "uniform collection of pious reading" (1992, xx, xix). The book is certainly a heterodox compilation of poetry and prose with few obvious connections across these two genres other than their generally religious content.[11] Like the Blickling collection, with which it is most frequently compared, the Vercelli Book features those narrative techniques that often characterize the anonymous corpus—straightforward narrative in both sermons and hagiography, and catechetical instruction on the general themes of Christian life. In addition, a number of the texts display "Irish" or "Insular" features of content and composition.[12] James E. Cross's identification of the Pembroke Sermonary as a major source for three of these homilies is also suggestive of a pastoral origin (1987).[13] The recurrent emphasis in the collection as a whole on Christian behavior, together with its interest in eschatology, however, accords equally well with its description as a manual for meditative reading. Meditative reading and pastoral concerns are not necessarily mutually exclusive.

If we agree that this anonymous collection, like Blickling, witnesses homiletic writing in the generation or so before Ælfric, then the reform itself was already under way. According to Scragg (1992, xli–xlii), Vercelli XIX–XXI, a set of Rogationtide homilies, may have been compiled in Canterbury during Dunstan's pontificate. By contrast, the events described in Vercelli XI, also for Rogationtide, are sufficiently vague that virtually any period of Anglo-Saxon history from Alfred onward would provide the appropriate context (indeed the parallels with Alfred's letter, attached to Old English copies of Gregory's *Pastoral Care,* are notable):[14]

Ðis syndon swares ꝺ geswinces dagas, swa we hit sylfe ongytan magon on þam manigfealdum unieðnessum þe dægwamlice on manna cynn fealleð on misgewidrum for manna gewyrhtum. Magon we nu ongitan, men þa leofestan, þætte ure ealra ende swiðe mislice toweard nealæceð. Nu syndon þa Godes cyrican bereafode ꝺ þa wiofeda toworpene þurh hæðenra manna gehresp ꝺ gestrodu, ꝺ þa weallas syndon tobrocene ꝺ toslitene, ꝺ þa godcundan hadas syndon gewanode for hyra sylfra gewyrhtum ꝺ geearnungum. ꝺ nalas þæt an Godes þeowas ane syndon, ac eac swylce cyningas ꝺ bisceopas ꝺ ealdormen, þa þe ðysse þeode rædboran syndon, hie habbað þa godcundan hadas ꝺ þæt Godes folc gestroden ꝺ bereafod for leasum tyhtum ꝺ lyðrum metsceattum. ꝺ we þonne nu for ure ealra gewyrhtum þas egeslican þing ꝺ þas ondrysenlican her on worulde þrowigað. (Scragg, 1992, 225/86–99)

[These are days of toil and strife, as we may ourselves understand from these manifold hardships that daily fall in storms on mankind for the deeds of men. Now we are able to understand, dearly beloved, that the end of all of us approaches swiftly and variously. Now are the churches of God robbed and the altars destroyed through the plunder and despoilment of heathen men, and the walls are shattered and broken, and the holy orders weakened by their own acts and merits. And not only are the servants of God at one in this but so too kings and bishops and ealdormen, those who are counselors to this people, have plundered and robbed the holy orders and God's people by false charges and hateful bribes. And we suffer now these terrible and dreadful things for all our deeds here in the world.]

Like the excerpt from Blickling XI, this passage uses homiletic conventions that generalize what might otherwise appear to be references to the years of the antimonastic backlash in the wake of the first phase of the Benedictine reform and to the upsurge of Viking raids from the 990s onward. Set in the now ("nu") of the Christian present, the style of Vercelli XI and its use of the topos of the end of the world suggests a causal relation among the destruction of churches and altars by the "heathens" ("ðurh hæðenra manna"); the complicity and laxness of kings, churchmen, and ealdormen (the leaders of the two estates); and "ure ealra gewyrhtum" ("all our deeds"). But the homily makes a moral point about collective responsibility for human events whose origin is sin (a point made at greater length by Wulfstan in his *Sermo Lupi*). In consequence, this catalog of events provides an example of the need for repentance, prayer, and worship in the three days of Rogationtide, as the conclusion to the homily stresses (225/103–7). The temporal world of the present is understood in the light of its future in "the end of us all." In Vercelli XI, the convention of the Last Days, which defies specificity (as the example of Blicking Homily XI also reminds us), combines with standard descriptions of decay and destruction (similarly common in Anglo-Saxon writing) and with the use of estates ideology to indicate the impossibility of a direct relation between text and event, as Scragg (1992, 220) also notes. That impossibility is governed by the operation of memory, will, and understanding in the structuring of Christian time. As the Vercelli homilist puts it, "[F]or þan we habbað mycle overþearfe þæt we ðas þing ealle mægene geþencen þe we nu hwile her ymbspræcon" (Therefore we have very great need that we should reflect with might on all these things of which we have now briefly spoken"; 225/100–101); memories of the past and expectations of the future are here enfolded into an understanding of a present always in need of moral reform.

Blicking XI and Vercelli XI are Rogationtide homilies, as already mentioned. This English season, like the other major Christian seasons, is particularly preoccupied with the performance of time. Rogationtide, Joyce Bazire and James E. Cross point out (1982, xv–xxiv), has its own liturgical readings, prayers, processions, and penitential practices, as well as its own history in the origins of the feast by Mamertus of Vienne. Indeed, both Vercelli XI and one of its companion pieces, Vercelli XII, for the second day of Rogationtide, supply another version of just such a history, claiming instead that Peter instituted the feast (Scragg, 1992, 219, 228). As a particular Christian season, memorialized by these liturgical rites and stories, the Old English Rogationtide homilies are at the same time markedly general, addressing familiar Christian themes that surface elsewhere in the corpus. Given this pressure to generalize in a season stressing the timeliness of Christian behavior, it is not surprising that what appear to be specific references to dates and events in both Blickling XI and Vercelli XI form instead particular instances of the universal. A similar technique is at work in Ælfric's writing, as his reference to the end of the world in the first English preface indicates; the genre of the preface is as universalizing as the season of Rogationtide in its representation of timeliness.

## Remembering the Reform

Like the earlier homilies of the Blickling and Vercelli collections, Ælfric's two series of *Catholic Homilies* pay as little attention to the Viking incursions as to the Benedictine reforms, in spite of their real effect on Ælfric's life. Nor do his homilies refer explicitly to his king, Æthelred II (the Unready), by name (though he is mentioned in the First Series English preface; see Clemoes, 1997, 174). It is worth pausing to consider Ælfric's reticence in more detail, precisely because it provides a sustained instance of what surfaces only occasionally in the earlier anonymous homilies. As in the case of Ælfric's traditional use of beginnings explored in chapter 2, conventions of Christian time and its meanings are fully assimilated in the *Catholic Homilies*.

The one compelling reference Ælfric makes to the troubling political circumstances of the decade of the 990s appears in his Latin preface to the Second Series of the *Catholic Homilies*, which expresses anxiety about the safe delivery of the First Series to Sigeric, archbishop of Canterbury, due to the activity of the "pirates":

> Et licet multis iniuriis infestium piratarum concutiebamur. postquam praefatum libellum tuae sanctitati transmisimus. Tamen nolentes repperiri falsidici promisores. dolente animo hoc opus perficimus; (Godden, 1979, 1/13–16)

> [And although we were being shaken by the great injuries of hostile pirates after we sent to your sanctity the little book mentioned before, yet not wishing to be found making false promises, we have completed this work with a grieving mind.]

Providing a crucial piece of supporting evidence for the dating of the *Catholic Homilies*, this brief though poignant passage is often cited as an indication of Ælfric's awareness of the political turmoil that beset southern England in the last decade of the tenth century (Godden, 1979, xci–xcii). In the immediate context of the highly rhetorical and formal genre of the preface, Ælfric's comments stand out in stark relief, especially if read with an eye for references to specific historic events. Yet the threat of the Vikings is encoded as a moral and psychological challenge for the faithful Ælfric; that a promise must be kept bears out the more general homiletic association between events and mindful behavior. Rarely, however, is it noticed just how isolated is this comment on the Danish incursions of the 990s in Ælfric's contemporary works. To be sure, Ælfric occasionally censors non-Christian practices and supersititions that could be imputed to the influence of Danish beliefs, as in the passage concluding his First Series homily on the Circumcision that censors several specific practices of divination "æfter hæðenum gewunan" (Clemoes, 1997, 229/163), but its context (discussed further in

86

chapter 4) strongly suggests that these are the practices of Christian, not necessarily Danish, English. A different aspect of tradition maintenance appears to be the concern of the *Catholic Homilies*, where the few references to the Danes are addressed in terms of pastoral matters of faith.

It could be argued, of course, that Ælfric, cloistered within the monastery, was largely insulated from the political world outside. Such an argument might harmonize with the fact that Anglo-Saxon homilies in general are studiously distanced from the historical events of their time. By the same token, however, English monasticism in general is not barred from participation in life beyond the cloister, and Ælfric's reformed Benedictinism in particular is predicated on extending its ideological principles beyond the monastery (as Clayton notes, 1985, 235–42). Ælfric's vision of English vernacular piety, though deeply informed by monasticism, cannot be seen therefore as a retreat from the world. According to his explicit intentions, the *Catholic Homilies* and the *Lives of Saints* that follows are not intended only for a monastic milieu.

In the instance of the *Catholic Homilies* and the Danish raids of the 990s, it is important to note that Ælfric's ecclesiastical dedicatee, Sigeric, archbishop of Canterbury, was central to the negotiation of the first two financial settlements with the Danes.[15] Moreover, his lay patron for these homilies (as well as for other later works) was Æthelweard, another member of the same negotiating party and ealdorman in charge of military organization for the south of England. Ælfric's relationship with Æthelweard and his family is a lengthy and sustained one, with a personal dimension far greater than that suggested by their patronage of his writing. Æthelmær, Æthelweard's son, founded Cerne Abbas, perhaps with his father, and later Eynsham in 1005, where Ælfric was the first abbot and to where he probably retired. Like his father, Æthelmær was a prominent figure in Æthelred's court. His family, moreover, had close contacts with that of ealdorman Bryhtnoth, memorialized in *The Battle of Maldon*.[16] The fact that the ignominious defeat of the English at Maldon in 991 is represented as a poetic triumph is therefore not altogether beside the point for understanding Ælfric's own attitude toward contemporary events. It is hard indeed to imagine that Ælfric managed to escape all but the most general knowledge of the Danes, even though he was sequestered in his monastery.

Both Sigeric and Æthelweard (d. circa 998) were probably older than Ælfric. Sigeric died shortly after the issuing of the Second Series of the *Catholic Homilies* (circa 994/95), and Ælfric's dedication of the collection to him may be simply the appropriate formal gesture for a junior monk to make to his senior colleague. Ælfric's relationship with Æthelmær was closer than that with his father, and Æthelmær's fall from grace at the turn of the century provides a plausible context for some of his later occasional writing (Clayton, 1993). Throughout his life, however, Ælfric maintained considerable contacts with other prominent figures. Influential early in his career were Ælfheah (bishop of Winchester and subsequently archbishop of Canterbury), who sent him to Cerne Abbas, and, of course, Æthelwold of Winchester.[17] All of his major works and correspondence are dedicated to figures with some importance in the ecclesiastical and aristocratic world. Apart from Sigeric, archbishop of Canterbury, and the family of Æthelweard, Wulfstan the homilist, bishop of London (996–1002), bishop of Worcester, and archbishop of York (1002–23) is the best known. But Ælfric also dedicated his Latin *Life of Æthelwold* (Lapidge and Winterbottom, 1991, 71) to Cenwulf, bishop of Winchester (1006), composed a homily for the installation of Æthelwold II as archbishop of Winchester (Assmann, 1889, IV; cf. Clayton, 1993), and wrote to Wulfsige, bishop of Sherborne (993–1002), within whose diocese fell Cerne Abbas (Wilcox, 1994, 54). His homiletic Letters to Sigefyrth (Assmann, 1889, II) and Wulfgeat of Ylmandun (Assmann, 1889, I), whose own political downfall is mentioned in the *Anglo-Saxon Chronicle*, together with the Letter to Sigeweard associated with his *Treatise on the Old and New Testament*, suggest other regional contacts, ecclesiastical and lay.[18] Prominent by virtue of its absence from this list is any mention of the royal family, especially when we recall that Æthelweard was related to Æthelred II (Keynes, 1980, 187–88) or when we contrast Ælfric's contacts with Wulfstan's activity on behalf of both Æthelred and Cnut. Malcolm Godden's suggestion (1991, 219) that Æthelred may have commissioned Ælfric's unfinished treatise on the role of the king in battle, *Wyrdwriteras Us Secgað* (Pope, 1967–68, XXII), itself a gloss on John C. Pope's own thoughts (1968, 726), has yet to be substantiated.

The discrepancy between the content of Ælfric's works and this list of his personal and professional contacts is nothing short of remarkable. The Letter to Wulfgeat (Assmann I) has only the baldest account of his political fall, and that to Sigefyrth (Assmann II) is equally frustrating for its brevity about Sigefyrth's circumstances (both are reedited by subsequent compilers as general homilies).[19] In short, when we seek to identify in his writing the history of specific events known to have occurred during Ælfric's life—monastic, military, or personal—we find only generalities. The problem of this lack of reference must therefore be considered at the level of the genre rather than solely on the individual instance. The terrain on which Ælfric formulates his response to the world of reform, politics, and the Danes is that of Christian discourse and its construction of time forged through the writing of the *Catholic Homilies*.

The paradoxes offered by this evidence are rich. While it is clear that the long history of the Benedictine reform in the tenth century is a major factor in the increased production of religious writing in the vernacular, a measure of the reform's impact on Anglo-Saxon Christianity in general is the way in which vernacular homilies thoroughly rewrite the historical moment as the Christian present. Religious writing washes away historical specificity. The task of associating text with event, the homilies with history, is made infinitely more complex by this successful incorporation of and mediation by Christian understandings of time. Moreover, although earlier homiletic collections such as Blickling and Vercelli are roughly contemporary with the first phase of the Benedictine reform, and although Ælfric's work is more firmly related to that of the postreform period, a closer look at the evidence of the reform suggests that homiletic production follows its spirit, not its letter.

The turning point in the history of the reform is conventionally associated with the accession of Edgar to the throne in 959 and his subsequent appointments of the three principal monastic reformers — Æthelwold, Dunstan, and Oswald — to the key sees of the English church at Canterbury, Winchester, and Worcester. Replacing the regular clergy and strengthening the observance of the Benedictine rule at the top of the institutional structure of the English church, the reformers capitalize on changes in monastic life begun earlier in the reign of Æthelstan. The refounding of the monasteries is one of the most remarkable and durable features of Edgar's reign. From the 960s on, reform is given greater impetus because of the new institutional prominence of the reformers. Change is initiated from the top down and derives its momentum from a unique power base; only the English reformers moved so strongly into the cathedrals. The key to understanding these events is the important relation between the reformers (especially Æthelwold) and Edgar, which results in a new definition of the relation between church (now theoretically, if not always practically, in the hands of the Benedictines) and the ruling family. That this relation is both political (in that it redefines land use and privilege for the church in relation with the royal family) and liturgical (in that it is based on a so-called return to Benedictinism) has long been known.[20]

The chief though belated and programmatic witness to this stage of the reform, the Latin *Regularis concordia* (probably compiled by Æthelwold in 971), makes plain the principal goals and the distinctive Englishness of this stage of the reform when contrasted with continental models.[21] The strengthened association between monastic church and the ruling family is signaled, for example, by the daily prayers to be recited for both king and queen, as well as by the ceremonies for the annointment of Edgar as king (Symons, 1953, 11–24; cf. Nelson, 1977). The symbolic representation of Edgar flanked by Æthelwold and Dunstan in the *Benedictional of Æthelwold* is a fitting tribute to reform ideology. The *Regularis concordia*, however, is primarily concerned with the regulation of monastic observance across both regular and monastic clergy. It appears to have had some success, as far as we can ascertain from the scant evidence for liturgical devotions in English books of the liturgy (Hill, 1992b; Gneuss, 1985).

Although the education of the clergy, both monastic and regular, is everywhere explicit in the program of reading and commentary of divine Scripture recommended in the *Regularis concordia* (following the rule itself), there is no mention of a broader pastoral mission of the kind that Ælfric, for example, promotes in the *Catholic Homilies*. Nor indeed is there any clear-cut reference to the practice of regular monastic preaching in the night offices that we might expect from a comparison with earlier Carolingian documents, such as the *Admonitio generalis* (which otherwise have an important influence on the English liturgical reforms). In fact, as Milton Gatch and Mary Clayton argue, references to English preaching throughout the period are not sufficient to sustain any argument about its institutional importance.[22] The language of the *Regularis concordia* is Latin, and, while it is tempting to see evidence for the dissemination of its wider aims to the regular clergy in its subsequent interlinear Old English glosses or in the translations into English of, for example, the Benedictine rule and the *Epitome* of Benedict of Aniane, the relation between Old English homilies and this stage of the reform remains provocatively elusive (cf. Lapidge and Winterbottom, 1991, li–lx; Hill, 1991). Put another way, preaching in English is not institutionalized by this phase of the reform. The Blickling and Vercelli homilies are indeed our best witnesses to the absence of a direct relation between vernacular preaching and the monastic reforms in its early phase.

These two principal features of the first stage of the reform—the close political associations of the reformers with Edgar and its concentration on monastic observance—are measures of its success. They also point, however, to an internal weakness: the lack of a policy for dissemination beyond the reformed cloisters and court.[23] To some extent, the unevenness with which the reform was received is predictable. The initial energy of the movement (in all regions except Winchester and to a lesser extent Worcester and Canterbury) dissipated with the death of Edgar in 975. Æthelwold died in 984, Dunstan in 988, and Oswald in 992. The retheorized relation between church and state—dependent as much on personality as it was on principle—was bought at the price of ignoring the conflicting economic interests of the regional ealdormen and the hostility or plain disinterest of the regular clergy. Reaction to Edgar's death in 975 was swift and resulted in certain areas in a backlash (Fisher, 1950–52). Internal factions within the ruling family combined with the external and increasingly dangerous Viking raids compromised the gains of the earlier movement. The pace at which monastic houses were reformed slowed, and the energy of the ruling class was channeled instead into controlling the Viking threat. There was a new caution in the air, even in the heart of the reformers' influence. Appointments to the Canterbury see in these later years, for example, remain in the sphere of Benedictine influence, but the appointments were conservative and ensured a fairly quick exchange of leaders with little time to institute or maintain long-lasting reform (Brooks, 1984, 255–310).

Æthelwold had effected substantial change at Winchester, however (Lapidge and Winterbottom, 1991, xxxix–clxxix; Yorke, 1988). Here, reformation was kept alive in part by the promotion of his cult and in part by the immense cultural activities of his school. Reform influenced every aspect of clerical and cultural life in this region: from the rebuilding of the monastic precincts, the development of artistic styles and scripts, and the revival of interest in Latin scholarship (and the school of Latin poetry) to the production of liturgical service books and the compilation and copying of key patristic texts. Yet the relation between such remarkable achievements in Latin Christian, largely monastic, scholarship and the corpus of the Old English homilies is by no means clear-cut even in the case of Ælfric, who regularly announces his own debt to Æthelwold. The regularization of language and liturgical practice at Winchester, for example, is not necessarily paralleled in anonymous Old English homilies copied during this period in other monastic scriptoria.[24] And Ælfric himself is clearly belated with respect to the reforming zeal of the first stage of the movement. Æthelwold died before Ælfric began writing in the early 990s, by which time the other figures of the earlier reforms were also dead. In addition, Ælfric's clerical appointments took him away from Winchester, first to Cerne Abbas and then to Eynsham. While he maintained a close relation with the ideology of the reform throughout his career, Ælfric is by no means a slavish student of its principles. As is well known, Ælfric distances himself from the ornate Latin style of the Winchester school in his own Latin and, while he appears to be one of the few promoters of Standard Late West Saxon outside Winchester, he remains idiosyncratic in other respects, pursuing an obsession with correct liturgical observance and maintaining an orthodoxy about the use of apocrypha that verges on the heterodox (cf. Clayton, 1990, 217–66; Hill, 1985).

How, then, are we to regard Ælfric's program of English homilies and saints' lives? As Clayton points out (1985, 229–30), the practice of compiling and composing homiliaries and homilies in English is less closely associated with the Winchester school than with the earlier English Vercelli and Blickling collections. The comparison with Wulfstan Cantor, who apparently wrote only in Latin, is instructive. Wulfstan Cantor remained at Winchester throughout his career, producing a body of highly accomplished Latin writing, which is, however, far more restricted to liturgical use than anything Ælfric ever wrote (Lapidge and Winterbottom, 1991, xiii–xxxix). Ælfric thus emerges as the only self-proclaimed student of Æthelwold with any interest in disseminating the reform beyond the small powerful monastic elite at Winchester. Not content with the Latin reform of the liturgy, Ælfric takes the necessary next step of structuring English preaching around the liturgical calendar. His achievement is the regularization of preaching according to the intellectual and theological principles of the reform, though in English and not in Latin. The trend toward vernacularization and pastoral care already existed outside the immediate sphere of the reforms, as indicated by the Blickling and Vercelli collections.

Unlike these earlier collections, Ælfric's three series of homilies (the two series of *Catholic Homilies* and the later supplementary works) offer a much more comprehensive program of preaching arranged, at least initially, in two annual sequences. These homilies, together with the *Lives of Saints*, Old Testament translations, letters, and miscellaneous texts, offer a clearly planned, regularly revised collection of religious writing grounded in Christian history that by far surpasses the earlier English works (Clemoes, 1959). Ælfric, in short, is to be credited with the most thorough and unique revisioning of past, present, and future in terms of the Christian present.

Three crucial points emerge from this discussion of the relation of the Old English homilies to historical events of the same period. First, what might appear to be references to particular events or dates in anonymous homilies such as Blickling XI and Vercelli XI are encoded according to Christian conventions of time that in fact resist specificity. Second, in accordance with these conventions, the text-external history of Ælfric's political and religious contacts throughout the period is at best a supplement to the text-internal contents of his writing, whose pastoral concerns are always much broader than references to their dedicatees suggest. Third, while the aims and principles of the Benedictine reform suffuse the homiletic writing of Ælfric, its history cannot be easily or glibly read back into the texts themselves. These three factors are strong indications of the internal cohesion of the genre. One measure of this cohesion is the consistency with which time is represented not as the history of contemporary events of the tenth century, but as the eternal present of Christian salvation history. This same evidence, however, viewed from another perspective suggests that the very success with which vernacular homilies deploy these conventions is itself historical; all are products of the same period that sees both the unfolding of the complex history of the monastic reforms and the Danish raids.

The Old English homilies, therefore, do participate in their historical moment, but not in ways which we expect. The homilists do not avoid history by retreating from their world into the monastery and into patristic tradition. Rather, the world of belief is brought to bear on that of human events; the historical present is mediated by belief. The faculties of memory, will, and understanding elucidate the homilies' deliberate use of conventions to construct a past, present, and future in harmony with the more general structure of Christian time as the story of salvation.

To view these strategies as traditional and therefore atemporal is to misread the transformative power of belief in late Anglo-Saxon England.

## The Past in the Present: History in Ælfric's *Lives of Saints*

Hagiography—often thought of as that typologically flattened and therefore nonhistorical genre—yields important evidence for contemporary Anglo-Saxon religious, political, and social life, as scholars increasingly appreciate. The burden of memory—of those objects worthy of memory, will, and understanding—is more obviously carried by hagiography and the cults of veneration that transfer the lives of the saintly figures from the past into the present than by the Rogationtide homilies in specific or by the homilies in general. Where the Benedictine reform is concerned, however, Anglo-Saxon writers venerate their leaders with Latin, not English, lives of their spiritual leaders, Oswald, Dunstan, and Æthelwold.[25] Ælfric himself wrote a Latin *Life of Æthelwold*, which may have been intended as prefatory to an English version that has not survived (Lapidge and Winterbottom, 1991, cxlix). Latin lives also formed a major component of cult activity centered upon the Anglo-Saxon royal dynasties of this period, with their saintly kings and religious mothers, daughters, wives, and sisters (Ridyard, 1988; Rollason, 1989a, 133–214). There are, by contrast, no vernacular lives of the ecclesiastical leaders of the reform, and the evidence of the few vernacular lives of royal saints barely matches the industry with which they are produced in Latin.

Ælfric's major vernacular hagiographical collection, the *Lives of Saints*, thus carries quite a different burden of memory, will, and understanding from that suggested by the evidence of contemporary Latin cults, which memorialize the reform and the piety of the West Saxon royal dynasties. The *Lives of Saints*, which includes both homilies and saints' lives, forms a body of pious reading dedicated to the aristocratic family of Æthelweard, whose prominence in late-tenth-century life has already been indicated. Pious reading is a medium for an advice literature, founded on scriptural and hagiographical precedent. Scripture, like hagiography, often provides Ælfric with the material whereby contemporary events may be recalled and understood. As for many Anglo-Saxon Christian poets, the sacred literature of the Old Testament invites "the reader to see imaginative parallels between moral truths and physical actuality, or between spiritual experience and historical events" (Godden, 1991, 208). In accordance with this general convention, the *Lives of Saints* are used by Ælfric to offer broad-based moral comment on the present. Indeed, one of the reasons why the *Lives of Saints* is not merely a collection of saints' lives but also of homilies is the collection's shared interest in the spiritual connections between past and present. The *Lives of Saints* are no *speculum principis*, but they do accommodate a view of Ælfric as priestly adviser or teacher—a role not dissimilar from that exemplified in his

Second Series *Life of Cuthbert* (Godden, 1979, X). In addition, this collection encodes a more specific vision of the English past in the present than that presented by the earlier and more pastoral *Catholic Homilies*, as Godden also notes (1985a, 94–97).

Ælfric's vision of the English past is heavily influenced by Bede, who also shaped the ways in which the saintly life became central to the Latin historiography of the church in England. Bede's *Historia* is in large measure a narrative of the saintly men and women (not all of whom became saints) whose lives are synonymous with the establishment and institutionalization of the English church. Hagiography provides a series of exemplary moments set within the larger typology of salvation history that grounds the *Historia* itself; the same strategy is deployed by the homilists, as we have seen. Nicholas Howe (1989) has investigated one aspect of this typology, which he terms the "myth of migration"; this myth is itself metonymous of the great pattern of fall and redemption that is everywhere implicit in the *Historia*. Bede's historical imagination is scriptural and therefore moral—"the vision of God in history," as Robert W. Hanning aptly terms it (1966, 90). The ninth-century Old English translator of Orosius's *Historiarus adversum paganos libri septem* holds a similar vision:

> Nu we *witan* þæt ure Dryhten us gesceop, we *witon* eac þæt he ure reccend is ꝺ us mid ryhtlicran lufan lufað þonne ænig mon. Nu we *witon* þæt ealle onwealdas from him sindon, we *witon* eac þæt ealle ricu sint from him, for þon ealle onwealdas of rice sindon. (Bately, 1980, 36/5–9; emphasis added)

> [Now we know that our Lord created us; we also know that he is our ruler and loves us with a truer love than any man. Now we know that all powers are from him; we know also that all rule is from him, because all power is from rule.]

In translating this passage from Book 2 of the *Historiarum*, the Old English writer has converted Orosius's rhetorical questions into statements of fact (cf. Hanning, 1966, 39). Creation, rule, and power all derive from God and form a body of knowledge (note how often the verb *witan* is used in this passage) that is the basis for wisdom. The wisdom that comes from knowledge, which is the wisdom of salvation history, governs the recording of history no less for this translator than for Bede. History reveals the presence of divine governance—a perspective that informs Bede's accounts of the saints in his *Historia ecclesiastica* as well as Ælfric's understanding of the politics of this world.

Although Ælfric uses Bede more than any other vernacular writer, he differs from Bede by structuring his writing explicitly on the patterns of fall and redemption that remain implicit in the *Historia*. For Ælfric, the lives of Bede's English saints form part of the sequence of scriptural history anchored by the traditions of the passional. They are not the high points of a narrative of the history of the church in England. This difference cannot be explained only as one of genre—of homilies as opposed to historiography—unless we also emphasize the difference in the objects of memory and veneration between these two genres. Bede's immediate object is the history of the English church; Ælfric's is God's rule as revealed by salvation history.

As discussed in chapter 2, salvation history explicitly structures the Christian cycle of worship and veneration in Ælfric's *Catholic Homilies* and his *Lives of Saints*. This move is governed in part by liturgical tradition, that is to say, by the structure of the homiliaries and passionals that form Ælfric's direct antecedents, and in part by his intention to reach and educate a wide English audience—a goal more easily served by vernacular preaching than Latin historiography. Bede embeds hagiography in history, albeit the history of the English church. Ælfric embeds history and hagiography in the story of salvation. History to a large extent is here hagiography, and hagiography is framed by the sequences of preaching and meditative reading that witness the central role of the liturgy in the Benedictine reform. The liturgy therefore structures the remembering of the past in the present in Ælfric's great sequences of homilies and saints' lives, and the subject of the divine reading and daily worship that is the work of the liturgy is God, from whom all power flows, to paraphrase the ninth-century translator of Orosius. To a far greater extent than Bede, in other words, Ælfric's vision of history is scriptural (that is, liturgical) and moral (that is, allegorical). In consequence, the *Lives of Saints* have important implications for the ways in which Anglo-Saxon vernacular religious writing reconceives its historic past. They also provide a medium within which Ælfric increasingly contests and debates political issues of his own time, though always from the perspective of his desire for the rule of God. The idea that the world of the spirit is distinct from that of history and politics is thus increasingly untenable in Ælfric's writing.

Saints' lives appear in both Ælfric's *Catholic Homilies* and in his later *Lives of Saints,* yet only one English male saint, the monk Cuthbert, is commemorated in the *Catholic Homilies* (Godden, 1979, X). Ælfric's ultimate source for this life is Bede, as it is for his *Life of Gregory* (Godden, 1979, IX), also included in the *Catholic Homilies.* Gregory is especially venerated by the English for promoting the mission of conversion. Also in this collection is Ælfric's *Life of Benedict* (Godden, 1979, XI), founding father of the Benedictines.[26] The saints whom we can identify with the English church in the *Catholic Homilies,* in other words, are associated with early monasticism, and all appear in the Second Series— the series that is apparently directed more at the clergy than at the lay congregation (Godden, 1973a).

The well-known group of English saints in the later *Lives of Saints* is equally retrospective and concerned with origins. The *Lives* of Alban and Æthelthryth (Skeat, 1, XIX, XX), together with those of the saintly English kings, Oswald and Edmund (Skeat, 2, XXVI, XXXII), can be read as forming a hagiographical account of the early days of the conversion and English monasticism. These *Lives* are also revisions from Bede.[27] Only the *Life of Swithun* (Skeat, 1, XXI) witnesses the reform itself, and here Ælfric makes a point of emphasizing the failure of the conventions governing the memory of the saints. Without a prior account of Swithun's life, Ælfric argues that he has to content himself with a list of miracles after Swithun's death (Skeat, 1, XXI, 442/9–20).[28]

To judge from the hagiographical evidence of the two series of the *Catholic Homilies* and the *Lives of Saints,* therefore, Ælfric offers in his "sweep of Christian history" a redaction of the early history of the English church, particularly from the perspective of monasticism, within which the story of the Benedictine reform and the events of the tenth century are symbolized by only one life, that of Swithun. This is an extremely selective gesture toward English hagiography as well as English church history.[29] Only in his emphasis on monasticism and English royal saints do we glimpse some of the major preoccupations of the Benedictine reform with its alliance between the ruling dynasty and reformed monasticism.

The audience of the *Lives of Saints* is not the reforming monks, of course, but influential lay aristocrats such as Æthelweard. Viewed from this broader perspective, the English lives offer Ælfric opportunities to model contemporary moral issues according to historic, that is hagiographical, precedent. The *Life of Æthelthryth,* for example, provides a sustained meditation on chaste marriage, as discussed in chapter 5. The *Life* of the ninth-century royal saint Edmund furnishes material with which to read the policies of Æthelred in dealing with the Vikings a century later.[30] The imaginative leap Cross (1965) made between the *Life of Oswald,* an early example of the conversion of a pious warrior king, and *The Battle of Maldon* reminds us of the efficacy of this particular saint as a model of royal governance in times of crisis. The *Life of Alban* stresses the early conversion of England to Christianity before the coming of the Anglo-Saxons and the importance of maintenance of the faith in times of persecution; it also finds, in the relation between the persecuted priest and Alban, a model for the social and moral significance of Christian teachers. A similar relationship pertains between Oswald and the saintly Aidan, of course. As these examples suggest, the objects of the past worthy of veneration furnish ways of understanding and intervening in the historic present through emphasizing chastity, the moral virtues of the ruling classes, and the importance of the priestly caste. Since these are general, symbolic models of behavior, the connections between idealized past and the contemporary present of the *Lives of Saints* always remains implicit; such moral parallels are nevertheless a form of advice for that present.

Ælfric's *Life of Cuthbert* in the Second Series of the *Catholic Homilies* (Godden, 1979, X), one of his earliest experiments in rhythmical prose, may also be an early experiment in the allegorical method later developed in the *Lives of Saints*. Cuthbert's ascetic monasticism, with its careful maintenance of a strict separation of the monastic order from regular and political life, is a useful English prototype to adapt to the ideals of monasticism enshrined later in the reform. Imaging Cuthbert as an Old Testament prophet and teacher, Ælfric emphasizes to a far greater extent than Bede Cuthbert's interpretation and prediction of events that straddle spiritual and political worlds. The ascetic Cuthbert is thus redefined to conform with reformed monasticism's emphasis on spiritual action in this world, offering Ælfric a pastoral model for his own careful interventions in postreform politics.[31] Images of the king or leader advised by his priest resonate both with the *Life of Alban* and with the *Life of Oswald*, while the *Life of Edmund*, wrongly advised by his bishop (Skeat, 2, XXXII, 318), offers the countertype.

The incidental references to the reform and its historical events in the *Lives of Saints* follow the same general pattern, which respects a careful distinction between strictly monastic domains and a secular audience informed by the reform's more general spiritual insights into the polities of church and state. The passage in his mid-Lent homily from the *Lives, De oratione Moysi* (Skeat, 1, XIII) for example, reveals the extent to which Ælfric manipulates homiletic conventions of time to make just such comments on the present:

Wel we magon geðencan hu wel hit ferde mid us.
þaða þis igland wæs wunigende on sibbe.
and munuc-lif wæron mid wurð-scipe gehealdene.
and ða woruld-menn wæron wære wið heora fynd.
swa þæt ure word sprang wide geond þas eorðan.
Hu wæs hit ða siððan ða þa man towearp munuc-lif.
and godes biggengas to bysmore hæfde.
buton þæt us com to cwealm and hunger.
and siððan hæðen here us hæfde to bysmre.
(Skeat, 1, XIII, 294/147–55)

[Well may we consider how well it went for us, when this island was living in peace, and monastic life was maintained with honor, and laity were ready against their enemies, so that our word spread widely throughout this earth. How was it then that men after cast out monastic life, and held in mockery God's servants, save that death and hunger came to us and after that the heathen force held us in mockery?]

Like the passage in Vercelli XI, Ælfric here appears to meditate upon the events of the antimonastic backlash in the aftermath of Edgar's reign as well as upon the Viking raids. But the real parallels with Vercelli XI lie in his equally studied avoidance of specific details. Ælfric's comments could apply (though they probably do not) to any "golden age" of English monastic history that was disrupted by the Vikings.[32] These incidental passages underline moral and collective responsibility for human events in the Christian present. For the Vercelli homilist and Ælfric, as for Bede before them and Wulfstan subsequently, the originary cause of these events is the failure of Christian will, not the heathen Vikings. The ideal Christian life outlined in this passage is one of peace and promotion of "ure geword," a state dependent on the maintenance of the mutual roles of the two estates—the warrior class and the monastic orders. Failure to respect these roles disrupts the social balance here just as it does in the Vercelli passage, and one consequence is the Viking raids. The duty of the religious orders is to pray and to promote God's word; this passage therefore provides an appropriate contemporary exemplum for the efficacy of prayer. Prayer, indeed, is the homily's main subject, as is illustrated by its series of Old Testament examples, central among which is the prayer of Moses.

Prayer and a reinstatement of the ideals of social harmony between the estates may strike a modern audience as an improbable response to the social crises of the late Anglo-Saxon period, until we recall that this is precisely what is called for in Vercelli XI, Blickling XI, and Wulfstan's *Sermo Lupi* (as well as in VII Æthelred, discussed in the introduction). In fact, Ælfric had already commented on the ideal orders of social and spiritual life in the *Catholic Homilies* (discussed further in chapter 4). In his later writing, however, as the examples of *De oratione Moysi* and the *Life of Edmund* indicate, Ælfric is increasingly prepared to apply his spiritual understanding of the past to more specific social debate through well-tried methods of allegory and allusion.

Thus, for example, references to the reforming king, Edgar, are exemplifications of God's grace as revealed by the correct ideological balance between church and king in both implicit and explicit contrast with the present. His *Life* of the Winchester saint, Swithun, opens and concludes with laudatory reference to Edgar and the flourishing of monasticism in his peaceful reign (Skeat, 1, XXI, 440/1–3, 468/443–53). The noble king fulfills his ideological bargain with the estates by establishing peace through political subjugation, thus creating the conditions for monastic life to prosper, as we have already seen from *De oratione Moysi*. Indeed, Edgar is credited in this *Life* with the recognition of Swithun's miracles and with ordering his translation (Skeat, 1, XXI, 450); Æthelwold's role, by contrast, remains firmly in the domain of the religious by implementing correct liturgical observance of rites to honor Swithun's miracles (454–59). The roles and responsibilities of reforming king and monastic

archbishop are thus carefully distinguished. The virtues of Christian kingship are similarly emphasized in Ælfric's *Epilogue* to his translation of
Judges, where Edgar is assimilated to a list of English kings victorious
by virtue of their devotion to God:

> On Engla lande eac oft wæron cyningas sigefæste þurh God, swa
> swa we secgan gehyrdon, swa swa wæs Ælfred cining, þe oft gefeaht
> wið Denan, oþ þæt he sige gewann ⁊ bewerode his leode; swa gelice
> Æðestan, þe wið Anlaf gefeaht ⁊ his firde ofsloh ⁊ aflimde hine sylfne,
> ⁊ he on sibbe wunude siþþan mid his leode. Eadgar, se æðela ⁊ se
> *anræda* cining, arærde Godes lof on his leode gehwær, ealra cininga
> swiðost ofer Engla ðeode, ⁊ him God gewilde his wiðerwinnan a,
> ciningas ⁊ eorlas, þæt hi comon to him buton ælcum gefeohte friðes
> wilniende, him underþeodde to þam þe he wolde, ⁊ he wæs gewurðod
> wide geond land. (Crawford, 1922, 416/78–417/87; emphasis added)

> [In England also kings were often victorious by means of God, as
> we have heard said; just so was King Alfred, who often fought against
> the Danes, until he won victory and defended his people. So too
> Æthelstan, who fought against Anlaf and attacked his forces and
> put the man himself to flight, and he remained in peace thereafter
> with his people. Edgar, the noble and single-minded king, raised
> praise of God everywhere in his people, more than all kings of the
> English people, and God always controlled his adversaries for him,
> kings and earls, so that they came to him without any fight seeking
> peace, submitted to him as he wished, and he was honored widely
> throughout the land.]

One of the select group of just English warrior kings, Edgar is here singled out for especial praise, once more for establishing peace.[33] Given
this idealization, it is not improbable that we are expected to hear in "se
anræda cining" the echo of Edgar's countertype—Æthelred "se unræd."
Ælfric's praise of Æthelstan's victory over Anlaf (memorialized in *The
Battle of Brunanburh* in the *Anglo-Saxon Chronicle*) and his emphasis on
peace in the two *Lives of Saints* passages that deal with Edgar's reign are
as eloquent as his studied avoidance of explicit comments on Æthelred,
in whose reign Ælfric composed his major works. Ælfric's brief descriptions of this ideal Christian king were influential. The poetic panegyric to
Edgar in the *Anglo-Saxon Chronicle*, possibly written by Wulfstan (cf.
Jost, 1923), reverberates with Ælfric's own epitaph.

The *Chronicle* poems are sometimes seen as nostalgic reminiscences
for the early glories of the West-Saxon dynasty, consolidating a past worthy of poetic memorialization (cf. Irvine, 1991, 202–8). Ælfric's use of
similar material is also multivalent, though in different ways. Edgar is
the ideal, saintly king—the Anglo-Saxon equivalent of the Old Testament
kings of Judges and of *De oratione Moysi*. It is precisely this equiva-

lence that enables him to use the Anglo-Saxon past as a vehicle for exploring ideologies of kingship and monasticism. Hence Edgar becomes an implicit *exemplum* for Æthelred. The point is made most elegantly and succinctly by Ælfric's unfinished extract on kingship: *Wyrdwriteras Us Secgað* (Pope, 1968, XXII). This short text uses scriptural and historical precedents to mount a persuasive case that a king should not lead his army into battle, but rely instead on his military subordinates. Arguing by example, as we might expect, this list is framed by Old Testament figures—David and Moses—into which are embedded New Law (to adopt Ælfric's own terminology) historical figures—Constantine and Gallicanus, Gratianus and Theodosius. These, too, are ideal types. Nowhere does Ælfric directly consider contemporary Anglo-Saxon practice, although the allusion to Æthelred's unhappy reign is as implicit in his remarks on the value of good counsel as it is in the *Epilogue* to Judges:

> Ure wissung and ure waru sceal beon of Gode,
> and we sceolon secan æt Gode sylfum urne *ræd*
> mid *anrædum* mode, and on eornost sprecan,
> þæt ure behat beon þe we behatað Gode
> fæste and getreowe, trumran þone stanweall;
> (Pope, 1968, 731–32/95–99; emphasis added)

> [Our guidance and our defense must be from God, and we must seek from God himself our counsel with a resolute mind, and speak in earnest that our promises be those which we promised God, firmly and faithfully, firmer than the stone wall.]

Ælfric looks to Scripture, as do the historians and prophets ("wyrdwriteras"), Bede, and the ninth-century translator of the Orosius, and finds God's rule and providence. Such passages sharpen our apprehension of the motive of his writing in general, which aims at nothing short of the establishment of the rule of God in this world. Debates about whether the king should lead in battle or whether the clergy should bear arms therefore take the shape of scriptural commentary and homiletic convention. At stake in such examples is a continual fine-tuning of homiletic precedent to account for and modify political practice. Present circumstances are accomodated within conventions such as *De duodecim abusiviis* (the so-called twelve abuses of the world), included in *De oratione Moysi*, and estate theory (the Three Orders), appended to the translations of Maccabees and also from the *Lives of Saints*.[34] Political theory is incorporated within the discourse of belief. It will be left to Wulfstan to develop a more coherent political theory in his Polity I and II (ed. Jost, 1950).

For Ælfric, however, the real point of such examples is the continual reminder of how God's law operates throughout time; so, too, the English saints join, in his writing, the universal ranks of the saintly. One aspect of tradition maintenance in Ælfric's later writing is therefore the encoding of a historically specific view—that of the relation between the two estates of clergy (read by Ælfric as specifically monastic clergy) and rulers—within a genre that presents a conviction in God's law as universal and communal. That aspects of this view—whether the king can fight, the correct balance between church and secular leaders, for example—are largely unique to Ælfric reveals the extent to which tradition maintenance is a selective ideological process.

Correct practice is also a matter for continual reiteration of the same belief in God's law, as argued in the case of Ælfric's *De falsis diis* in chapter 2, one of the texts that concludes the *Lives of Saints.* There whatever interest contemporary readers may have in Danish practices is firmly deflected to a revelation of God's truth across time and culture. The same holds true for the better-known account of pagan practices in *De auguriis* (Skeat, 1, XVII), where incidental reference to Danish beliefs is firmly grounded in a general text on divination and related practices for the universal Church, taken from a variety of Christian sources (Meaney, 1985). These short excerpts emphasize Ælfric's studied avoidance of the topic of the presence of the Danes in England, their beliefs, or their threat to political stability. This technique of reticence makes perfect sense. The topic of the Vikings will not stand up to scrutiny according to the tenets of desire, memory, and understanding that inform Christian representations of time as a repository of moral standards for the Christian of Ælfric's society, whether or not a Dane. In Wulfstan's *Sermo Lupi,* by contrast, it is the non-Christian Dane who furnishes the ideals of moral behavior so lacking among the English in the early decades of the eleventh century.

## Reinventing Tradition: Wulfstan's *Sermo Lupi*

Faced with Ælfric's complex, demanding, and allusive approach to the present, which is itself only one manifestation of a much broader medieval interest in allegory, modern commentators are unanimous in their relief in finding a sermon that addresses that present more directly. Wulfstan's *Sermo Lupi* is probably the best known of all Anglo-Saxon sermons precisely because it addresses in urgent and powerful prose the contemporary events of the interregnum in the year 1014 and the failure of the royal, religious, and secular worlds to respond appropriately to the Danish incursions. Critical delight in the *Sermo Lupi,* however, should not obscure the oddity of the choice of this work as canonical text. Although Stephanie Hollis (1977) and Godden (1994) have both made strong cases for the integrity of the homily within Wulfstan's eschatological discourse, the compelling absence of this kind of "historical" writing otherwise in the homiletic corpus makes it desirable to reexamine this particular howl of the Wolf.

At issue is the not the *Sermo*'s claim to historicity—the case for its authentication is impeccable—but the extent to which critical interpretation of the *Sermo* rests only on our apprehension of a close fit between text and event. The unique circumstances of this singular public address to the English people could not be plainer, although the number of its versions, Latin and English, should give us sufficient pause for thought. Three of these versions are different enough to merit separate editions, to which we can now also add a Latin version.[35] Such reusability indicates at the very least a certain fluidity and adaptability in both content and context for the *Sermo*.

Moreover, the *Sermo* is a masterpiece of generalities that purport to document the devastating breakdown in social and religious life among the English. Some examples of this breakdown in the *Sermo* are analogous with the accounts of these years in the *Anglo-Saxon Chronicle*, even to the extent of echoing the language of specific entries, as Dorothy Whitelock notes (1976, note to line 59). There can be little doubt, then, as to the general accuracy of the text's representation of English life in these crucial years. But what this analysis leaves out is the question of genre. Religious writing represents time by means of conventions that indicate its mediation by belief. The *Sermo Lupi* is no exception, although its use of convention and conviction amounts to a reinvention of the tradition. The *Sermo Lupi* offers no eternally present world of ideal beliefs, but a powerfully negative account of its present failures.[36]

Most commentators, positioning the *Sermo* in relation to other works by Wulfstan, have rarely considered its genre in relation to English homiletic writing more generally.[37] As a result, passages from Vercelli XI and Ælfric's *De oratione Moysi*, for example, which use shorter versions of the same topos of the ills of contemporary life, have been dismissed from analysis because they are based on thematic similarity alone (cf. Whitelock, 1976, 35–36). It is precisely thematic similarity, however, that is important for understanding the *Sermo*'s relation to homiletic tradition. As I have already argued, the moral energy of Vercelli XI and the works of Ælfric resides in their desire for an understanding of the present that will reinstate the rule of God, by inducing penitence and by modifying the behavior of the English. Both Vercelli XI and *De oratione Moysi* are written for the penitential seasons of Lent and Rogationtide. That Wulfstan prescribes three-day penitential fasts for national terrors in his laws is consonant with this penitential discourse and its use in the *Sermo* (cf. Whitelock, 1976, 24, and the discussion of VII Æthelred in my introduction). Moreover, the primary cause of English disarray in all of these examples is not the Viking invasions, but God's anger at English moral laxity: itself a well-known genre from Bede onward. This may in part account for Wulfstan's incorporation of Alcuin's version of this theme (as Howe notes, 1989, 8–22) in the conclusion to the *Sermo*. What is striking about Wulfstan's use of this topos is indeed its position in the *Sermo*. Wulfstan works from present situation to past analogy, which fortifies his reading of the present; by contrast, Ælfric works firmly within the ideals of the past that imply the present.

Wulfstan's powerful evocation of the failures of the Christian present tends to minimize critical apprehension of his adaptation of other homiletic conventions. The topos of the opening lines of the *Sermo*—the familiar belief that Christians must hold themselves in readiness for the Last Days—gains a specific temporal urgency, which most other vernacular writers resist. The cleansing-of-sins topos is another convention in penitential homilies, reanimated here by its particular relevance to the contemporary present (cf. Bethurum, 1957, 336, note to lines 23–25). Even the breakdown of social bonds, so powerfully itemized by Wulfstan, is anchored in part by the same scriptural reference, Matthew 10:21 (Whitelock, 1976, line 62) used by Ælfric in his *De oratione Moysi* (Skeat, 1, XIII, 304/296–98); so, too, familiar analogies to Paul's Epistles appear in both works (cf. Godden, 1994, 154).

Wulfstan has learned the lessons of tradition well. Several of the most powerful lists in the *Sermo* derive from his own earlier sermons and laws (lines 55–61, 137–48, 166–73). In fact, the specific abuses that Wulfstan details, most notably in his repeated stress on the decay of loyalty and the breaking of social bonds, can all be paralleled and exemplified from his own law codes (as Whitelock's edition elegantly and decisively proves). The creation of a new text by incorporating and rewriting several old ones is a mainstay of homiletic composition. What *is* new in the *Sermo* is not the genre, but Wulfstan's use of the particulars of legal discourse rather than the general rule of God; this is in fact a general feature of his writing. While we would not argue that the Old English laws are a direct reflection of Anglo-Saxon society, this is precisely the rhetorical claim of the *Sermo*.

The *Sermo* thus conforms closely to the general use of time in English homilies, but by negative association. The events of 1013–14 provide an *example* of the need for repentance. Although it's a very good example, Wulfstan does not stress its exemplarity, but its specificity. By using convention to represent the present, the *Sermo* remains firmly within the homiletic domain, but reverses its premises. What makes the *Sermo* unusual, therefore, is the close fit between our apprehension of historical events and their remodeling in homiletic discourse, creating an effect of an intimate relation between text and event not found in other homilies.

Wulfstan works hard to maintain this effect of intimacy. The *Sermo*'s compelling claim to contemporaneity rests as much on Wulfstan's style as it does on its content. The hammering repetitions of pronouns, the reiterated calls to the English people, the cumulative nature of the lists, and the breathiness of its alliteration, for example, are all general features of English homiletic writing, compactly and consistently applied in this particular case. Whence Wulfstan's incessant use of the present tense to mean *this* present historical moment, rather than a generalized Christian present. In sum, the *Sermo*'s claim for critical attention rests on its ability to deploy the rules of convention, genre, and style so effectively that it appears unique. This uniqueness, however, is the product of the influence of English homiletic writing in general and of Ælfric in particular on its author.

Theories of literary influence are rare in Anglo-Saxon studies and tend to assume that influence is a matter of resemblance: of copying and imitation. As already argued, this is not necessarily the case for Ælfric, who was certainly deeply influenced by his teacher, Æthelwold, though not to the point of imitation. A similar relationship prevails between Ælfric and Wulfstan, as even the barest comparison between the howl of the Wolf in the *Sermo* and Ælfric's serene, confident distance from similar subjects implies. To argue that Ælfric, the earlier writer, was not faced with the pressing force of historical events to the same extent as Wulfstan is certainly valid,[38] but inadequate when we consider the literary relation of these two writers. Everything Wulfstan writes can be read as a response to Ælfric and is one measure of the known relationship between the two men. Most critics respond to this relation by explaining their differences in terms of their careers — Archbishop Wulfstan as opposed to Abbot Ælfric — but this, too, is an inadequate measure of their literary relationship.

Where Ælfric writes exegetical homilies, Wulfstan rarely does. Where Ælfric argues strongly for the separation of the religious orders from the other estates in his homilies, Wulfstan responds with a whole new theory in his legal texts (Polity I, II) in terms not synonmous with Ælfric's position. Where the abbot attempts to define the power of the bishop, the archbishop quite naturally tries to extend it.[39] Where Ælfric develops one style of rhythmical prose, Wulfstan develops another. Wulfstan makes a practice of rewriting Ælfrician texts, often ignoring the intent of his original, as his *De falsis deis* illustrates. And where Ælfric offers an idealized portrayal of human affairs, Wulfstan gives us his most masterly negative account, the *Sermo Lupi*. If the immediate context for the *Sermo* is the historical events of the Danish raids, then its immediate literary context and unconscious antagonist is Ælfric.

Nicholas Howe (1989, 13) sees the conclusion of the *Sermo Lupi* as witnessing the last great flourishing of the migration myth. As Bede's *Historia* itself demonstrates, this myth is a metonym for salvation history. Nor is it the case that Exodus provides the only sacred frame for the ancestral history of the Anglo-Saxons, as Howe suggests in his reading of the Old English poetic *Exodus* (1989, 72–107). Ælfric's rigorous deployment of salvation history in homiletic discourse witnesses to a far greater extent than Wulfstan the shaping of history according to the theme of salvation. The literal subject of *De oratione Moysi* and *Wyrdwriteras Us Secgað* is Scripture. The liturgical structure of salvation history grounds his series of homilies and saints' lives, providing a discursive frame for the interpretation of contemporary events that, for Ælfric at least, is paradoxically far more real than what we would now call his historical present. After all, the *Lives of Saints* is much more than just a handful of lives of English saints. Scripture and the sacred history of the saints, structured by the operation of memory, will, and understanding, is the key to understanding the historicity of Old English homilies as exemplifications of divine providence, and Ælfric is its best practitioner. The *Sermo*'s reticence where Scripture is concerned is as striking as Ælfric's general reticence about contemporary events. By the same token, where the *Sermo* remembers only one particular moment in history and reads it eschatologically,[40] Ælfric's works are intended to recall the whole pattern of salvation history.

Far more central to Ælfric's work than to Wulfstan's is the concept of sacred history: the Word assumes a transcendent reality that subsumes contemporary actuality, as Ælfric points out in *De oratione Moysi.* Here, the main point of the reference to a "golden age" of monasticism is that it provides the appropriate conditions for the dissemination of "ure word." Understanding of the Word, moreover, is not simply a vehicle for reinstating the principles of contemporary political debate, such as the ideals of kingship and its relation to the estate of the clergy. Rather, by reinstating those ideals of responsibilities and duties of the estates that enable monasticism to flourish, Ælfric gets to the heart of the didactic function of the homilies. Images of Christian teachers, models of ideal Christian communities, and the ideals of salvation history are closely related.

CHAPTER 4

❖

# Didacticism and
# the Christian Community
## The Teachers and the Taught

"Scholarly tradition," remarks Roberta Frank, "wants us to speak well of the works we study; there would be little point in talking about something that was not beautiful and truthful, not 'interesting'" (1991, 88). As for works, so, too, periods. Although Anglo-Saxonists may disagree about the emphases of their interpretations of the Benedictine reforms, the late tenth century is usually characterized with good reason as a "golden age."[1]

The contribution of the vernacular homilies to this "cultural renascence" (Greenfield and Calder, 1986, 68) of the intellectual and cultural achievements of the Anglo-Saxons, while appreciated, is nonetheless underestimated. As the preceding chapters demonstrate, the homiletic corpus offers the strongest evidence in the period for the maintenance of a Christian discourse in the vernacular. This discourse has its own tradition-dependent rules that reiterate the truth of the faith, its aesthetic conventions, and its use of time. That is, this discourse has its own history. At the same time, vernacular religious writing offers a specific perspective on the events of the tenth century; past, present, and future are located within the moral frame of the Christian present. That present is in harmony with a Christian worldview, which is a product of, and comment on, the events of the age of the vernacular homily. Homiletic discourse not only has its own history, but that history is itself part of the history of the late Anglo-Saxon period. As the preceding chapter indicates, Ælfric is in large measure responsible for the perception of the mid-tenth-century phase of the reform as a "golden age."

The relation of homiletic discourse to the "golden age" of the late Anglo-Saxon period centers on its didacticism, yet the moral ideals and performativity of this writing appear to stand in the way of understanding its particular historical nature. At its most superficial, didacticism is taken to mean moral teaching; the prior views and behaviors of the taught are assumed to be modified by the teacher in the process of instruction. For homilists and hagiographers alike, Christian didacticism and its traditions offer the only view, the only legitimate perspective on truth, and thus the only moral paradigm for behavior. Outside Christianity lies heresy, apostasy, paganism, and error. In other words, didacticism operates from within the traditions of this discourse to maintain and apply its truths, which are those of the Christian Anglo-Saxon world of the late tenth and early eleventh centuries. To underestimate the importance of this discourse to the "golden age" of its period is thus to underestimate the social power of its truth claims, and thereby to ignore a large body of evidence for how the Anglo-Saxon Christian elite viewed and represented their world.

Two other, broader perspectives that cross the divide of the late Anglo-Saxon and post-Conquest periods nuance our understanding of the implications of vernacular didacticism for assessing the "golden age" of late Anglo-Saxon England. First, for historians such as R. I. Moore, the years 950 to 1250, which incorporate a substantial part of the late Anglo-Saxon period, see the formation of a persecuting society across Western Christendom.[2] Second, in even conventional accounts of the Middle Ages, these same years are singled out as witnessing the beginning of the formation of concepts of the individual (cf. Colin Morris, 1972). Such conventional accounts have been taken further in recent, hotly debated, scholarship that identifies the Gregorian reforms and those of the Fourth Lateran Council of 1215 as witnessing a historical shift in the formation of subjectivity. From the twelfth century onward, in short, we begin to recognize the characteristics of the modern subject.[3] These two "master narratives" of the formation of a persecuting society and of the invention of the subject are not mutually exclusive (they are in fact interdependent), and both have considerable implications for our understanding of late Anglo-Saxon England.

By including late Anglo-Saxon England by date if not by detailed analysis in the emergence of persecution evidenced across medieval societies, Moore challenges us to refine notions of the late Anglo-Saxon "golden age," but not without reason. On the one hand, fears of Arianism haunt the period, and the laws (secular and canonical), the penitentials, and the homilies all regularly proscribe heresy and heathenism while prescribing chaste heterosexual behavior.[4] On the other, this period can hardly be documented as one of systematic, habitual, or widespread persecution of individuals and groups according to the familiar later medieval formulation of unbelief (Jews, heathens, and heretics); sexuality (for example, sodomites); or physical disease (lepers). But, Moore argues, neither can the persecution so characteristic of later medieval societies be ascribed only to a sudden increase in the numbers of Jews, lepers, or sodomites in the West or to a concomitant rise in popular discrimination against these groups. Moore suggests instead that the conditions governing the emergence of systematic persecution in the later medieval period should include the exercise of political opportunism by the ruling classes and the reformation of the institutional structures of the church (1987, 66–99 and 124–53). In this regard, the ecclesiastical reforms of the tenth century lay the groundwork for the later Gregorian revolution and the rise of the persecuting society. As we have seen, these later reforms also lay the groundwork for the formation of the modern subject, especially in their emphasis on confession.[5]

Late Anglo-Saxon England is thus located at the intersection of two contrasting narratives: the first celebrates the achievements of the English church as part of a cultural "golden age," and the second regards these very achievements as symptoms that help predict the later formation of a Western Christian society characterized by persecution. This second narrative intersects with a third, which currently disregards the Anglo-Saxon period altogether by locating the emergence of the modern subject in the twelfth century and later. The rise of vernacular didacticism in late Anglo-Saxon England provides important evidence for rethinking the interrelation of these narratives by concentrating on the regulatory function of Christian teaching.[6] Instruction in the vernacular homilies maintains the idea of a Christian society in England largely by means of systematic classification of groups and by definitions of knowledge, behavior, and identity. These definitions, which are included in the necessary conditions for the emergence of persecution according to Moore, provide the cohesive forces of an English Christian society, within which the subject is located and identified as Christian and from which all other subjects and forms of knowing are expelled.

Narratives about the persecuting society and the formation of the subject also ask Anglo-Saxonists to reflect on the discipline's assumptions about patterns of cultural assimilation and identity more generally. Following Bede, who takes his cue from Gregory's guidelines for the conversion, critical accounts of the long history of the English church are narratives of assimilation and integration, whereby paganism is smoothly if unevenly converted to Christianity. This developmental model culminates in the Benedictine reforms and the "golden age." As Bede also emphasizes, however, religious assimilation, whether of non-Christians or of different modes of Christianity, causes both real and symbolic violence. The roles of conflict and of social power in producing cultural syncretism merit closer analysis. In the early period of Anglo-Saxon history, the massacre of Welsh monks at Bangor and the controversy over the dating of Easter are classic examples of the clash of religious traditions.[7] The conversion of Danish leaders after the Viking incursions in the ninth and tenth centuries; the notorious, though often ignored, massacre of Danes on Saint Bride's Day in the early eleventh century; and the conflicts within the clergy over the Benedictine reforms themselves should also give us pause for thought.[8] These conflicts are radically different from the systematic pursuit of heresy in the later medieval period, however. With the exception of the specters of Pelagianism and Arianism, the social fact of heresy is famously absent from the history of the Anglo-Saxon period, although canon law, the penitentials, and, as we shall see, the homilies bear witness to its symbolic importance.[9] The project of Anglo-Saxon Christianity primarily addresses the dangers of heathenism and apostasy, as my study of Ælfric's *De falsis diis* and Wulf-stan's *Sermo Lupi* has already indicated. As far as we know, vernacular discourses of the other—the Jew, heathen, or heretic—are largely symbolic and ideological methods of educating a Christian society.[10] Since the place where these ideologies are both explored and maintained is the vernacular homilies, their didactic purchase on the Christian subject is of major importance.

This chapter begins, therefore, with an examination of didacticism and its production of the Christian truths whereby both community and individual subject are defined. There is only one law, to which all Christians are subject, and there is only one faith in which all participate. Such a reading of the homilies qualifies and historicizes contemporary critical assumptions about popular religion in late Anglo-Saxon England, as exemplified by Ælfric's homily for the Feast for the Circumcision in his First Series of the *Catholic Homilies* (Clemoes, 1997, 224–31). Fidelity to the law of Christianity necessarily defines the other as abject. The abjected Jew, leper, heretic, or sodomite is associated by scholars of the later medieval period both with systemic persecution and with the invention of the modern subject. The final section of this chapter argues that Anglo-Saxon homilies, however, bear witness to the formation and regulation of a moral discourse about community, identity, and subjectivity largely ignored by both Anglo-Saxonists and later medievalists.[11] The interest, as Frank might put it, of the Anglo-Saxon "golden age" in relation to the homilies resides in the emergence of institutional discourses about Christian community and identity.

## Didacticism and Christian Reason

Fundamental to homiletic writing is its pastoral intent. The pastoral mission informs the didactic aesthetic of religious prose and its use of conventions of time, both of which frame notions of moral knowledge and behavior, as demonstrated in the preceding chapters. But aesthetics and salvation history only begin the project of understanding didacticism as a mode of instruction. Religious didacticism encodes several assumptions about its intended audience, conceived both as a social group—the Christian community—and as individuals belonging to that group—the Christian or "Christianus." Didacticism assumes that the individual—literate or illiterate—is educable, and that education is a socially and institutionally regulated process of conscious rational instruction in the traditions of Christian knowledge. In Anglo-Saxon England, this method of instruction in the vernacular has its origins in the Alfredian reforms of the ninth century, which are aimed largely at the upper classes and the clergy. Vernacular religious writing of the late tenth and early eleventh centuries is more ambitious: by intellectual argument and moral practice, it aims to direct the behavior of all Christians, who are defined as individual subjects by virtue of their relation to the Christian community. Didactic writing in Anglo-Saxon England addresses the individual as a moral actor amenable to reason to a more complex extent than any other discourse of this period. It is the use of Christian reason in addressing this moral agent that is most at odds with modern understandings of the educational process.[12]

One major barrier to understanding the role of didacticism in a traditional society like Anglo-Saxon England is historical. Modern theories of education, like modern practices, are not articulated with reference to one single tradition of knowledge and one system of reason (quite obviously, there is now no such unified tradition within Christianity). Nor is education conceived of as primarily moral. In Anglo-Saxon England, formal Christian education is restricted to the clergy and the aristocracy; as a privilege of the few, instruction is socially stratified and predominantly in Latin. Apart from the evidence for monastic and court schools, the only institutional provision for vernacular education and the only conceptualization of its necessity occurs within the vernacular homilies.[13] Vernacular education is a matter of assimilation into the ideals of a Christian society and is aimed at a much wider social segment than Latin education—a necessary consequence of the pastoral mission. Ælfric is alone among the vernacular writers in realizing the scope, though not necessarily the importance, of this mission.

Vernacular homilists like Ælfric are not primarily educational theorists, nor are they theologians, politicians, or even, for the most part and excepting Wulfstan, lawmakers. The homilies offer no full-fledged theory of didacticism, nor is Anglo-Saxon England the age of the *ars praedicandi*.[14] A sensitive reading of the homiletic corpus, and of Ælfric's works in particular, however, enables the reconstruction of the importance of moral education from a variety of perspectives. The homilies are very explicit about their intentions, even if hard evidence of how the homilies were received is slender and limited only to copying, editing, and manuscript reception. Nevertheless, to emphasize the educational content of vernacular sermons makes sense only if its goals are also emphasized. These are directed toward understanding God and the necessity of worship in a process that hinges on the relation between forms of knowing and forms of action. Hence the emphasis in the homilies on the individual as a rational actor. As Ælfric comments in one of the Easter sermons from the Second Series of the *Catholic Homilies* (*Alius sermo de die Paschae*), Christian knowledge brings understanding, but that understanding must be transformed into action:[15]

Be ðison we magon tocnawan. þæt us is twyfeald neod on boclicum gewritum; Anfeald neod us is. þæt we ða boclican lare mid carfullum mode smeagan. oðer þæt we hi to weorcum awendan. (Godden, 1979, 162/55–58)

[Regarding this, we may know that there is for us a twofold need in scriptural writings. Our first need is that we consider with careful mind bookish doctrine; the other is that we turn it into works.]

The dual goal of understanding and acting is the major contribution of vernacular religious writing to the continuing project of maintaining a Christian society in England. This goal is quite distinct from those supported by the canons, laws, and penitentials. The aesthetics of religious prose and its structuring according to Christian notions of time also serves these objectives. For a writer like Ælfric, vernacular prose style is modeled on and revelatory of the divine order of the world. As Ælfric here suggests, Anglo-Saxon Christian didacticism is performed within a framework of knowledge, belief, and action.

Alasdair MacIntyre's study of justice and reason in tradition-dependent systems of knowledge helps define more precisely the historical difference of Christian education in the early medieval period. Within this system (heavily dominated by Augustinian Christianity), reason is a process of justification (MacIntyre, 1988, 146–63). As Ælfric's *De falsis diis* demonstrates, belief is confirmed by a reasoning process that refers back to those beliefs and judgments about knowledge and action that have already been produced by the tradition. Belief is prior to reason, which reason confirms with the aid of divine grace. Reason supports, directs, and continues to direct belief by means of a process that aims to deepen apprehension of the divine. Reason thereby defends the mysteries central to Christianity. Knowledge so produced confirms the truth of belief, as defined against falsity, and demands obedience to it.

In this pre-Cartesian world of Anglo-Saxon preaching, Ælfric is exemplary only to the extent that he rationalizes and maintains the preaching mission more systematically than any other vernacular writer. It may be that he was uniquely situated to do so. As monk and later abbot, Ælfric did not attain the institutional prominence of his teacher, Æthelwold, within the church, nor did he enjoy the status of official royal adviser, as did Wulfstan. Neither engaged on the momentous tasks of reforming monastic practice, ecclesiastical administration, and the liturgy nor burdened by legislative administration and the vexed political situation of the early eleventh century, Ælfric appears to have embraced his Christian mission enthusiastically and obediently. English preaching is shaped by Ælfric's historical situation, confirming the more general insight that traditions are produced by specific sociocultural formations. How Ælfric conceptualizes preaching and how he produces Christian knowledge in accordance with his understanding of the pastoral mission have radical consequences for our understanding of religion in Anglo-Saxon England.

Ælfric's English homilies, like other vernacular homilies of the period, provide access to the body of knowledge that is Scripture, but that access is limited. Scriptural lections are recited in Latin before translation into English for commentary in the homily or sermon, although this practice is hardly systematic.[16] Translations from Scripture outside the homiletic tradition, such as Ælfric's own translation of parts of the Heptateuch (ed. Crawford, 1922; cf. Marsden, 1995) or the anonymous West-Saxon Gospels (ed. Liuzza, 1994), are the exception rather than the rule. Debates about the implications of a vernacular Bible for a lay audience have yet to be widely articulated, although Ælfric expresses concern about these implications for a clerical audience in his preface to the translation of Genesis (Wilcox, 1994, 116–19; cf. 37–44). In the homilies, however, interpretation of Scripture in the vernacular is strictly controlled by the preacher, who is himself governed by the rules whereby knowledge is produced in a tradition-dependent system. Ælfric's evident fidelity to the prior authority of the Latin exegetical tradition (Hill, 1992a) is again unique only in the extent to which he pursues and demonstrates that fidelity with his systematic exploitation of his sources.

The art of exegesis is that interpretation is endless, of course, but it is misleading to view spiritual interpretation as analogous to literary interpretation. All meanings are directed toward knowing a God who is finally unknowable. Moreover, Christian learning in the homilies is produced by a system of sharply defined reciprocal hierarchies that bind teacher to taught. In drawing on these conceptual hierarchies to structure his implied vernacular congregation, Ælfric is indeed extending the reach of Christian knowledge beyond monastery and court but, *pace* Jonathan Wilcox (1994, 21), he is no democrat. Spiritual interpretation produced by a tradition-dependent system of knowledge rationalizes belief, which it mandates as true and which provides the matrix for behavior. Obedience to the truth that is Christian law limits interpretation by defining all other interpretation as false—heathen or heretical. Reason is not only a process of justification, but of defining and enforcing the limits of Christian knowledge and action.

The homilies situate both community and individual subject as Christian by means of didactic instruction in rational belief. Instruction is not merely intellectual but psychological, dependent on the faculties of memory, will, and understanding, as argued in chapter 3. Desire for Christian knowledge, which is both assumed and created by the homilies, is governed by a prior understanding of the will (in the Augustinian sense); education of the will directs the believer toward God and thereby toward obedience to God's truth in thought and deed. The individual cannot advance along the path toward God on his or her own, however, because the will is understood to be irreparably fallen. Only God's grace can repair the will. Understood in this light, Ælfric's comment that he translates the teachings of the Church Fathers into English trusting in divine grace ("ic truwige ðurh godes gife"; Clemoes, 1997, 174/48–49) is utterly conventional, but no less true. His homilies construct a community of learning in which training the individual will is the primary concern.

Didacticism in the homilies is therefore a discipline guided by tradition-dependent knowledge of Scripture and aided by grace. This discipline is active, embracing mind and body, understanding and action, as Ælfric reminds us, and focuses on the apprehension of a truth that is always beyond the self. Alien to the post-Cartesian mind in its insistence that false beliefs represent, in MacIntyre's words, "a failure of the mind, not of its objects," Christian education in the homilies rests on the premise that it is the "mind which stands in need of correction" (1988, 357). Teaching corrects ignorance, which can otherwise lead to false truth. Ælfric summarizes the position neatly (and alliteratively) in his Second Series homily for Rogationtide, *Feria secunda. Letania maiore:*[17]

> Læwede menn behofiað. þæt him lareowas secgon. ða godspellican lare. ðe hi on bocum leornodon. þæt men for nytennysse misfaran ne sceolon. (Godden, 1979, 180/1–3)
>
> [Layfolk require that teachers tell them the gospel doctrine, which they learned in books, so that men should not err through ignorance.]

Teachers learn from books their doctrine and instruct the taught through the oral genre of preaching—learning becomes telling. This justification of the hierarchical process of didactic instruction is derived in the homily from Christ's discussion of the first two commandments (Matthew 22:36–40; cf. Godden, 1979, 180–82). Both teacher and taught are enjoined by the first commandment to love God, despite their different duties and responsibilities within the Christian hierarchy. Obedience to God's truth holds the Christian community together by means of the virtue of humility. Humility is central to the process of instructing the fallen will. The second and complementary commandment— "Lufa ðinne nextan. swa swa ðe sylfne" (Love your neighbor as you do yourself; 180/4–5)—relates the ethical obligations of the Christian community to love one another to teaching's emphasis on action: "Ne fremað cristenum menn. þeah he fela god wyrce. buton he symle hæbbe. ða soðan lufe on him" (It benefits not a Christian man, though he performs many good works, unless he always has true love in him; 180/16–18). Love and humility—the products of the Law—are the prerequisites of successful learning and action. How far these virtues extend is one way of defining the limits of Christian community, as we shall see.

Ælfric's emphasis on the virtues of love and humility in acquiring knowledge and acting on its basis indicates that the transmission of Christian knowledge entails a psychological transformation of what we now call the self. Humility is incumbent upon both preacher and congregation in their reciprocal relation toward knowledge. An ignorant preacher cannot correct an ignorant believer, as Ælfric is fond of saying, and teaching is useless unless the mind of the believer is ready to receive it (Clemoes, 1997, 360/150–52). Ælfric's homilies, according to the Latin preface to the First Series, are written with the explicit intention of reaching the hearts ("ad cor peruenire; Clemoes, 1997, 173/9–10) of the believing English for the benefit of their souls. These are not empty conventions. Vercelli VII, for example, for which no Latin source has yet been identified, leaves us in no doubt of the significance of learning for the Christian self:

> Butan tweon, lar is haligdomes dæl, ⁊ ealles swiðost gif hio hyre gymeleste framadrifeð ⁊ ælce gitsunge afyrreð ⁊ þyssa woruldlicra þinga lufan gewanige ⁊ þæt mod to Godes lufan gehwyrfeð, ⁊ gedet þæt hit ealle ða lustfulnesse þysses andweardan lifes onscunað. Soðlice sio lar mid geswince hio sceal þa forenemnedan þing forðbringan. (Scragg, 1992, 134/1–6)

> [Without doubt, learning is part of holiness, and most of all if it drives away carelessness, expels every avarice, diminishes love of worldly things, turns the mind toward love of God, and brings it about that we shun all the desires of this present life. In truth, with work learning shall bring forth all these aforementioned things.]

Learning is defined here as an active sacred labor, couched in the conventional terms of patristic pyschology; the lesson of virtue leads one toward the love of God ("to Godes lufan") and away from sin and worldly desires.

The English homilies offer ample evidence for this psychic disciplining of mind and body. The most frequent analogy is that of food, so clearly mediated by the importance of the Eucharist. Food serves the body as instruction feeds the soul; without instruction, the will fails in its search for God, as exemplified in Ælfric's First Series homily for the first Sunday in Lent:[18]

> Swa swa þæs mannes lichama leofað be hlafe: swa sceal his sawul lybban be godes wordum: þæt is be godes lare. þe he þurh wisum mannum on bocum gesette; Gif se lichama næfð mete. oððe ne mæg mete þicgean. þonne forweornað he ⁊ adeadað: swa eac seo sawul gif heo næfð þa halgan lare: Heo bið þonne weornigende. ⁊ mægenleas; þurh þa halgan lare. heo bið strang ⁊ onbryrd to godes willan; (Clemoes, 1997, 267/52–268/57)

> [Just as man's body lives by bread, so shall his soul live by God's word, that is by God's doctrine, which he has set in books through wise men. If the body has not food, or cannot eat food, then it weakens and dies: so too the soul, if it has not holy doctrine, it will be

weakening and without virtue. By holy doctrine it will be strong and stimulated to God's will.]

The homology between body and soul—feeding and regulating the body and feeding and regulating the mind—is fundamental to Anglo-Saxon didacticism, and a reminder that both body and soul are the material effects of specific practices. Just as the body is perfected after death by resurrection, so too will be knowledge and wisdom, Ælfric points out in his First Series homily, *De Dominica oratione* (Clemoes, 1997, 332/ 195–200). Perfect wisdom is the goal of the didactic process, which cannot be attained before death and without grace. The believer strives to perfect the body in emulation of Christ; so too must the acquisition of learning, of the Word itself, be right, correct, and without blemish.

The historical difference of Anglo-Saxon Christian teaching thus resides not merely in its vehicle—preaching—nor in its psychology, but above all in its rationale for transmitting the truth of its knowledge, which is the basis for belief and action.

## Popular Religion: Ælfric's First Series Homily on the Circumcision

Unquestioning obedience to the truth of one particular belief system looks suspiciously irrational to a modern, post-Enlightenment mind. MacIntyre (1988) reminds us, however, that reason has its own history. Ælfric's reformist emphasis on the cohesion of obedience, love, and truth in teaching—a product of his monastic training—can be matched by less systematic, though no less commonplace, remarks about teaching throughout the homiletic corpus. As will be abundantly clear by now, it is precisely the commonplace nature of these remarks that is important as an index of the traditions of didacticism. The homilists tell us no less than we expect (and scholars trained to enjoy the understatement of the poetry may balk at the explicitness of the prose).

Ælfric's First Series homily on the Circumcision (Clemoes, 1997, 224–31) provides an exemplary opportunity to observe Christian teaching in action, confirming the general observations about didacticism with which this chapter began. The purpose of didactic writing is to offer a rationale for Christian knowledge and action. Each feast day provides analogous rationales, which are specific to the liturgical readings for that day. These rationales are produced from the meanings for that day generated by traditional Christian exegesis. The homilies both elaborate and exemplify that knowledge for the vernacular congregation and provide the framework whereby truth is discerned and falsity defined. All knowledge and action is governed by this process, which situates the individual in relation to truth and, as a result, produces the Christian subject in terms of a communal identity. There is thus only one subject in

Christian didacticism—the believer, who is subject to the continuing discipline of believing, and hence knowing. The nonbeliever—heathen or Jew—is abjected by this same process, as are his or her practices.

Charms, medicinal recipes, poetry, and other material artifacts, by contrast, offer evidence for a more culturally diverse world of belief than the Christian homilies. This evidence appears to confirm narratives of cultural assimilation built upon the evidence of the conversion. In pursuit of the details of this syncretism, Karen Jolly argues for a model of popular religious belief that integrates the world of the homilies with that of the charms (1996, esp. 71–95). That Anglo-Saxon culture has room for a variety of beliefs and practices, however, is less important—because well known—than how we analyze the relation between them. This relation is above all a matter of perspective, as Jolly points out. In constructing a model of popular religion that incorporates the charms with the evidence of the homilies (though not the laws or penitentials), Jolly's perspective is both synthetic and symbiotic. Diversity and contradiction live side by side in a strikingly modern way in this "holistic worldview" (19) of popular beliefs. Accommodation of non-Christian beliefs turns out to be the achievement of the English church. Yet before we turn from the homilists to other cultural sources for their evidence of religious practices not quite so dogmatically Christian, we need to be confident of the homiletic evidence itself. What Jolly's argument downplays is the homiletic emphasis on the truth of its beliefs.[19]

Viewed from the perspective of the homiletic evidence, two issues reframe this debate about the popularity of popular religion in Anglo-Saxon England. Both issues hinge on the didactic nature of the homilies. The first involves analysis of the relation of the homilies to what Jolly calls formal religion and I have been calling the institution of the church. Homilies in general are aimed at an audience broader than that of the upper reaches of the clergy and aristocracy, but this does not mean that their audience is conceived as an undifferentiated "mass" or populace. Nor can we usefully include the institution of the church in a larger pattern of cultural belief without also emphasizing the power of this institution to create and govern those beliefs.[20] As I have already argued, the homilists present their pastoral mission as a hierarchical and unequal relation of knowing, however reciprocal this relation may be. That is, didacticism is based on an unequal power relation. This ideological view of the Christian community complements what we know of Anglo-Saxon society in general, with its sharp differentiation between class or rank and its definitions of the duties and responsibilities appropriate to each.

The second issue of didacticism in relation to the popularity of Anglo-Saxon beliefs involves the homilists' commitment to reason and the Christian truth it confirms—a force radically underestimated by Jolly. For the homilists there is one truth and one rationale for it. Logically, therefore, there is only one popular religion — that of Anglo-Saxon Christianity. All other beliefs are necessarily false, even when presented as mere practices. From the perspective of the homilies, an alternative model of popular religion makes no sense. In consequence, the relation of Christianity to other beliefs of the period must be understood as dialectical and conflicted.

Ælfric's homily on the Circumcision usefully demonstrates how late Anglo-Saxon didactic writing contests belief in terms of the truth of Christian knowledge and practice. This homily for New Year's Day, as those familiar with *Sir Gawain and the Green Knight* will also recall, is often cited for its evidence of popular, nonorthodox Anglo-Saxon Christian practices also associated with the first day of the new year. Such a reading, however, ignores the main body of the homily, which is in fact one of Ælfric's more characteristic texts in terms of genre.[21]

The Circumcision homily begins by rehearsing the lection for the day in both Latin and Old English — Luke 2:21, on the circumcision and naming of Christ — and then offers a commentary on it, derived largely from Bede's homily for the same day, as Wilcox notes (1994, 26). The circumcision of Christ recapitulates in the New Testament the covenant of God with Abraham in the Old — the first man circumcised by God's command. The distinctions between the Old and the New, between literal and spiritual observance of the law, and between Jew and Christian are thus the homily's main themes. Reason is the process by which such distinctions are made, and it is these distinctions that provide the intellectual justification for Ælfric's rejection of nonorthodox beliefs and practices in the latter part of the homily (Clemoes, 1997, 228–31). In short, the truth-value of Christianity in the homily is contested on the efficacy of its knowledge as opposed to the knowledge of other practices, which include those of the Jews as well as those of non-Christian Anglo-Saxons.

In the exegetical tradition, the circumcision of Abraham is a literal sign ("tacen"; 224/22) of the covenant. Circumcision for all boys on the eighth day after their birth fulfills the covenant, enabling the house of Abraham to flourish in its generations. This first marking of the body as God's is accompanied by the practice of divine renaming: Abram ("healic fæder," high father) is renamed Abraham, father of nations ("manegra þeoda fæder"); Sarai, meaning "my leader" ("min ealdor"), is renamed Sarah ("Sarra"), "leader" ("ealdor") and mother of all believing women (225/33–40). God's blessing on the house of Abraham is signified by a mark, a new name, and the promise of genealogy and generation. The circumcision of Christ, which manifests Christ's fidelity to the Old Law, heralds the transformation of that law and the accompanying shift in spiritual interpretation and observance, which ushers in Christianity by rejecting Judaism (225). Baptism and the practice of spiritual circumcision fulfills for the New Law the promise of circumcision in the Old (225–26).

Ælfric is at equal pains in this section of the homily (224–28) to explain what circumcision means in the Old and New Law, using the familiar exegetical modes of literal and spiritual interpretation. Although literal circumcision is forbidden under the New Law, only by reference to its practice can the practice of spiritual circumcision—its spiritual analogy—be understood. This point requires patient explication of the processes of spiritual signification, which provide justification for fidelity to the law: "ac gif hit him dyslic þince þonne cide he wið god þe hit gesette: na wið us þe hit secgað" (but if it seem foolish to anyone let him chide God, who established it, not us, who say it; 226/85–227/86). Human reason ("menniscum gesceade"; 227/91) is the rationale for obedience to God's law: "For ði sealde god mannum gescead þæt hi sceoldon tocnawan heora scyppend: ꝺ mid biggenge his beboda þæt ece lif geearnian" (Therefore God has given men reason, so that they should acknowledge their Creator, and by obedience to his commandments, earn eternal life; 227/95–97).

Circumcising the body as a literal sign of the covenant is replaced by the spiritual, though no less material, discipline of excising vice from both body and mind in the New Law. This exhaustive regulation of the self is programmatic and transformative. Only once achieved can the believer merit the name of Christian (cf. Isaiah 65:15, 62:2) and join the family of Abraham in true faith ("æfter soþum geleafan"; 228/114):

Ne sceole we for ði synderlice on anum lime beo ymbsnidene: ac we sceolon ða fulan galnysse symle wanian. ꝺ ure eagan fram yfelre gesihðe awendan. ꝺ earan from yfelre heorcnunge: urne muð fram leasum spræcum. handa fram mandædum: ure fotwylmys fram deadbærum siðfæte: ure heortan fram facne; Gif we swa fram leahtrum ymbsnidene beoð þonne bið us geset niwe nama. swa swa se witega isaias cwæð; God gecigð his þeowan oþrum naman; Eft se ylca witega cwæð; ðu bist geciged niwum naman. þone ðe godes muð genemnode: Se niwa nama is cristianus. þæt is cristen; (227/102–10)

[Nor should we be circumcised in only one limb, therefore, but we must continually diminish foul lust, and turn our eyes from evil sight, and our ears from evil hearing, our mouths from false speaking, hands from wicked deeds, our footsteps from the deadly path, our hearts from guile. If we are thus circumcised from sins then will a new name be given us; as the prophet Isaiah said, "God will call his servants by another name." Again the same prophet said, "You will be called by a new name that the mouth of God has named." That new name is "Cristianus"; that is, Christian.]

To be Christian is to be thoroughly circumcised from sin in a process that enacts to excess the circumcision or marking of the body under the Old Law. The practice of spiritual circumcision replaces the visible sign with the invisible, and signals Christian identity by means of a new collective name and a new family in the kin of Christ. Ælfric thus uses the Feast of the Circumcision to explore how Christian identity is maintained by the excision of sin — a practice that depends on redefining Jewish practices. Spiritual circumcision anchors how divine law resignifies identity and family.

As the second half of the homily (228–31) demonstrates, spiritual knowledge derived from an exegesis of scriptural circumcision does not tolerate other meanings and practices associated with this day. Supplementing his primary source, Bede, with Bede's scientific teaching (Smetana, 1959, 185), Ælfric begins this section with a discussion of when the new year should commence. Correct knowledge is thus the overarching theme of the homily, whether it be the correct meaning of circumcision or of when the year begins. The custom that holds that the Feast of the Circumcision on New Year's Day (January 1) is also the first day of the year is contested by Christian knowledge, which offers custom no basis in tradition. Here Ælfric swiftly demonstrates the application of Christian learning by surveying the evidence for the various dates of the beginning of the year among the Romans, Hebrews, and Greeks, as well as in Anglo-Saxon calendars and liturgical books. He thereby distinguishes between rational knowledge and customary practice, both Christian and non-Christian. Correct Christian knowlege demands that the first day be that when the world was created. That day, according to the traditions of the Bible and its Christian exegesis, is March 18. The creation of the seasons on the fourth day is calculated as March 21 — the Feast of Saint Benedict — and is confirmed by natural knowledge of the rebirth of the seasons. Nature is also subject to God's law.

This remapping of the seasons by the processes of Christian reason and knowledge is analogous to the remapping of the body in the first part of the homily. In the first part of the homily, the body of the Jew is replaced by that of the Christian; in the second, all calendars are replaced by the Christian. Knowledge is governed by analogy and similitude — by microcosm and macrocosm — and Ælfric's thematic emphasis on reason connects what initially appears to be two disparate parts of a homily associated only by date.[22]

Reiteration of the calculation of the Christian calendar by tradition and the subjugation of natural law to that calculation, moreover, provides Ælfric with the most correct justification for arguing against non-Christian Anglo-Saxon practices for the same day.[23] Divination, regulation of travel and action according to the lunar calendar, observance of Monday as the first day of the week, and the distinction between those animals that enjoy God's blessing and those that do not are all antitheses of Christian observances for the same day (229–30). Ælfric is firm on this point. Christian belief is the only rational knowledge, and the law of divine creation demystifies the rule of nature such that Ælfric imputes natural phenomena associated with the lunar calendar to its work-ings, rather than to the power of non-Christian charms.

By these arguments, Ælfric continues the emphasis in the first half of the homily on what it means to be Christian by outlining what it means to be Christian and Anglo-Saxon in the second: "Nis þæs mannes cristen-dom naht þe mid deoflicum wiglungum his lif adrihð: he is gehiwod to cristenum menn. ˥ is earm hæþengylda" (The Christianity of the man who drives his life according to devilish charms amounts to nothing; he has the form of a Christian but is a wretched heathen; 230/186–88). The crucial distinctions in the homily are thus those between Christian and Jew, Christian and heathen, where Jew and heathen are synonymous. In-deed, it is these analogies that also account for the elision of women in the process of exegesis; their role in the restructuring of the Christian family is only briefly mentioned. Sarah, Abraham's wife, is a figure for female obedience, humility, and modesty (228/118–20), yet this figure is undeveloped, subsumed instead under the more general interpellation of the Christian.[24] In short, by exploring the role of reason as a faculty that perceives distinctions, Ælfric leaves us in no doubt of the extent and limits of Christian knowledge and identity.

To speak of a popular religion in Anglo-Saxon England that accom-modates both the Christian subject and the abjected other, who may en-tertain a variety of beliefs and practices, is thus nonsensical (that is, ir-rational) from the perspective of the homilists. This is not to deny the existence of such subjects, of course, of whom the evidence of the charms, material culture, and the poetry leaves us in no doubt, but rather to em-phasize that the attitude of Ælfric toward them is rational (in the tradi-tional Christian sense), uncompromising, and contestatory. Just as the Jews are rejected by Christianity, as is abundantly evident from this homily, so too are all other formations of belief. Equally important, the homily offers us a glimpse of the processes of definition and distinction whereby Christian identity is formed and maintained. Crucial to these definitions is the contrast between those groups of abjected others and the collectivity of Christian identity-as-community. Ælfric follows stan-dard homiletic practice in referring to the Christian group as "we," con-trasted with the third-person pronouns used to refer to Jews and hea-thens alike. The vernacular homilies in general are rich in such evidence for how Christianity interpellates the Christian.

## Christian Community, Family, and Didactic Identity

*He that loveth father or mother more than me is not worthy of me: and he that loveth son or daughter more than me is not worthy of me. And he that taketh not his cross and followeth after me is not worthy of me.*
—Matthew 10:37–38

As Christ points out to his disciples in the context of the injunction to preach (Matthew 10:7), Christianity commands the reorientation of familial bonds toward God. Ælfric's Circumcision homily turns on the significance of this reorientation. Through the practice of spiritual circumcision and baptism, the believer joins the Christian family in fulfillment of the covenant between Abraham and God and receives a new name. By these means, the Christian subject enters history.

Ælfric exemplifies the transformation of the individual into a believing subject in his First Series homily on John the Baptist: "Ac se þe his þeawas mid anmodnysse þurh godes fylste swa awent. he bið þonne to oþrum menn geworht: oþer he bið þurh godnysse: ⁊ se ylca þurh edwiste" (But he who with the help of God so changes his practices with a resolute mind, he will be made another man; another will he be in goodness, and the same in matter; Clemoes, 1997, 385/166–68).[25] Belief in Christianity makes a new subject through the acquisition of virtue ("godnysse"), which entails mental discipline in the presence of God's grace; the material body, however, remains the same. Underlying this process are the distinctions between the visible and the invisible, the literal and the spiritual, the Old and the New, also used by the Circumcision homily. These distinctions chart the significatory process of Christian typology. In fulfillment of the pastoral mission, didacticism endlessly emphasizes the spiritual power of language under the New Law. Rituals such as baptism and the mass also offer ample evidence of this power, where what is real is defined by the presence of God's grace and the Word incarnate.

The implications of this process of relocating the literal within the spiritual are profound for understanding the analogies between Christian body, self, family, and community, which have been already discussed as conventional analogies for the didactic process. When Ælfric speaks of believers united in Christ's body (following Paul), as he does repeatedly in the homilies, this is no mere metaphor, but a description of the Church itself. The world of the spirit redefines that of the letter; the metaphor of incorporation shifts and amplifies the referent. Unity in Christ's body *is* unity in the Church, and the Church is no metaphor. At the heart of didacticism is the Word incarnate, Christ, in whose body all faithful are joined. Fidelity to the Word identifies the individual with a community of learning, which embraces both literate and unlearned in their pursuit of God's will. The knowledge desired by this community is the attainment of wisdom, aided by the gift of the spirit — "for þan ðe word is wisdomes geswutelung" (because a word is a sign of wisdom; Clemoes, 1997, 384/140–41). In consequence, Anglo-Saxon homilies chart the familar process of distinguishing social and familial bonds from Christian ones, which are similarly social and familial, but are located within institutional structures of belief. Extensive obligations to kin, so treasured by students of the poetry and so evident from the secular laws, take on a different character in the light of Christian meanings for family.

By sublating the family into the Christian "familia," concepts associated with family and body are resignified. Ælfric addresses his brothers in Christ as "mine gebroðra" (my brothers) and uses the pronoun "we" to refer to this Christian family, which redefines and transcends other familial bonds according to the obligations of love or "caritas." Ælfric elucidates these meanings in his First Series homily on the Lord's Prayer, *De Dominica oratione*:[26]

> God is ure fæder þi we sceolon ealle beon on gode gebroþru. ⁊ healdan þone broþerlican bend unforodne þæt is þa soþan sibbe. swa þæt ure ælc oþerne lufige swa swa hine sylfne. ⁊ nanum ne gebeode þæt he nelle þæt man him gebeode; Se þe ðis hylt he bið godes bearn ⁊ crist ⁊ ealle halige men þe gode geþeoð beoð his gebroðru. ⁊ his gesweostru; (Clemoes, 1997, 327/47–52)

> [God is our father; therefore we must all be brothers in God and keep the brotherly bond unbroken, that is, the true peace, such that each of us love another as himself, and command to none that which he would not that another command to him. He who obeys this is a child of God and Christ and all the holy who thrive to God are his brothers and his sisters.]

This extract from Ælfric's *De Dominica oratione* offers a compelling vision of the idealized Christian community, which incorporates all ranks of society: "for ði nu ealle cristene men ægðer ge rice. ge heane. ge æþelborene ge unæþelborene. ⁊ se hlaford ⁊ se ðeowa ealle hi sind gebroðra ⁊ ealle hi habbað ænne fæder on heofonum" (and so now all Christians, whether high or low, noble or ignoble of birth, and the lord and the slave, all are brothers, and all have one Father in heaven; 326/40–42). Membership in this fraternal community, however, is limited, as Ælfric stresses when he discusses the second commandment in his Second Series homily, *Letania maiore* (Godden, 1979, 181/10–12): "On ðam oðrum bebode. we habbað gemet. þæt we oðerne lufian swa swa us sylfe. þa ðe þurh geleafan. us gelenge beoð. and ðurh cristendom. us cyððe to habbað" (In the second commandment we have a limit, that we love another as ourselves, those who through faith are related to us, and through Christianity have kindred with us). The virtue of charity, in other words, applies only to those who believe and are known to believe. Charity is a measure of the Christian community, and does not extend beyond it (as is equally clear from Ælfric's Circumcision homily).

These representations of the Christian family, subject to the law of belief, incorporate but do not dismantle social hierarchies. The inequalities of Anglo-Saxon society remain intact, strengthened by the ideals of a community of believers that is defined repeatedly as hierarchical and unequal. The possibility of a more equitable redistribution of social power is uncountenanced precisely because of this hierarchy, within which only moral change is articulated. Social and familial relations within Anglo-Saxon Christianity are conceived of as a series of fixed states or ranks, each with their own moral duties and responsibilities, specific to secular or ecclesiastical spheres. Moral responsibility is classified according to rank, gender, and marital state. When morality colludes with political fact, powerful mystifications are operating.

As *De Dominica oratione* and *Letania maiore* spell out in their representations of the social vision of the Christian community, the rich remain rich, the poor, poor. Enumerating the states or ranks of society, *Letania maiore* goes further (Godden, 1979, 183–89): both rich and poor are bound to one another by their obligations of charity in the case of the former and patience in the case of the latter; similarly, the slave serves his master, the married man is faithful to his legal wife, the wife obeys her husband, and the child obeys its parents (while punishment is an appropriate method of teaching virtue); a good king has a benign paternal relation to his people and is responsible for their moral well-being, but this homiletic enumeration of social roles and responsibilities offers no role for a queen. Reasonable moral behavior—the virtue of moderation—binds one group to another.

Such preaching promotes a conservative social vision elaborating a Pauline view of Christianity, as Godden points out (1990, 56–57). It is also Paul's teaching, whether directly or indirectly, that lies behind much of Ælfric's preaching on marriage and chastity, as explored in chapter 5. Similarly, Paul's influence on Christian meanings for circumcision is a strong reminder of how Christian society is constructed by resignifying Jewish practices while expelling Judaism itself. The Christian community is thus regulated from without as well as from within, as is equally evident from Ælfric's discussion of the healing of the leper (Matthew 8:1–4) in his First Series homily for the Third Sunday after Epiphany.[27]

The leper's disfigured body is a mark of a disfiguring faith: "laðlic bið þæs hreoflian lic mid menigfealdum springum. ⁊ geswelle. ⁊ mid mislicum fagnyssum: ac se inra mann þæt is seo sawul bið micele atelicor gif heo mid mislicum leahtrum begriwen bið" (loathsome is the body of the leper with many ulcers and swellings, but the inner man, which is the soul, is much more terrible, if it is steeped in various vices; Clemoes, 1997, 242/44–47). Like the diseased body, which is expelled from the community until it is healed, so too the diseased soul must be healed through confession and penitence. Only Christ may heal, and only the priest may regulate inner and outer health, whether by spiritual cure or excommunication: "Swa sceal don se gastlicra sacerd. he sceal gerihtlæcan godes folc ⁊ þone ascyrian. ⁊ amansumian fram cristenum mannum þe swa hreoflig bið on manfullum þeawum þæt he oþre mid his yfelnysse besmit" (So must the spiritual priest do, he must put right God's people and separate and excommunicate from Christian men he who is so leprous with sinful practices that he soils another with his wickedness; 244/79–82).

As these examples suggest, Ælfric's Pauline vision of Christian society as the Body of Christ is a strong moral endorsement of the social inequities of Anglo-Saxon society, maintaining its fixed boundaries by reference to the abject figures of Jew, pagan, or leper. The church supports social inequities by regulating moral behavior within a society already conceived of as hierarchical and Christian; that is, not Jewish or pagan. The homiletic vision of the Christian community holds in place the harsh realities of Anglo-Saxon life, however charitable its moral discourse.

The example of the sacerdotal power of confession also reminds us that teaching is similarly reciprocal and hierarchical; Ælfric in particular is sensitive to the limits and asymmetries of this relation between teacher and taught. His homilies repeatedly guard against heterodoxy, heresy, and heathenism, and draw a line between that knowledge which is appropriate for the laity and that which is inappropriate.[28] At the same time, none of the homilists exclude the ranks and duties of the clergy from their descriptions of the Christian community — they are, after all, integral to it. Preaching is the duty of bishops and masspriests, as the homilies repeatedly emphasize, and the role of preacher is held up to scrutiny as a moral ideal within homiletic discourse. "Lange sceal leornian. se ðe læran sceal. and habban geðincðe. and þeawfæstnysse. þy læs ðe he forlæde. ða læwedan mid him" (Long shall he who shall teach learn, and have authority and obedience, lest he mislead the laity along with himself), as Ælfric puts it in *Letania maiore* (Godden, 1979, 183/111–13) — a homily that particularly stresses the importance of correct learning for the clergy. While Ælfric does not elaborate upon the specific duties of the clergy in regard to preaching to the extent that he does in his Pastoral Letters (cf. Hill, 1992b, 106–16), he leaves his homiletic congregation in no doubt of the dangers of clerical ignorance.

Justice, however, belongs to God (and the church). Ælfric tends to avoid in his homilies the somber accounts of the fates of the fallen teachers in hell so vividly depicted by the homilist of Blickling Homily IV (for the Third Sunday in Lent). In the Blickling version of the apocryphal *Visio Pauli*, the priest who is slow to perform his duties is condemned to "þære fyrenan ea, & to þæm isenan hoce" (to the fiery river and the iron hook), and the bishop who fails in charity is bound with chains of fire, thrust into the river of hell, and denied God's mercy (Morris, 1874–80, 43). By contrast, Ælfric's analogous account of hell, the vision of Furseus authorized by Bede, does not focus quite so explicitly on the tortures of fallen clergy.[29] In general Ælfric promotes instead the positive ideals of preaching and the sacerdotal duties of the priesthood, fortified by images of the Old Testament prophets and the evangelism of Christ, the apostles, and the early martyrs such as Stephen. Whether by reference to apocryphal stories of hell or by homiletic reinforcement of the didactic ideals of the clergy, the homilies avoid explicit mention of the regulation of clerical abuses by the church, evident from canon law and the Pastoral Letters. The obligations of tithing, almsgiving, fasting, and confession are similarly regularly mentioned by both reformist and anonymous homilists, especially in the Lenten homilies and often in contexts that emphasize the mutual obligations of priest and community, but specific details of these practices are sparse.[30] The reciprocal relation between teacher and taught represented in the homilies does not disturb or analyze the balance of power, whether in secular or clerical spheres; it maintains it.

Definitions of the roles of Christian teacher in relation to the broader meanings of Christian community have the added felicity of bringing into focus Ælfric's own self-presentation as a preacher. As is well known, Ælfric is rare among the vernacular writers of the Anglo-Saxon period for his provision of prefaces, in Latin and Old English, to his major works: the *Catholic Homilies,* the *Lives of Saints,* his *Grammar,* his translation of Genesis, the *Admonitio ad filium spiritualem,* the *Vita S. Æthelwoldi,* and his Pastoral Letters (all in Wilcox, 1994). Not since the vernacular letters and prefaces of Alfred, whom Ælfric expressly admired, is an "I" identified with a particular individual used with such authority and apparent selfhood. Joyce Hill has recently pointed out, however, that the Pastoral Letters were not issued in Ælfric's name, but were composed for the secular clergy on the authority of the bishops acting in the tradition of the Benedictine reform. She concludes that "in consequence Ælfric avoided the process of self-identification within the public text through which, as we have seen, he laid claim to the tradition elsewhere" (1994, 183). The point is well taken. There is a startling difference between the conventions of authority used by Ælfric in the letters and in the homilies.

In addition, the unique information that Ælfric offers about himself in the prefaces to the *Catholic Homilies,* for example, does not identify him with modern ideas of authorship, but with those associated with the patristic concept of an "auctor," whose work as writer and translator has the authority of tradition and thus commands respect and obedience (cf. Wilcox, 1994, 70–71)—whence Ælfric's concern with theological accuracy, the avoidance of error, and his insistence on accurate copying in these prefaces. What bears further emphasis, however, is the extent to which Ælfric fashions his identity in the *Catholic Homilies* from longstanding conventions about preachers and teachers in the Christian tradition more generally. While Ælfric's concern with orthodoxy sets him apart from the homilists of collections such as Vercelli and Blickling and his opening sentences in the prefaces to the *Catholic Homilies* proclaim his affiliation with the reform tradition, Ælfric is nevertheless working within the general didactic conventions shared by other vernacular homilists. Seen in this light, Ælfric does not stand within one tradition (the reformist) so as to comment upon another (the anonymous), but uses homiletic tradition to embrace, incorporate, and thereby naturalize any sense of competition and conflict within it.³¹ The identity of Ælfric as preacher is subject to this idea of tradition, and his self-representation is therefore alert to the nuances of institutional authority and genre.

It is perhaps because of Ælfric's alertness to genre and authority that the English preface to the First Series of the *Catholic Homilies* begins in a manner reminiscent of the later *accessus ad auctores*.³² The preface identifies the author, his authority, and his reasons for undertaking the task of composition—the dangers of ignorance—and locates this task in the tradition of moral education in English first undertaken by Alfred (Clemoes, 1997, 174). Yet, within the space of some fourteen lines, the preface shifts genre by turning into a homily, thus appropriately introducing the homiliary itself. Indeed, this section of the preface was reissued as a separate (short) homily on the end of the world and the coming of the Antichrist, a theme common throughout the homiletic corpus (as discussed in chapter 3).³³ In the context of the preface, however, this "homily" has different work to do: it is a sustained examination of the importance of preaching in relation to the preacher himself.

The theme of the Last Days, composed of a pastiche of verses from the familiar scriptural source (Matthew 24:21, 5, 24, 22), elaborates the rationale for teaching: "Gehwa mæg þe eaðelicor þa toweardan costnunge acuman ðurh godes fultum. gif he bið þurh boclice lare getrymmed. for ðan ðe ða beoð gehealdene þe oð ende on geleafan þurhwuniað" (Everyone can withstand the coming temptation more easily, if he is strengthened by scriptural learning, because those who persist in faith until the end shall be preserved; 175/67–69). Indeed Matthew 24:14 urges preaching in the Last Days and may well be the impetus for Ælfric's associations here. Instruction in the interpretation of the scriptural signs of the Last Days enables the believer to distinguish between the true (Christ) and the false (Antichrist). But competence in interpretation is always mediated by the clergy, who enact the gospel injunction from Christ to instruct and to provide by their behavior an example of that instruction. This urgent, ever-present need for doctrinal instruction produces the teacher as a matter of necessity. However, the teacher is neither unique individual nor specific author in either medieval or modern senses, in spite of references to an "I" or "we." Ælfric represents himself instead as an exemplary teacher supported by his affinities with scriptural tradition, which he underscores (175–77) with references to both Old Testament prophets (Ezekiel 3:18–19 or 33:8–9 and Isaiah 58:1) and New Testament apostles (1 Corinthians 3:9). Using such affinities, Ælfric is indeed the teacher as obedient to the tradition:

For swylcum bebodum wearð me geðuht þæt ic nære unscyldig wið god. gif ic nolde oðrum mannum cyðan [oþþe þurh tungan] oþþe þurh

gewritu ða godspellican soðfæstnysse þe he sylf gecwæð. ⁊ eft hal-
gum lareowum onwreah; (176/119–21; cf. Wilcox, 1994, 110/76–80)

[From such commands it seemed to me that I should not be guilt-
less before God if I did not wish to make known to other men [either
by voice] or by writing the evangelical truth that he himself said,
and then revealed to holy teachers.]

It may well be that this conclusion to the preface, with its series of quotations on the moral importance of teaching from both Old and New
Testaments, is aimed specifically at the clergy. Ælfric's own identity is
similarly informed by the same traditional expectations. Nothing in the
preface contradicts the general representation of the preacher outlined
in the other homiletic examples already discussed. In the homilies, that
representation is primarily the moral ideal of the instructor specific to
ecclesiastical rank, whose knowledge is matched by his actions, and it
is in the light of such a conventional ideal and with the support of God's
grace that Ælfric's homiletic identity is constructed. The rationale for
preaching and the conceptualization of the preacher as holy teacher
emerge in performance — as the preface becomes homily.

## Acting Christian?

The differences between Ælfric's authorial personae in, for example, the
prefaces to the *Catholic Homilies* and in the Pastoral Letters might lead
us to assume a distinction between self and representation, between an
authentic personhood and convention. In one guise or another, whether
as a concept to be dismantled, challenged, or affirmed, the notion of the
self as a marker of an authentic, true, or natural identity is foundational
in modern Western culture,[34] whence the seemingly endless debates about
identity politics that inform much recent thinking. Ironically, in recon-
ceptualizing the subject as performative, postmodern critics such as Judith Butler (1993) have arrived at a notion of the self not dissimilar from
Ælfric's own representations. Modern sensibilities can therefore accommodate the possibility that there is no self that hides behind an assumed facade of convention; in fact, we might say that Ælfric's personae
are authentic in their conventionality. In his prefaces, Ælfric always
names himself in relation to networks of authority and in terms of generic
conventions of letters or prefaces — "alumnus adelwoldi beneuoli et
uenerabilis presulis" (student of the benevolent and venerable prelate
Æthelwold; Clemoes, 1997, 173/3) or "Ælfric gret eadmodlice Æðelweard
ealdorman" (Ælfric humbly greets Æthelweard ealdorman; Skeat, 1, 4/35,
cf. Wilcox, 1994, 120/1), for example. These personae, however, are rare
in Anglo-Saxon religious writing. Far more troubling to modern theories
of identity is the dominance of the first person plural, "we," in the hom-

ilies. The believer is not interpellated by personal name in the Circumcision homily, but by the collective noun Christian. The homiletic use of the Christian "we" suggests that, in the history of subjectivity, there are periods when concepts of self are not synonymous with those of individual identity; rather, individual identity is located within social systems of class and community. In the late Anglo-Saxon period, neither the self nor the individual are the foundational categories for what is deemed true, essential, or authentic; that category is inhabited instead by God.

The project of didacticism in the homilies is the maintenance of the Christian as Christian—as a member of the Christian community. This project is achieved by instruction in a body of knowledge (Scripture and patristic commentary), which defines the Christian against the non-Christian, and by the exercise of virtue, which defines Christian behavior as a continual process of the attainment of belief in thought and deed. Didactic teaching, in short, is aimed at an intellectual apprehension of a preexisting system of knowledge, which is maintained by action and defines identity. Although these actions are performed by individuals, their meaning and validity as authentic and true Christian actions are conferred on the individual only in relation to the congregation or community. Ritual actions—baptism, attendance at mass, prayer, confession, penance, and charity (in the specific senses of almsgiving and tithing)—are central to Christian identity and therefore central to the pastoral mission.

Obedience to God's law is manifested by the maintenance of Christian rituals and is the justification for them. Despite the fact that we may prefer other, more immediately material, explanations for the practice of tithing, for example, the homilies make it clear that the ideology of tithing is obedience to the law.[35] Obedience is the hallmark of Christian identity; as both origin and consequence of knowledge, and both justification and form of action, obedience is an enactment of a truth not grounded in an individual, but in a socially structured system of belief.

The social nature of ritual is emphasized throughout the homilies by denying the tremendous barriers between lay and clerical participation in terms of liturgical and pastoral roles. Vercelli Homily XII for the second day of Rogationtide, to take one example, demonstrates the powers of incorporation into the community invested in ritual behavior.[36] A season for tithing, fasting, and prayer (as also outlined in chapter 3), Rogationtide in this homily is distinguished by specific communal actions that manifest service to God:

Þonne wið þon gesette us sanctus Petrus syðþan ⁊ oðerra cyricena ealdormen þa halgan gangdagas þry, to ðam þæt we sceoldon on Gode ælmihtigum þiowigan mid usse gedefelice gange ⁊ mid sange ⁊ mid ciricena socnum ⁊ mid fæstenum ⁊ mid ælmessylenum ⁊ mid halegum gebedum. ꝺ we sculon beran usse reliquias ymb ure land, þa medeman Cristes rodetacen þe we Cristes mæl nemnað, on þam he sylfa þrowode for mancynnes alysnesse. (Scragg, 1992, 228/12–18)

[Then later Saint Peter and leaders of other churches established for us the three holy Rogation days, so that we should serve Almighty God with our fitting procession and with songs and with attendance at churches and with fasting and with alms and with holy prayers. And we should carry our relics around our land, the worthy crucifix of Christ which we call the cross of Christ, on which he himself suffered for the redemption of mankind.]

Individual actions such as prayer, fasting, alms — none of which are specific only to Rogationtide — combine with communal action appropriate to this liturgical season — the processions, singing, attendance at church, and the carrying of relics. These behaviors mark individual church and geographic place with the universal symbols of Christian history and worship. The conventional signs of Christianity — the cross, the Gospels, relics, litanies of the saints (228/18–29/39) — derive their meaning in relation to the specific rituals of the season, located in time and place. Worship of the saints offers protection "ge on þas tid ge on aeghwylce" (both at this time and at all time; 228/38–39), and the carrying of the Gospels symbolizes knowledge of Christ's story, his conquest of the devil through fasting, and the mysterious (that is to say, mystified) power of the Christian knowledge, which is greater than "ænig man æfre aspyrigan mæge oððe gecnawan mæge" (any man may ever explore or know; 229/28). In the same way, the offerings of cattle, land, wood, and goods at this season signify worship, honoring God for the salvation of those in the past, present, and future (229/33–37).

These ritualized actions, which enact belief in the forms of Christian knowledge both specific to this feast and to Christianity in general, ensure the presence of the divine in each and every congregation at the moment of enactment. That is to say, worship in the name of God sanctions and transforms the communal instant into a moment of divinity, recalling and reworking the words of Christ himself: "We þonne syndon nu gesamnode. We gelyfað in dryhtnes naman. He is us betweonum on andweardnesse" (We are now gathered together. We believe in the Lord's name. He is among us now; 229/49–50; cf. Matthew 18:20). Like the homiletic section of Ælfric's first preface to the *Catholic Homilies*, this homily is performative; it gathers together all the behaviors appropriate for this day into one text and restages them for and in the presence (and present) of the congregation. The homily's rhetorical power culminates in this transformative moment of divine presence, which structures its emotional charge as a form of the "timor Domini," the fear of the Lord. Quoting from Psalm 110:10 (228/54) for its scriptural authority, "timor

Domini" is the origin of wisdom, of scrutiny of the self, and of desire. Desire is transformed into zeal ("onbyrdnes"), through which virtue flourishes and vice is conquered (229/51–58). Fear of the Lord is thus the foundational emotion produced by ritual behaviors for Rogationtide and its guarantor, as the conclusion stresses:

> Nu we gehyrdon, men ða leofestan, hu god is þæt we hæbben dyrhtnes egesan. Secan we symle mid ondrysnum egesan þa halgan reliquias dryhtnes ⁊ þyllicre gesamnunge. ⁊ þonne huru getilien we þæt we þonne ða halgan lare godspelles gehyren þæt hio fæste wunige on ussum modgeþancum. (230/72–76)

> [Now have we heard, beloved men, how good it is that we have fear of the Lord. Let us always seek with venerable fear the holy relics of the Lord and such gatherings. And then indeed let us so strive when we hear the holy teaching of the gospel that it remain fast in our minds.]

Ritual action in the presence and place of the congregation is fostered by learning to produce, maintain, and celebrate the individual believer as member of a socially stratified community whose ideological reach transcends both space and time. But the individual, though subsumed into the Christian community, remains a moral agent, whose mental discipline is entailed by these continual reenactments of belief. The Christian is always in performance, in the act of becoming.

Acting suggests a role assumed by the individual for a specific purpose. Ritual similarly implies a sense of self separated from and transformed by action. As many anthropologists argue, social meanings and named emotions forged in the process of ritualized behavior are distinct to that ritual and not to the individual.[37] Acting Christian in the homilies, however, does not permit such distinctions between self and society. There is no identity beyond the community, which liturgical ritual confirms, or beyond the Christian behaviors that ritual maintains. Nor is there a concept of self that authenticates ritual, which is instead authenticated by Scripture, its liturgical enactment, and God. In Vercelli XII, it is the presence of God that ushers in fear; fear, the "timor Domini," structures pyschic identity and the struggle of the soul for virtue. Acting Christian is thus synonymous with being Christian.

This interpellation of the Christian by ritual and knowledge is thus closer to Butler's sense of the performative processes by which identity is assumed than to concepts of acting or anthropological theories of ritual.[38] There are, however, key differences. Christian identity is produced by belief in God, which both structures and confirms the individual as Christian. Vercelli Homily XII reminds us that belief is a continous psychic process, or struggle, which is fortified by zeal, humility, and obedience and which maintains Christian identity in the face (or fear) of a transcendental subject, God. Failure to believe results in abjection, both within the moral individual and without, where reside the pagan, the excommunicant, the leper, or the Jew. In short, the making of a Christian is a highly conscious social process, which is the result of training, discipline, and learning—the product of Christian didacticism so evident in homiletic literature. It is crucial to grasp that identity so produced is essentialist in terms of belief rather than privileged in terms of performances of sex or gender, as Butler argues. Belief is therefore foundational to identity in the homilies, which has important consequences for our understanding of sex and gender in the concepts of the Christian explored in chapter 5.

What does the project of Christian didacticism in the Anglo-Saxon "golden age" offer students of the later medieval phenomena of the persecuting society and of the formation of the modern subject? First, these homilies confirm that being Christian is intimately bound to not being Christian—didacticism is aimed at the incorporation of the believer into the Christian community and the abjection of other forms of belief. This same ideological process is later used to persecute the Jews and to prosecute heresy. In Anglo-Saxon England, however, the abjection of the Jew is a figure for the abjection of the pagan, just as the prosecution of the sodomite in the penitentials is a means of maintaining chaste heterosexuality, as Frantzen (1996a) points out. At the same time, it is clear that these structures of belief are emergent in late Anglo-Saxon England, whose symbolic project is more the establishment of a Christian society in England than its defense against other ideological challenges. The signal achievement of the homilies is thus to persuade their audience of the truth of Christianity by means of traditional forms of reason and knowledge; this is a truth increasingly taken for granted (and thus increasingly threatened) by later medieval formations.

Second, there is an identity assumed by the Christian prior to the twelfth century. Christian identity in the homilies is, however, communal to a radical extent; it contests traditional Anglo-Saxon communities of kinship obligations, while reconfirming the sometimes threatening social hierarchies of service to lord or superior by reference to their Christian equivalents. Church or congregation replaces hall, and the social power of king or lord is annexed to that of Christianity, whose moral and intellectual strength becomes a principle of social organization by virtue of this relation. Being Christian—acting in its name—entails duties and responsibilities appropriate to social rank or class. The insistence on classification and division of identity in the homilies confirms social hierarchies—being Christian means being Christian and a king, thane, or slave. Christianity is a thoroughly social system. The imbrication between social inequities and Christian responsibilities predicts the essential conservatism of Anglo-Saxon Christian society, and thus obscures the fact that there is a choice. As later Christian communities, and individuals, discover, there are other ways of organizing Christian society, other, sometimes more utopic, "golden ages."[39]

Moreover, by virtue of membership in Christian community — a community that subsumes the ties founded on place and time — the individual is both produced and authenticated, though this authenticity must be tried time and again on moral grounds. The homilies are fundamental evidence for the formation of the Christian as moral agent in the early medieval period. This final point has been obscured, I think, by the insistence of interiority as a defining moment in the formation of the modern subject. Individuals, however, live in groups and identify with them; the collective Christian community in the homilies rests on the formation of a collective moral conscience in which all, as individuals, share. The vocabulary of this moral conscience is that of sin and virtue, and no homily is without it (Vercelli XII is exemplary in this regard). To argue that there is no interiority in the Anglo-Saxon period is to argue that the language of sin and virtue resists internalization, which is equally belied by later developments such as the importance of confession in the history of the formation of the subject. One measure of the "golden age" of Anglo-Saxon Christianity, therefore, is the extent to which the Christian Anglo-Saxon subject is interpellated and maintained as a member of a group with his or her own moral conscience; these are the preconditions for the later "invention" of the individual.

# CHAPTER 5

# Chastity and Charity
## Ælfric, Women, and the Female Saints

*for ðan ðe ðam luste and geswencednysse naht eaðe on anum timan ne gewyrð;*

*[for desire and trouble do not go together easily at one time.]*
 —Ælfric, Second Series homily, *Dominica in Sexagesima*

Homiletic ideals of Christian community and identity are constructed as a socially structured system of belief. Belief defines social and familial bonds in an educational process that emphasizes Christian knowledge and action, made manifest in the responsibilities pertaining to rank or state. This ideal community and the obligations of the Christian individual relative to it appear, on the face of it, strikingly disinterested in issues of gender. Ælfric's First Series Circumcision homily, for example, pays scant attention to the specific roles and duties of women within the Christian community, while other examples explored in chapter 4 recognize the Christian as universal and transcendental; that is, implicitly masculine. Gender in the homilies is not used as a boundary that identifies the Christian from the non-Christian in a process of exclusion and abjection, like the figures of the Jew or the pagan. How women figure in the homiletic ideals of Christian society of the late tenth and early eleventh centuries is thus a legitimate question.

For many historians of women, the "golden age" of Anglo-Saxon women resides in the earliest centuries of Christian Anglo-Saxon England, not in the time of the Benedictine reforms, discussed in chapter 4. This other, earlier "golden age" is synonymous with the remarkable female religious of the *Historia ecclesiastica,* as evidenced by aristocratic dynasties of royal wives and saints, female governance of double monasteries, and above all, perhaps, by Abbess Hild. Recent criticism has qualified this view, partly by reassessing the cultural record itself and partly by drawing attention to the historiographical model of the golden age, with its implicit structure of rise and fall.[1] Whatever the value of structuring the late Anglo-Saxon period as an inevitable decline from the early "golden" years, an emerging body of evidence suggests that this later period, itself so often characterized as a "golden age" (though on different criteria), is hardly "golden" for all women (cf. Schulenburg, 1989;

Stafford, 1994, 1997). The Benedictine reform, with its partner in the royal dynasty of the West Saxons, is heavily monastic, aristocratic, and, hence, masculine in character. The pace at which female houses are reformed slows as that of the monasteries increases, and refoundation is accompanied by a stricter separation of the sexes within monasticism, a new emphasis on clerical celibacy, and a tightening of royal and monastic hold on church land and, hence, economic resources (as outlined in chapter 3). At the same time, the enhanced dynamics of royal power, which are so much a feature of late-tenth-century life, register a new emphasis on the royal wife and queen, especially in her role as patron of monasticism. While royal wives such as Emma occupy a place in the cultural record that indicates her considerable exercise of power, it is equally evident from marital patterns in the royal families that even the royal bride could be exchanged at the whim of, or according to the political opportunism of, her king (cf. Stafford, 1990, 1997).

Such complex shifts in relations between male and female religious, and between male and female royal power, are evident in the late-tenth-century liturgical customary and major witness to the Benedictine reforms, the *Regularis concordia*. Here, the explicit division of the sexes in monastic life is underlined by the fact that overall supervision of the monks is the responsibility of the king, while the queen oversees that of the nuns, so as to avoid any scandal (Symons, 1953, esp. 1–9).[2] This same document leaves us in no doubt, however, of both royal and monastic masculine authority. By the late tenth century we are a long way indeed from the dual monasteries of the age of Bede. And yet, the evidence of the conversion of masculine to feminine pronouns in the glossing of the *Concordia* suggests that some nuns followed its rules as eagerly as their monkish counterparts (Hill, 1991). The ideology of the *Concordia* suggests a tightening of institutional structures, a hardening of definitions of monasticism, and a concomitant shift in the relations between the sexes. Women emerge as both the same as and yet different from the men, by whose power, whether monastic or social, they are increasingly defined.

As products of this same era, with its active didactic interest in the forging of a Christian society for the late Anglo-Saxons, the homilies also participate in the structuring of these relations between gender and social power. The homilists' superficial disinterest in matters of gender, apparently evident in homiletic descriptions of the ideals of community and identity, dissolves on closer examination. The homilies do not avoid issues of gender or indeed sexuality; these emerge instead in the intersection between the doctrines of charity and chastity—between the imperatives of Christian love and the disciplining of desire. This chapter explores further the relation between religious desire and knowledge (the goal of didacticism) by examining its boundaries with discourses of women, sexuality, and the body. It concentrates exclusively on the Ælfrician evidence, largely because it has yet to be fully assessed, and moves from a discussion of the *Catholic Homilies* (especially the First Series homily for the Feast of the Purification of Mary and the Second Series homily for Sexagesima) to the lesser-known *De doctrina apostolica* (Pope, 1968, XIX), concluding with a discussion of Ælfric's female saints in his *Lives of Saints.* What emerges from this analysis is Ælfric's construction of a discourse of chastity as an exchange system. This spiritual discourse, which advances the intellectual authority of the church, accommodates gender, but in ways that mystify the asymmetric relations of power between the sexes in Anglo-Saxon England.

## Women's Place?

In a familiar Anglo-Saxon formulation, Anglo-Saxon homilists generally identify both gender and sexuality with marriage, reproduction, and hence with women. Women are associated, in other words, with the control of resources within a Christian society, and with the kinds of knowledge or ideologies used to justify that control. Explored through the lens of gender, the discipline of both body and mind that binds community comes into sharper focus. Women, subject to the same structures of belief and class as their male counterparts (though, as we shall see, differently), are also the subject of considerable anxiety and ambivalence. This anxiety in turn registers an anxiety about the kinds of knowledge about desire, the body, and sexuality available throughout the Anglo-Saxon period (as Magennis, 1995, also notes).

Ælfric's discussion of marriage in the homiletic enumeration of social roles and responsibilities found in his Rogationtide homily, *Letania maiore* (Godden, 1979, XIX), also discussed in chapter 4, is characteristic. Here, the rank or estate ("had") of marriage appears among a list of other estates that includes kings, bishops, masspriests, children, slaves, masters, and merchants (Godden, 1979, 183–87). These states, which are hardly synonymous with modern definitions of class, are structured in binary terms that highlight the reciprocal responsibilities of the individual elements of the pair: the king has responsibilities to his people, the people to the king; the slave to his master, and vice versa. Moreover, these binary pairs confirm an unequal distribution of power, as already discussed. Within the estate of marriage, a familiar and heavily Pauline hierarchy of the sexes prevails; married men are enjoined to love their wives, while wives are counseled to obediently honor their husbands (185/ 153–59). Separation is forbidden, unless accompanied by the practice of chaste marriage: "Twæming is alyfed. þam ðe lufiað swiðor. ða healican clænnysse. þonne ða hohfullan galnysse" (Separation is permitted for those who love more exalted chastity than anxious fornication; 185/ 166–68). Marital intercourse is procreative and governed by reason. "Ne sæwð nan yrðling. ænne æcer tuwa; Ne nan wer ne sceal. his wife genealæcan. siððan heo mid bearne. swærlice gebunden gæð. ðe læs ðe hi amyrron. heora gemæne cild" (No farmer sows a field twice, nor shall a man approach his wife, after she is heavily bound with child, unless they destroy their common offspring; 185/181–84), as Ælfric puts it.

Having raised the issue of the female body, however, Ælfric, in a moment of characteristic Anglo-Saxon reticence, pulls back: "[Þ]is is swiðe hefigtyme. eow to gehyrenne. gif we hit forsuwian dorston. ne sæde we hit eow" (This is very tiresome for you to hear; if we had dared forswear it, then we would not have said it to you; 185/184–85).[3] The point is, of course, that Ælfric cannot avoid addressing women (and their bodies) even if he wishes, ambivalently, that he could. The paradox of Christian attitudes toward women and marriage, long agonized over by the Church Fathers, is in full force here. Christianity, as Dyan Elliott points out, is caught in a double bind in its emphasis on chaste religious desire as well as the necessity for procreation, not merely because it is enjoined by Scripture, but because of the political necessity to reproduce Christianity itself (1993, 38–93). Unregulated desire causes trouble or, to paraphrase the epigraph for this chapter, lust and trouble do not sit well together. Women's place in late Anglo-Saxon Christian society is thus indelicately (for Ælfric at least) an embodied one, synonymous with desire and reproduction and raising the anxious issues of marriage and chastity. Ælfric resolves these troubling issues of desire and bodies in *Letania maiore* by both addressing and avoiding the subject of women.

Indeed, the principal focus or subject of Ælfric's proscriptions in *Letania maiore* is not women, but married men (it is, for example, the farmer who does not sow the same field twice). Within such homiletic enumerations of the Christian community, women's place is overdetermined and elusive, governed both by class or estate and relative to men, who are themselves subject to the universalizing imperatives of Christianity. On other occasions in his homilies, Ælfric displays a similarly complex and conflicted attitude toward women. In *De Dominica oratione* (Clemoes, 1997, 327/52), for example, women are included in the Christian "familia" as sisters—the complement of the fraternal bonds between men that occupies most of Ælfric's discussion—but do not merit a full discussion. In his First Series mid-Lent homily, the feeding of the five thousand is gendered explicitly masculine, into whose company women are accepted if they be like men: "Þeah gif wifmann bið werlice geworht. ꝺ strang to godes willan: heo bið þonne geteald to ðam werum þe æt godes mysan sittað" (Though if a woman be made manfully, and be strong to God's will, she will then be counted among those men who sit at God's table; Clemoes, 1997, 279/115–17).[4] The classification of the chaste—as virgins, wives, and widows—applies to both women and men, as we shall see; so too Ælfric's lives of female saints appear to offer ideals for worship for both sexes. At the same time, however, Ælfric's women remain firmly female—a place dictated by social, theological, and economic imperatives whereby men produce and women reproduce.

Prompted by this attitude toward both the difference (marked by separation) and similarity of the sexes in secular and religious spheres, and the anxiety it generates, the question of Christian identity explored in chapter 4 in terms of belief can be reposed as an inquiry into the possibility of its relation to gender. What kinds of subjects are Ælfric's Christian women, given the overdetermined and ambivalent placing of women in homiletic discourse?

Ælfric's developing discourse about chastity, marriage, and female sanctity intersects with a dominant cultural discourse about the body, which I have explored more fully elsewhere (Lees, 1997b). This discourse is characterized by restraint in the secular sphere and by the metaphoric operation of the cultural practice of "translatio" in the spiritual. As the case of the saintly body so neatly illustrates, the translation of the saint enacts the relocation—the replacing—of the body and of desire. Ælfric both restrains and cannot restrain himself from mentioning female sexuality and its place in *Letania maiore*; so, too, his representations of female sanctity both address and deny the body of the saint and her desires. Ælfric thus reenacts the paradoxical attitude toward the female body as a resource so characteristic of medieval Christianity, while also highlighting Anglo-Saxon cultural ambivalence about the body in general. More specific to Ælfric, however, is the precise logic of chastity and charity that informs his discourse about women and Christian knowledge; chastity and charity, like women and their bodies, are involved in complex systems of translation and exchange.

## Chastity and Its Rewards

Chastity is a dominant discourse within the church throughout the Anglo-Saxon period. The form that this discourse takes, however, is heavily dependent on genre and institutional function. This point is clarified by examining briefly the discourse of chastity within the regulatory literature of the Anglo-Saxons as a prologue to its use by the homilists.

For Bede, the origin of regulatory literature in the Anglo-Saxon church is synonymous with the conversion, as is illustrated by the *Libellus responsionum*. Inserted toward the end of the first book of the *Historia ecclesiastica,* the *Libellus* comprises Gregory's replies to Augustine's questions about institutional and social conflicts that surfaced during the conversion of Kent. Where the issue of chastity is concerned, the *Libellus* focuses on two bodies in relation to the rituals of worship: that of the woman and that of the man and cleric (Colgrave and Mynors, 1969, I:27). Augustine's eighth question addresses the sexed, maternal, and menstruating female body in relation to sacred space and ritual: how soon after menstruation or childbirth can a woman approach the altar; when can a married couple resume sexual relations after childbirth? His ninth addresses, by contrast, the moral dilemma confronting men as a

137

consequence of impure dreams in relation to a similar concern with sacred practices, whether those of the man about to receive the sacrament or the man about to administer it.[5]

The *Libellus* reminds us that Christianity brings a religion not only of the book but also of the body to Anglo-Saxon England. That body is sexually differentiated and gendered. The rituals of approaching the altar and the mass in Augustine's eighth and ninth questions emphasize that Christianity has a repertoire of practices centering on the body in relation to sacred space and liturgical rite. Hence the emphasis on the literal and spiritual cleansing of the female body after birth and on the purification of the male body after an impure dream. These familiar rituals of the body, which are central to Christianity, are constructed by the doctrines of cleanliness and uncleanliness: chastity and sin. Sin and chastity binds body and soul together in a paradox: the pure body is only pure because it embodies denial, because it denies the flesh.[6]

Not just about sexuality or even the body, therefore, the *Libellus* addresses marriage, kinship, law, and the regulation of the emergent institution of the church. Gregory's replies urge restraint, tolerance, and flexibility about the implementation of Christianity, paving the way for the distinctively syncretic, and thus contestatory, model of English Christianity that is the hallmark of Anglo-Saxon culture. The delicate balance between restraint and proscription in Gregory's *Libellus*, for example, shifts in favor of proscription in the later Anglo-Saxon regulatory literature, although it is impossible to gauge the extent to which the Anglo-Saxon penitentials modified practice, within and without the church (cf. Hollis, 1992, 27–40; Frantzen, 1996a). Nevertheless, the discourse of the later penitentials remains pretty much the same as that of the *Libellus*, moving freely between subjects now considered theoretically distinct, such as theft, heresy, drunkenness, marriage, and, of course, sexual behavior. In the penitentials, the sins of the flesh provide an epistemology of sex closely connected with social formations such as class and gender, but chastity, and Christian behavior in general, is a practice regulating desire, of which sexuality is but one expression.[7]

Anglo-Saxon laws also make regular provision for the regulation of sexual transgression, including adultery and rape. Marital status, that is, sexual status as virgin, wife, or widow, combines with rank to provide Anglo-Saxon women with their legal identity (Richards and Stanfield, 1990). The regulation of sexual behavior, in other words, is one expression of the often conflicting social practices centered on the family in both secular and spiritual domains, as is witnessed by the fairly extensive Old English vocabulary for cohabitation, marriage, concubinage, polygamy, and spiritual marriage (Ross, 1985; Fischer, 1986; Coleman, 1992). In such binary, heterosexual examples, it is hard to escape the suggestion that sexuality is identified with women. Anglo-Saxon women have sex and rank; men have rank and weapons, as the common terms for male and female indicate: "wæpned" and "wif."[8] Anglo-Saxon homilists make a similar identification, as we have already seen. It is equally clear from the homiletic descriptions of Christian community already surveyed that issues of the body, marriage, sexuality, and regulation are not exclusive to the regulatory literature. Like the regulatory literature, chastity in the homilies manifests obedience to the law. Unlike the penitentials and the laws, homiletic discussion of chastity is not structured only according to the logic of penance or punishment, but also to that of reward and offering (gift or sacrifice).[9] While the homiletic structuring of the Christian community according to state or rank emphasizes moral responsibility in this world, the familiar threefold structuring of chastity according to "had," or state—that is, virginity, widowhood, and marriage—promises a reward in the next world for behavior in this. That this reward is God's gift to the chaste, and that the chaste are both male and female, is stressed in Ælfric's First Series homily on the Purification of Mary (Clemoes, 1997, 249–57).[10]

The nature of gifts, or sacrifices-as-offerings, is in fact a dominant theme of Ælfric's homily, which begins as an exegesis of Luke 2:22–32 (to which is later added Luke 2:32–40). Mary's obedient presentation of Christ in the temple is accompanied by a gift ("lac"), as required under the Old Law. The spiritual meaning of these offerings—of a lamb, a pair of turtledoves, or pigeons (cf. Luke 2:24)—occupies the middle section of the homily. These gifts are interpreted variously as innocence, goodness, purity, or the dual affection of love and awe (251–53), all of which parallel the discussion of the ranks of chastity and their rewards in the latter part of the homily, and all of which are symbols of possessions, or "æhta" (252/102). Yet it is not only the spiritual significance of the offerings that Ælfric explores; it is also the nature of their exchange.

This exchange is based neither on the need of the receiver nor on reciprocity between gift-giver or receiver. "Nis gode nan neod ure æhta" (God has no need of our posssessions; 252/95), Ælfric points out. Rather, the act of giving signifies the neediness of the giver—not only of Mary but of all mankind—for God's recognition (252/97–100). By acknowledging God through the gift of possessions, the giver is also acknowledged, and it is the giver who will be rewarded in heaven. The offering is thus a material object (a lamb, a pair of doves, or pigeons) and a symbol (of innocence, love, and purity), as well as an obligation required by law, hence a practice, and a choice (governed by the will) signifying faith. In the course of the explication of the gift, moreover, the narrative of the homily has moved from Mary's purification, and an emphasis on women, to the universal law of this gift for all Christians.

The same conditions govern the listing of the chaste in the next section of the homily (254–56). The homily's beginning (the giving of gifts) and its end (the rewards of the chaste) are governed by the same narrative structure. The rituals of purification with which the homily opens, so reminiscent of Gregory's and Augustine's concerns about female purity in the *Libellus*, illustrate the observances required of all women, who are implicitly identified as mothers, for whom the chaste and suffering Mary is the exemplar (249/4–14; cf. 254/169–80). In the middle of the homily, picking up Luke 2:32–40, Anna is an example for all chaste widows, who are explicitly identified as women, as Ælfric stresses in one of his few direct addresses to women, "Behealde ge wif" (Behold, you women; 255/188; cf. 196–97). Both Mary and Anna are granted the power of revelation as a result of their behavior, yet on each occasion the explication moves away from this emphasis on women to focus on mankind in general and their relation to Christ. In fact, Ælfric's explication of the significance of Christ and Simeon occupies the center of the homily (252–55), framed on one side by a discussion of Mary and her offerings and on the other by Anna and her chaste widowhood.

Furthermore, like the analysis of the offering in the early section of the homily, the list of the chaste, with which Ælfric interrupts and thereby universalizes his analysis of Anna and widows, is structured as a series of practices that involve an exchange. Virginity, symbolized both by Mary and John the Baptist, receives a hundredfold reward "on þam ecan life" (in eternal life; 255/208); marriage, symbolized by Zacharias and his wife, a thirtyfold reward; and widows, symbolized only by Anna, a sixtyfold reward. The states of chastity in both sexes are thus material disciplines of the body symbolizing the life of the spirit, obligations governed by law, and also choices, which are gifts or offerings characterizing the Christian condition. Those who choose libidinousness are like "nytenum Ᵹ na mannum" (animals and not men; 256/214).

Mary Clayton (1990, 222) observes that Ælfric's homily for the Purification is Christocentric rather than Marian, and indeed, Christ is the literal center of the homily, as already noted. But this homily also focuses explicitly and unusually on the subject of women, figured by both Mary and Anna and underlined by direct addresses to women. At the same time, as we have also seen, women's place in the homily is a slippery one, which is a direct result of the ways in which women feature in both metaphoric and literal exchanges. By using Mary and Anna as types, their signification slides from an emphasis on women to one on men: from Mary to Christ; from Anna and widows to all the chaste. In this process, the female first signifies the feminine condition, but then the masculine and thus the universal. This process of metaphorization is one of translation, or "translatio." Gender is here subordinated to conventional patterns of exegesis, and, in this particular case, these patterns are explicitly structured around patterns of exchange. The only way these patterns can hold women in place is by an insistent reiteration of type, which steadies their exchange. Both Mary and Anna are characterized as iconic images of endurance and suffering—symbols that condense both charity and chastity in images that immediately recall the arche-typal female saint.[11]

Charity and chastity are equally closely associated in Ælfric's Second Series homily for Sexagesima (Godden, 1979, 52–59), a homily that com-pletely reverses, however, the emphases of the earlier Purification homily and, as a result, eliminates the focus on women as exchanged subjects.[12] Ælfric's exegesis of the parable of the sower, taken largely from Luke 8:4–15, concentrates on analogies between God and the sower, the earth and the human mind. The seed or word of God that falls on good ground will bear the fruit ("wæstm"; 56/107) of patience and heavenly reward, while that which falls on stony or thorny ground will yield only false riches, cares, lust, or the trouble of temptation:

Woruldcara and welan. and flæsclice lustas forsmoriað ðæs modes ðrotan. and ne geðafiað godne willan infaran to his heortan. swilce hi ðone liflican blæd forðræstne acwellon; Twa wiðerræde ðing geþeodde drihten on ðisum cwyde. þæt sind ymhidignyssa. and lus-tas; Ymhidignyssa ofðriccað þæt mod. and unlustas tolysað; þwyr-lice ðing. ðe heora hlafordas doð geswencte fram carum. and slipere þurh unstæððignysse. Witodlice on oðrum timan hi geswencað heora hlaford þurh ymhidignysse heordrædene. and on oðrum timan þurh oferflowednysse to unlustum gehnexiað. for ðam ðe ðam luste and geswencednysse naht eaðe on anum timan ne gewyrð; (55/94–56/105)

[Wordly cares and riches and fleshly desires choke the throat of the mind, and do not allow good will to enter the heart, as if they killed by crushing the living fruit. The Lord joined two oppositions in this speech, which are anxieties and desires. Anxieties oppress the mind and false desires loosen it. Perverse things, which make their masters troubled with cares, and slippery through unsteadiness. Certainly at one time they trouble their master through the anxiety of watchfulness while at another time, through excess, they soften him for false desires; for desire and trouble do not go easily together at one time.]

This remarkable passage, which describes so clearly the complex interi-ority (so often denied to the Anglo-Saxon period) constructed by a psy-chology of sin, associates desire and anxiety with unsteadiness, softness (a mental state inviting seduction), and slipperiness. These conditions, which argue for a system of control, offer analogues to dynamics of chastity and reward in the Purification homily. Note, however, that the subject of this passage is male; the master ("hlaford") governs the mind, not the mistress. Desire and anxiety are states of busyness (55/93), or restlessness, to paraphrase Augustine. Their counterparts are patience and steadfastness, love and single-mindedness ("soðan lufu and anræd-nysse"; 55/88). Recall that the reward granted to the gift-giver in the Purification homily is "ecere reste" (eternal rest; Clemoes, 1997, 252/92). The solution to, and resolution of, wayward desire is patience, love, and chastity with its fixed rewards. It is no surprise, therefore, that the next section of the homily deals with the states of chastity, even though Ælfric has interrupted his major sources in order to do so.

Ælfric's account of chastity is here facilitated by a reference to Matthew's account of the same parable, with its enumeration of the thirtyfold, sixtyfold, and hundredfold fruits (Matthew 13:8; cf. Godden, 1979, 56/115–58/166). This switch in scriptural reading is fully integrated into the narrative of the homily. The focus on men noted earlier is maintained throughout discussion of the states of chastity, even though Ælfric insists, conventionally enough, that chastity is a condition characterizing both sexes. Nevertheless, men—and clerics above all—are his subjects. Thus Ælfric begins by restating the law of marriage among laymen, continues by elaborating the rewards of widowhood for men, stressing the shame of those impotent and exhausted men who still desire the gifts ("gifta"; 56/130) of marriage, and concludes with the rewards of virginity, which belong especially to the servants of God, both male and female (57/130–35). Even after this nod in the direction of female religious, however, Ælfric's emphasis on the male clergy persists. While chaste marriage here is permitted to the regular clergy, the law of chastity governs all other ecclesiastical orders, enforced by canon law, and exemplified by the practices of the Apostles (57/136–58/166).

In the course of Ælfric's discussion, the rewards of chastity are fiercely countered by the dangers of transgression and the threat of punishment. Ælfric modulates this punitive emphasis by concluding with the example of the patient and chaste Servulus, rewarded by the miracle of literacy and the death of a saint, who then went on to the field ("æcer") of reward (58/166–59/198).

Ælfric's inclusion of the discussion of the chaste in the Sexagesima homily is an interpolation from his other sources, as already noted. Such a manipulation of sources tends to suggest that the association between desire and chastity is distinctively Ælfrician (at least in this particular case).[13] There are many reasons why Ælfric might turn in his second full discussion of chastity in the *Catholic Homilies* from an emphasis on women to one largely on men. Ælfric had already made this move in the Purification homily, of course, but the Sexagesima homily is manifestly more focused on male behavior. The Second Series Sexagesima homily is thus the counterpart to his First Series Purification homily—Ælfric, as is well known, disliked repeating himself. As is equally well known, the Second Series increasingly takes its readers to be clerics, and the clerical emphases of his account of chastity are clear enough. Finally, the parable itself, with its subject of the sower, seems to implicitly dictate a masculine perspective. All of these explanations are perfectly acceptable when judged on their individual merits, but we might note, too, that in their sum there remains a hint that Ælfric has moved away from the subject of women. Indeed, the primary distinction between the chaste in the Sexagesima homily is not between male and female, but between lay and cleric, married and unmarried. Gender, in other words, is here subordinate to rank and state, and in the marital place women are subordinate to men.

The contrasting practices of chastity between lay and cleric also occupy Ælfric's most extensive and most heavily Pauline discussion of marriage and virginity in his later homily, *De doctrine apostolica* (Pope, 1968, XIX). This homily pulls together most of the themes of the Purification and Sexagesima homilies but resituates them firmly within the obligations of Christian law. Ælfric's discussion of the chaste has moved from the feminine to the masculine and now on to the universal identity of the individual as Christian. "On manega wisan lærð Godes lar þa Cristenan" (The Christian learns God's law in various ways; 622/1), the homily begins, and Ælfric proceeds to explore these ways by categorizing them according to mental condition.

To those unfamiliar with his earlier Sexagesima homily, these mental conditions or states of softness and hardness ("liðnys ge stiðnyss"; 622/2) are surprising; such conditions of mind are hardly familiar from either the poetic corpus or other Ælfrician discussions. Softness, however, is a quality of mind associated with seduction and perversity, as the passage from Ælfric's Sexagesima homily, quoted earlier, confirms. Since the subject of softness in that passage is male (the "hlaford"), we may be only a short step from identifying softness with the Anglo-Saxon gender continuum for masculinity. Allen J. Frantzen's discussion of the "hnæsc," the soft womenly men or sodomites in the Old English translation of Theodore's penitential, would seem to confirm this association (1996a, 277–80). The evidence of *De doctrina apostolica*, however, complicates the discussion considerably. Conditions, whether of mental or social states, are its main theme. These states illustrate the many ways in which doctrine is learned by the Christian. While we might argue, therefore, that these conditions are aspects of a universal Christian identity that is implicitly masculine, Ælfric makes no such identification.

Instead, the homily unfolds as a sequence of analogies, which are themselves structured as a series of complementary progressions — from soft to hard, from young to old (here hardness and softness find their counterpart in milk and meat, following Paul's own analogy for the carnal and the spiritual in 1 Corinthians 3:1–2), from secular to religious, from chaste marriage to chastity, and from sinner to penitent. In this progression along the path to the Christian good, Ælfric carefully respects the moral qualities of each condition. It is in the nature of water to be soft ("hnesc") and of stone to be hard ("heard"), he points out, "ac swaþeah

þæt wæter foroft dropmælum þyrlað þone heardan stan" (but nevertheless water very often pierces drop by drop hard stone; 623/30–32). Softness as a condition has here a moral quality that contrasts with the gendered evidence of softness in the penitentials.

At the same time, the homily leaves us in no doubt about the relative
values of each state weighed on a Pauline scale of carnal and spiritual.
Appropriately enough, the homily's discussion of marriage begins with
the Old Testament commandment to be fruitful, multiply, and fill the
earth (623/34–624/35; cf. Genesis 1:28), but moves swiftly into the laws of
the New Testament (624/35–628/118), using Christ's commandments regarding marriage (Matthew 19:9–12) and Paul's First Letter to the Corinthians (1 Corinthians 7). Here, Ælfric addresses more fully than in his earlier
*Catholic Homilies* the conditions governing specific marital practices —
infidelity, childlessness, widowhood, death of a spouse, marriage to a
nonbeliever, separation, and intercourse (624–28). This discussion, which
was probably written just before the composition of the *Lives of Saints*
and is certainly one of his most legalistic, was clearly both needed and
timely. The catalog of marital states, characterizing both the man and the
woman, is taken largely from 1 Corinthians 7 (though not in sequence),
supplemented by a sermon by Caesarius of Arles and Augustine's *De
bono coniugali*, as Pope's edition points out. And, following Paul, Ælfric's best advice for the Christian is to remain stable within whichever
state of chastity is given. "Ælc man hæfð synderlice gife fram Gode,
sum swa, sum elles" (Each man has his own gift from God, some this,
some that; 627/105–6), says Ælfric, quoting Paul (1 Corinthians 7:7).

Like Ælfric's earlier discussions in the *Catholic Homilies*, therefore,
the conditions of chastity are gifts practiced by the giver, although the
emphasis of *De doctrina apostolica* remains firmly on the gift. The system of chastity as exchange and reward is not explored, and there is no
analysis of the threefold division of the chaste. What is emphasized instead is that chastity, as a gift given by God, is also a gift given to God.
Chastity is a choice, not a command, and virginity is the purest offering. Just as hardness is for the few who take up higher things (623/
11–14), virginity is "seo clæne lac" (the pure offering), which must be
given to God without prior command (624/50–52).

As both gift given to and choice made by the chaste, chastity is regulated by a network of practices central to the church, whose specific disciplining of conditions of mind and body is most fully explored in *De
doctrina apostolica*. These rituals of discipline take a form and a practice appropriate to mental state, marital condition, and social situation —
secular or clerical. The homily concludes with two exemplary stories
from Bede that, in a familiar Ælfrician move, reverse its dominant emphasis on the maintenance of a condition by illustrating instead a will-
ful refusal to accept the discipline of penitence and reformation (631–
35; cf. Colgrave and Mynors, 1969, V:13–14). These two stories, placed

consecutively in Bede, feature first an upperclass secular man and, second, a monk.

Taken as a whole, however, the evidence of *De doctrina apostolica*, will not support the implication that by concluding with two stories that feature men, his subject is itself primarily masculine. The only time gender is explicitly stressed in this homily is when Ælfric categorizes the male and female condition within the state of marriage. Ælfric's primary subject is the conditions by which Christian law is maintained and implemented. Of these conditions, secular and religious are uppermost, and the concluding exempla conform to this pattern by illustrating the state of impenitence in both social and religious spheres. By so doing, the homily has also succeeded in relating two central doctrines of the church: chastity and penitence.

That Ælfric is concerned to clarify the relation between states and practices in this homily is underlined by the transitional passage between the discussion of marriage and the concluding exempla (628/115–30). Here, laymen who choose to practice the restraint of the pure are urged to fortify themselves with alms, penitence, and regular participation in church services. In case we miss this crucial point, Ælfric underscores it by providing a full account of when the lay should attend church and the minimal requirements for mass (628/119–24). As a ritual of body and mind, chastity is thus directly embedded into the other central observances. A similar point was made by Ælfric early in the *Catholic Homilies*. In his First Series homily for the First Sunday in Lent, Ælfric stresses the relation between chastity and tithing: "Swa swa godes .æ. us bebyt þæt we scolon ealle þa ðinc þe us gescotað of ures geares teolunge gode þa teoðunge syllan: Swa we scolon eac on ðisum teoðingdagum urne lichaman mid forhæfednysse gode to lofe teoðian" (Just as God's law commands us that we must give the tithe of all things that accrue to us from our yearly tillage, so too we should tithe our body by abstinence on these tithing-days for the praise of God; Clemoes, 1997, 273/196–99). The association between chastity and tithing also accounts for the structure of what otherwise seems a rather curious late compilation of extracts from Assmann II (the Letter to Sigefyrth) and *De doctrina apostolica*. This compilation, *From De virginitate* (Pope, 1968, XXX), links chastity to tithing by stressing obedience, whose first model is Christ. Tithing, almsgiving, and chastity are examples of sacrifice—gifts to God.

Tithing and almsgiving, however, are also ecclesiastical manipulations of economic resources, encoded by the homilists as conventional practices signifying faithful behavior and obedience. Like chastity, tithes are gifts; like tithes, chastity is a way to regulate the resources of the Christian, both mental and physical. *De doctrina apostolica*, when viewed in relation to Ælfric's other discussions of chastity, thus offers a glimpse of a spiritual economy centered on the Christian, who is both subject and object of its practices. Given such a sophisticated array of interconnecting practices that produce and maintain the Christian, it is hardly surprising that gender disappears from view. Gender has its place within this economy, but that place is deliberately circumscribed, that is, mystified, within the dynamics of its universalizing discourse.

Analysis of gender in Ælfric's homilies thus complicates the kinds of models for the gender system offered by, for example, the poetry, laws, and penitentials. The spiritual economy of chastity is not governed by a binary system of heterosexuality, nor does it appear to conform to a single-sex, masculinist model (though there is no doubt that the universal Christian is first male and only secondarily female). It does not even appear to conform to a system of differentiation based on the binaries of hard and soft that Carol J. Clover (1993) detects in the Norse literature and that Frantzen (1996a) sees in the Anglo-Saxon penitentials. Rather, the discourse of chastity and its states produces and subsumes gender as one of its effects. In consequence, any discourse of gender is intentionally vague; that is, contingent. Dependent on the particular emphases of chastity that Ælfric chooses to explicate, his homilies can be suggestive of all three models of gender differentiation. The significance of these models can be clarified, relatively speaking, only by recourse to other kinds of evidence, such as the laws and the penitentials. That Ælfric gives us contradictory, ambivalent, overdetermined messages about gender and women's place, therefore, is perfectly consonant with this discourse. Thus chastity conceals from itself its own ideologies.

## Female Bodies, Female Saints

There is, however, one place in homiletic discourse where gender comes firmly into view—the female lives of saints. In this particular place, the female body is both subject and object of the spiritual economy of chastity. This economy is not focused on disciplines that regulate and produce the ideals of a Christian society in its entirety, however. Hagiography offers instead narratives that represent female chastity as a lived spiritual resource; the saint makes a sacrificial gift that signifies ultimate obedience. In the female lives, the dynamics of chastity-as-exchange focus on the struggles of one body to transcend its worldly place and achieve the life of the spirit. The female saint is a condensed icon of chastity, symbolizing both gift and gift-giver, who plays out in representational terms the discourse of chastity explicated in the homilies. That descriptions of Anglo-Saxon marriage enact a similar ideology, whereby the bride is given to the spousal family and is represented as a freely chosen gift, is entirely to the point.[14]

Sainthood is a spiritual drama played out on the physical body, and it addresses the problems of the flesh and the relationship between the body and desire with particular clarity. Consonant with early medieval Christianity and with the social gendering of the sexes, the relation between the body and sexuality is focused on the female (the "wif") in Anglo-Saxon culture. Female saints confront and overcome the deadliness of their bodies and the deadliness of their sexuality time and again. In representing the desire to transform the pleasures of the sexed body into those of the spirit, Anglo-Saxon Christianity demonstrates an intimate acquaintance with the problems of the flesh, its desires and vicissitudes. The eight prose female lives in the late-tenth-century collection of Ælfric's *Lives of Saints* (two of which are not by Ælfric) offer the most distinctively English expression of this genre.[15]

Hagiography centers on death, passion, whereby the saint transcends his or her body. Predicated on the *imitatio Christi,* not all transcendences are the same, however. Ælfric's male saints take many paths to that *imitatio;* the female saints in the *Lives of Saints,* however, live lives testing the sexed body—their virginity and chastity—whether as Brides of Christ (Agatha, Agnes, and Lucy), monks (the two transvestite saints, Eugenia and Euphrosyne), chaste wives (Æthelthryth and Cecilia), or ascetics (Mary of Eygpt). The transformation of sexuality into the gift of chastity is the prime component of the female saint's life. Women have sexuality where men don't, and women who become saints redirect it toward God. Thus the repeated motifs throughout the *Lives* are the failed or redeemed marriage, the brothel scene, the attempted seduction scene, the torture scene, and so on. The problem that transcendence offers the female saint and her hagiographers is delicate, therefore. Sexuality is what matters in the female life, but as a source of temptation it must be seen to be understood and therefore denied.[16] When the female body is thus brought into view, it is accompanied by the kinds of cultural ambivalences and evasions that characterize Ælfric's discussion of the place of the female body in the marital estate, discussed earlier.

Critics and hagiographers alike seem aware of the problems of representation and reception that the female saintly body offers. In an insight that few have bothered to explore, Rosemary Woolf nearly three decades ago commented that poetic lives such as *Juliana* and *Judith* might offer a model of identification for Anglo-Saxon nuns:

> While no Anglo-Saxon nun need expect to endure such persecutions, there was a model for them in Juliana's rejection of a prosperous lover and committal of her virginity to God. The pleasures to be derived from the text are perhaps equally obvious. In the description of the tortures there was certainly an element of the sensational. (Woolf, 1966, 45)

Woolf's linking of pleasure, sensation, and torture provides an intriguing point of departure for an analysis of readerly identification with hagiography, even though the issue of who read (or listened to) Old English poetry is controversial. The *Lives of Saints* collection, however, offers us some slightly clearer ideas of audience.

Saints are not the subjects of their lives; sanctity is, and sanctity is the product of the relationship between the saint and the perception of saintliness. In demonstration of this point, the *Lives* offer internal evidence for the monitoring of audience and reception. The *Life of Agnes* (Skeat, 1, VII) is by that of Constantia; that of Agatha (Skeat, 1, VIII) inspires Lucy (Skeat, 1, IX), and Lucy her mother; Eugenia's example (Skeat, 1, II) inspires her mother, Claudia, her two eunuchs, Protus and Iacinctus, and Basilla; Cecilia (Skeat, 2, XXXIV) is charged with the conversion of her husband, Valerian, and his brother Tiburtius; Æthelthryth (Skeat, 1, XX) remains improbably chaste through two marriages and ends her life as abbess to a female community; Euphrosyne's story (Skeat, 2, XXXIII) is a lesson both for her literal father (Pamphnutius) and her spiritual father, the abbot; and Mary of Eygpt (Skeat, 2, XXIIIB), the archetypal "fallen" woman, is the object of Zosimus's quest for spiritual perfection. Negative examples are also proffered: the seductress Melantia in the case of Eugenia; the prostitute Aphrodosia [*sic*] and the tyrannical Quintinianus in the case of Agatha. The embodied spiritual struggles of the female saint transform male and female, familial and marital relations around her, sometimes political life, and often religious life itself, since many of these saints found or preside over female communities.

External evidence, in the form of Ælfric's preface to the collection, also fills out our sense of reception. Dedicated to his aristocratic male lay patrons, Æthelweard and his son, Æthelmær, the preface states quite clearly that Ælfric is translating into English those lives commemorated in monastic circles (Skeat, 1, 2/5–9, 4/41–45; cf. Wilcox, 1994, 119–21). Continuing his plan to extend the purchase of monasticism into secular circles (which first began with the *Catholic Homilies*), Ælfric is also aware of the dangers of this move, stating that he has suppressed certain elements of the lives for fear of lay misunderstanding (Skeat, 1, 2/9–14; cf. Wilcox, 1994, 119/9–120/15). While he does not explicitly refer to the female lives as a locus for such misreadings, their repetitive staging of conventional scenes testifies to Ælfric's general concern. What is at stake in hagiography is the *meaning* of the saint, as the preface suggests. This meaning is bound particularly to the female saint's sexuality, which has to be transformed in order to offer an exemplary life: the transformed body, not the sexed one, is the exemplar.

As a result, Woolf's suggestion that women (or men) would identify with the sensational tortures of these saints requires modification. The tortured saint offers an ideal that is highly defended against. The saint inspires others, though not to emulation. Never are the struggles of the sexed saintly body a focus for imitation; Constantia learns from Agnes, her exemplar, to resist marriage, but does not endure her agonizing death

(186–95). The act of looking at the saint is also carefully censored: sexual knowledge is a dangerous matter. Consider the nakedness of Mary of Eygpt, protected from the eyes of Zosimus (Skeat, 2, XXIIIB, 14/ 204–20), or the nudity of Agnes, concealed miraculously by her hair and then by an angelic light that protects her from sight and touch in the brothel:

Hi tugon ða þæt mæden to þæra myltestrena huse.
ac heo gemette þær sona scinende godes encgel.
swa þæt nan man ne mihte for ðam mycclum leohte
hire on beseon. oððe hi hreppan.
for þan ðet hus eall scean. swa swa sunne on dæg.
and swa hi hi gearnlicor sceawodon. swa scimodon heora eagon
    swiðor.

(Skeat, 1, VII, 178/148–53)

[They dragged that maiden then to the house of prostitutes, but she at once found there shining an angel of God, so that no man was able to look at her because of the great light, or touch her, because the house all shone, like sun in day, and the more eagerly they looked at her, the more their eyes were dazzled.]

Consider also the cases of Eugenia and Euphrosyne, each of whom assumes male disguise rather than stand trial as a Christian woman.

Uncannily aware of the process whereby the sexed body is presented so as to be exchanged, hagiography is at pains to make sure that what we see is what we should see. The point is made succinctly by Agatha's breast. The first reference to her breast is metaphoric: no attempt to alter Agatha's will can modify the faith that resides in her breast (Skeat, 1, VII, 196/30–31). The second is to her literal breast, which is cut off by her torturers, and prompts Agatha's comment on her spiritual wholeness:

... Eala ðu arleasosta
ne sceamode þe to ceorfanne þæt þæt ðu sylf suce.
ac ic habbe mine breost on minre sawle. ansunde.
mid þam ðe Ic min andgit eallunga afede.

(202/124–27)

[Oh, you most wicked, are you not ashamed to cut off that which you yourself have sucked? But I have my breast in my soul, whole, with which I shall completely feed my understanding.]

In a miraculous gesture, an angel heals her, alone in her prison cell, in a blaze of light that blocks the gaze of her torturers (204/144–48). As a sign of her faith, Agatha's breast is thus reliteralized but remains defended from sight. It is essential that the interiorization of the breast be rendered accessible as a sign for others, but the careful screening of the body part from sight stresses that her breast is a sign not of the flesh but of its conquest. Similarly, the two transvestite saints, Eugenia and Euphrosyne, both of whom remain in monasteries undetected for many years, are finally revealed as women: on each occasion, the woman-as-man is unveiled, unclothed, her flesh on view against her will, not as a sign of fallen humanity but of the redeemed sexed body (Skeat, 1, II, 38/232–36; 2, XXXIII, 354/313–20). The act of looking, always problematic in Anglo-Saxon culture, is indeed a potent moment in these lives, with the acquisition of correct knowledge its correlative: even when naturalized by the ideology of spiritual love, the dangers of the unspiritual gaze, the pleasures of eroticized scopophilia, sadism, and masochism, lurk everywhere.[17]

The renunciation of her material sexual body is therefore emphatically the privilege of the female saint and no one else. Saintly bodies are cleansed and purified from filth (a common motif, but particularly literalized in rites of washing in the *Life of Æthelthryth*, Skeat, 1, XX), interiorized (as in the peculiarly dramatic case of Agatha's breast), or sex-changed (as in the case of the transvestite saints). Female desire is transformed into spiritual discourse (the *Life of Agnes*, for example, opens with a lengthy, deeply sensual rejection of her suitor that is modeled on *The Song of Songs* and echoed by her follower, Constantia; cf. Skeat, 1, VII, 170/25–172/62 and 188/330–32) or rewritten as texts (as with the miraculous inscription that instructs Zosimus about where to bury Mary's body; cf. Skeat, 2, XXIIB, 50/748–54; and the golden message that confirms, or rather consummates, the chaste marriage of Cecilia and Valerian; cf. Skeat, 2, XXXIV, 358/56–360/64). But there is a catch. These saints, seemingly represented as not-sexual, not-women, even not-human, in fact remain female, sexed, and human, especially at moments of transcendence: Agatha's breast remains a sign of her sex.[18]

## Virginity and Marriage

In contrast with the view that saintly transcendence is a process that subsumes sexual differentiation (cf. Szarmach, 1990), the examples of the female lives indicate that it is essential that these saints remain representations of the feminine. Ælfric is no different from other Old English hagiographers in this regard, although his explication of the gifts of chastity and the rewards of the chaste offer further support for his position. Chastity is a discipline whose practices are dependent on the condition or state of the individual; women's state is female, and Ælfric's female saints offer a particular example of the conditions of marriage and virginity elucidated more generally in *De doctrina apostolica*. The purest gift is virginity, not marriage, as the lives make plain. At the same time, it is also clear from Ælfric's homily on the Purification that particular examples are instances that can always be generalized. Mary and Anna offer individual instances of practices available to all. These two conflicting patterns of an emphasis on the female and on the universal come together in the spiritual economy of chastity in the hagiography. Here the gift and giver of chastity is a woman; she is a sacrificial object, situated within complex negotiations of exchange and reward, whereby marriage is exchanged for virginity. As a result, the female lives play out the tensions and connections between marriage and virginity, as well as those between the individual and the exemplary, with particular clarity.

Fulfillment of the theology of virginity is also fulfillment of that of marriage. Virginal saints such as Agnes resist non-Christian marriage, while others from the same collection live out the doctrine of spiritual or chaste marriage: Cecilia (Skeat, 2, XXXIV) and Æthelthryth (Skeat, 1, XX), Julian and Basilissa (Skeat, 1, IV), and Chrysanthus and Daria (Skeat, 2, XXXV). We see in such examples the use of the female body as a resource for both sanctity and marriage. Elliott notes how the benefits of spiritual marriage — the extension of marriage beyond death, the tentative freedom of the woman from the realm of secular marriage politics in which she features largely as an object for exchange, the insulation of the male from the dangers of sexuality — often conflict with the church's teaching on secular marriage and chaste procreation. She suggests that Anglo-Saxon England is particularly enamored of the concept of spiritual marriage, basing her comments on the earlier period of monasticism (particularly Bede) and on the later Latin cults of royal women (Elliott, 1993, 16–131). Ælfric's treatment of spiritual marriage, indeed his attitude toward marriage in general, has yet to receive detailed examination. In general, however, it is clear that Ælfric favors clerical, monastic, and saintly chastity (male and female), praising those virginal saints, monks, and clerics who avoid women at all cost and also those who practice more sociable forms of mixed sex cohabitation.[19] As we have already seen, he recommends chastity in the secular realm, too, and insists on the sacrament of marriage. Rightful marriage gets its fullest exposition in *De doctrina apostolica*, which enumerates all the conditions by which this sacrament is obediently maintained.

Taken together, Ælfric's discourse of chastity, marriage, and virginity in the *Lives of Saints* offers no single recommendation, even in its focus on the ideals of virginity. His lives are thus consonant with the teaching of the church in general and with the explications of the states of chastity offered by his homilies. His female saints demonstrate time and again that chastity is a discipline of restraint ("forhæfednyss"), to paraphrase *De doctrina apostolica* (Pope, 1968, 628/116), characterized by struggle. The focus of that struggle, represented as an exchange of the torments of pain for the rewards of the spirit, centers on the maintenance of the state of chastity by the female saint; chastity is given by God to the saint and returned by her to God. At the same time, these women offer ultimate ideals — models of states — to which the Christian community more generally can aspire.

The *Life of Æthelthryth*, for example, concludes with an exemplum about a secular couple who, having fulfilled their procreative duties, adopt chastity within marriage for thirty years, after which the husband enters monastic orders (Skeat, 1, XX, 440/120–35). This brief exemplum reverses the emphasis of the life itself on Æthelthryth's own miraculous virginity, and demonstrates the ways in which the individual woman — as saint — is at the same time a figure of sanctity. As a figure of chaste sanctity, Æthelthryth's life is thus generalized as a model for all Christian behavior. In generalizing, Ælfric exchanges a woman for a man (a pattern seen earlier in his Purification homily). His focus in the exemplum is primarily on the married man; the wife of this particular chaste couple is subject to his authority. Moreover, the thane ends his life in a monastery — in a striking parallel to Æthelmær's own retirement in Ælfric's monastery at Eynsham. Æthelthryth and the exemplum of the thane thus chart the ways in which monasticism deploys the discourse of chastity as both spiritual and socioeconomic resource.[20]

Ælfric's female lives are written at a time when clerical hostility toward women is increasing across Christendom and when religious women are being enclosed in their convents while their monastic brethren, by contrast, are extending their influence in the secular world, as already indicated. In a culture wary both of the body and of women, the female body is a double threat, to be guarded against and contained, but Ælfric may also be commenting on more specific marriage practices within his culture. There is some evidence that secular marriage embraced forms of cohabitation broader than those of the Christian couple, particularly in the earlier Anglo-Saxon period, and perhaps Germanic in origin. Syncretism may explain why evidence for concubinage and serial polygamy surfaces from time to time throughout the period in cultural competition with an emphasis in the clerical material on the moral duties of the Christian couple. In the tenth and eleventh centuries, syncretic practices become intriguingly concentrated on the royal dynasties. Serial polygamy and concubinage seem to be the prerogative of the ruling family of the West Saxons (Stafford, 1990). The vexed marital histories of Edgar and his three wives (Æthelflæd, Wulfthryth, and Æthelthryth), or Æthelred II (the Unready) and his two wives (Ælfgifu, daughter of Thored of York, and Emma), or Cnut and his two wives (Ælfgifu of Northampton and Emma), provide a social context for Ælfric's emphasis on monogamy, chaste marriage, and chastity. Ælfric's interest in marriage is in part a tightening up of monastic and clerical chastity in the period of the Benedictine reform. The female lives also offer Ælfric a vehicle for an oblique comment on the behavior of his rulers as well as advice on the practices of chastity for his male patrons.

That vehicle, moreover, is the genre of hagiography as it is informed by the broader discourse of Christian chastity. As in the case of Ælfric's discussion of the ranks and conditions of the chaste, he respects the conventions of this genre and its boundaries. Ælfric's women are saints, ideals of chastity as lived by women, and exemplary figures within a spiritual economy characterized by exchange and translation. In such an economy, women have their fixed place as wives, widows, and virgins. Women are held here by constant reiteration of the conditions of chastity and by re-iteration of the conventions of sanctity (it is no accident that the female lives act out the same scenarios time and again). At the same time, as wives, widows, and virgins, Ælfric's women are types of chastity, which Ælfric repeatedly stresses are available to men and women—to all Christians.

Viewed overall, Ælfric's discourse of chastity is governed by a finely tuned process of intellection and abstraction, within which women are defined as both female and not female at the same time. To read chastity and the Christian identity it maintains through the lens of gender is thus no easy matter, since it reverses the priorities of the discourse it-self. The process by which chastity is the subject of its own discourse, rather than men and women, ironically (that is, ideologically) facilitates a freeing up of the gendered positions that we expect from other forms of cultural evidence. Women signify as subjects of chastity in texts that emphasize their relation to sanctity, femininity, and masculinity (as in the case of the transvestite saints), all of which are incorporated within Christian identity. Put another way, the performativity of gender within the discourse of chastity is a moving target.

Ælfric's writing on and about women thus testifies to the powerful ideologies by which Anglo-Saxon Christianity evades discussion of the real conditions of women's lives. The extent to which criticism on women and gender in this period is still engaged in a dispute about their relative sociocultural power is in part a measure of the hold of such ideologies on contemporary discourse. From the perspective of the religious evi-dence, the view that Anglo-Saxon women have more power than their Anglo-Norman sisters reads history according to its ideologies, rather than distinguishing the ideological from the historical. While it is clear that only further detailed analysis of the cultural record will elucidate the hold of such ideological constraints, the evidence of Ælfric demon-strates how sophisticated are its intellectual rationales. One of the first historians of women, Christine Fell, dismissed religious evidence from her analysis of women in Anglo-Saxon England because its "anti-female propaganda" seems "to have been ineffectual in practice" (1984, 13–14).[21] In fact, Ælfric's discourse of chastity as an ideology within the prac-tices of the church seems to have been extremely effective in keeping gender in its (mystified) place.

# Conclusion

❖

Homilists and hagiographers produced in late Anglo-Saxon England a corpus of texts that created a tradition of vernacular Christian teaching unique in Western Europe. That corpus is internally consistent, unified, and cohesive to the extent that differences between individual perspectives measure the success with which it negotiates its own tradition-dependent conflicts. As a result, Anglo-Saxon homilies and saints' lives in English present an image of a devout Christian society as a living institution, with its own practices, rituals, and intellectual rationale, whatever the real circumstances of its reception. The work of culture that this material argues for and performs is unparalleled in its ambition. Few critics would argue for such cohesiveness or social ambition on the basis of the corpus of Anglo-Saxon poetry. It is a salutory reminder, however, that so much of the vernacular prose of this period is the product of one man, Ælfric. The tradition of vernacular religious writing in late Anglo-Saxon England does not originate with Ælfric, but it is Ælfric who realized its ideological importance by shaping and rationalizing it such that the newness of this corpus appears governed by the age-old conventions and rituals of the church. In Ælfric's writing, belief in Christianity is a traditional, foundational truth holding together English society.

*Tradition and Belief* has examined only a few aspects of the religious work of late Anglo-Saxon culture that this tradition performs. I have explored the role of aesthetic pleasure, use of conventions, construction of time, didactic rationales, and discourses of charity and chastity in this writing in order to open the corpus to an analysis that moves beyond the kinds of source-dependent critique that more often characterize its study. By so doing, *Tradition and Belief* places late Anglo-Saxon religious writing firmly on the agenda in the continuing project of understanding medieval religious culture in general. It also uses this writing to put pressure on models of cultural studies currently prevalent in the academy that oversimplify the work of culture by ignoring the important relation of culture to belief.

Within the Anglo-Saxon period itself, however, much remains to be done. Homilies and saints' lives have more to tell us about the law of Christian obedience in relation to a culture heavily dominated by a general ethic of social fidelity and the giving and receiving of oaths, for example. The material relation of religious vernacular writing to other forms of cultural evidence manifested by such writings as the laws and penitentials has yet to be fully explored. How far the cultural capital of this writing intersects with the economic power of the church in the period is an important question for future research. The model of Christian society that religious discourse works so hard to promote requires testing against the material record of wills, foundations, endowments, and patronage, even as we explore further its own discourse. Within that discourse, the centrality of the Eucharist and of its connection to the powerful relation between knowledge and belief demands greater attention than I have given it here.

At the same time, each chapter of *Tradition and Belief* opens up new avenues of investigation into the Anglo-Saxon cultural record. The ideological power of the aesthetics of religious prose suggests that we need to take a clearer look at the cultural work of the poetry and its own ideological investment. The homiletic construction of time within a matrix of Christian origins demands a reassessment of the hold of ethnic origins and identities on the Anglo-Saxon cultural imaginary. The work of the homilists in producing and maintaining a Christian "we" argues for a rethinking of the characteristics of identity across the period; this project takes its place at the intersection of psychoanalytic, material, and historicist approaches to the study of culture. Moreover, the extent to which the success of the homilists in maintaining Anglo-Saxon society as Christian is evaluated by means of the "golden age" of the Benedictine reforms prompts a reexamination not only of this important period and its cultural achievements, but also of its relation to later English and continental formations. Finally, the conceptualization of chastity and charity as systems of exchange merits further analysis in its own right. This evidence casts light on the ways in which gender functions and fails to function in late Anglo-Saxon culture; it also clears the way for a reassessment of conventional views of Anglo-Saxon culture as a gift economy—a view held largely on the basis of the poetry.

*Tradition and Belief* thus uses late Anglo-Saxon religious writing to prompt new ways of looking at old material. The avenues I suggest here will clarify further the interrelationships of forms of cultural evidence only if they also continue to respect the specificity of particular instances, genres, and evidence. This book offers a way of thinking about cultural power as a dynamic network of interconnecting practices and discourses. Religious writing provides ample evidence of such cultural power, the centrality of which in late Anglo-Saxon culture has been radically underestimated. The challenge that remains is to assess how this important facet of Anglo-Saxon culture relates to and intersects with other forms of cultural evidence, such as the poetry, whose traditional centrality in the critical record is beyond dispute.

# Notes

## Preface

1. "I began with the desire to speak to the dead," begins Stephen Greenblatt (1988, 1). For psychoanalytic theories of loss and their relevance to the study of medieval literature, see Fradenburg, 1990 (esp. 172–77). Margherita (1994, esp. 100–112) pits historicist theories of medieval culture against psychoanalytic ones, although Aers points out in his 1995 review of her book that a rapprochement between these two approaches is not merely possible, but desirable from both psychoanalytic and historicist perspectives. Such a rapprochement is explored by Brennan, 1993. For a powerful outline of Aers's views, see Aers, 1996.

2. For a preliminary introduction to Ælfric's life, see Hurt, 1972; more reliable are Clemoes, 1966, and Wilcox, 1994, 1–15. Ælfric's major works are cited by editor; for the First Series of *Catholic Homilies,* see Clemoes, 1997 (which replaces the earlier edition and translation by Thorpe, 1844–46); for the Second Series, see Godden, 1979; for the Supplementary Series, see Pope, 1967–68; for the *Lives of Saints,* see Skeat, 1881–1900 (cited by volume and text number). I have followed the editors' decisions in all regards, with the exception of "þ" in Clemoes, 1997, which has been silently expanded to "þæt." All translations are my own, unless otherwise indicated.

3. As Asad (1993) also argues. Mann (1986) similarly emphasizes that the history of religion is an important component in the history of power in the West. For a study of contemporary beliefs and practices in North America, see Kintz, 1997.

4. Bethurum, 1957, 54–68, and Whitelock, 1976, 7–17, have useful introductions to Wulfstan's life. All references to Wulfstan's homilies are to these editions, unless otherwise specified; all translations are my own unless otherwise indicated. For the dating of his clerical appointments, see Whitelock, 1937.

5. Although both Wulfstan and Ælfric also wrote in Latin and are thus connected to other Anglo-Latin writers of the Benedictine reform, I am specifically interested in their vernacular works. A good introduction to the Anglo-Latin works of the reform period is Lapidge and Winterbottom, 1991, xiii–clxxxviii; and for Anglo-Latin in general, Lapidge's chapter in Greenfield and Calder, 1986, 5–37.

## Introduction

1. VII Æthelred, ed. and trans. Whitelock, Brett, and Brooke (1981), 373–82, with the Old English from Cambridge, Corpus Christi College 201, as VIIa, at 379. See also Liebermann, 1903, 260–61, with the Old English at 261. The Old English version is also translated by Whitelock (1955), 409–11 (at 410).

2. "...when the great army came to the country" (Whitelock, Brett, and Brooke, 1981, 379).

3. Napier, 1883, XXXIX, is the English version of the code. See Bethurum, 1957, 38, for Wulfstan's authorship of these homilies (which is less probable in the case of Napier, XXXVI).

4. For brief discussion, see Frantzen, 1983, 146–47. IV Edgar (c. 963) begins by identifying the causes of a recent pestilence with the sins of the Christians and their failure to

tithe (Whitelock, Brett, and Brooke, 1981, 102–9). A penitential ordinance was later placed on all those who had fought in the Battle of Hastings (Stafford, 1989, 155). Ælfric's *Life of Edmund* reports that Theodred ordered a three-day communal fast for the wrongful execution of three thieves who broke into Edmund's shrine (Skeat, 2, XXXII, 330–31). My thanks to James W. Earl for directing my attention to this example.

5. See Heslop, 1990, for a measure of his cultural success. Although the myth of Cnut's attempt to turn back the tide had yet to be articulated, Lawson (1993, 133–34) argues that there may be a grain of truth in this story of Cnut's piety (where later popular accounts see only a failed king).

6. Quoted from the Old English version in Corpus Christi College 201 (Whitelock, Brett, and Brooke, 1981, 431–34, at 433–34). Compare I Cnut, dated 1020/22 (Whitelock, Brett, and Brooke, 1981, 471); for the dating of this later code, see Whitelock, 1948.

7. "Wulfstan was the last expression of the tenth-century English phase of the alliance between church and king, a phase similar to the Carolingian model in which law was seen as the fundamental instrument of ruling" (Stafford, 1989, 138).

8. Frantzen (1990, 22–95) points out, however, that debates about Christianity have been fundamental in the history of Anglo-Saxon studies.

9. This project is treated with considerable sophistication from a psychoanalytic stance in Earl, 1994; see also Hill, 1995, and Hermann, 1989.

10. The classic study is Gatch, 1977; see also Clayton, 1990; Grundy, 1991; and Wright, 1993. For essay collections, see Szarmach and Huppé, 1978, and Szarmach, 1986a, 1986b, 1996b. Broader in conception and analysis is Frantzen, 1983, with a discussion of the homilies at 150–74.

11. This methodology is institutionalized in two sources projects: *Fontes Anglo-Saxonici* and SASLC (Sources of Anglo-Saxon Literary Culture); see Biggs, Hill, and Szarmach, 1990. For the lively debate about source study, see Frantzen, 1990, 83–95; Lees, 1991; O'Brien O'Keeffe, 1994; and Scragg, 1997.

12. Stafford, 1989, is a good general introduction to the period.

13. For the Benedictine reform, see Lapidge and Winterbottom, 1991, li–lx.

14. As Godden (1973a) argues in the case of the Second Series of the *Catholic Homilies.*

15. Representative is Blair, 1977, which discusses the prose at the end of the book (350–63).

16. How the prose is defined as literary is usually fudged by even the most sympathetic critics. Bately's comment is representative: "One of the most significant literary achievements of the Anglo-Saxons was the establishment of vernacular prose as an acceptable medium both for the dissemination of knowledge on a wide range of subjects and for the provision of moral instruction and entertainment" (1991, 71). Students of sociolinguistics, by contrast, have long been familiar with the social implications of literary style; for a useful introduction, see Hodge and Kress, 1988, 79–120.

17. In fact, the two genres are more often kept rigorously apart, as is the case in Greenfield and Calder, 1986, which nonetheless has the fullest introduction to the vitality and range of the prose (38–121).

18. Although this transparency is notoriously difficult to define. Few critics have assessed the alterity of Old English poetry, but see the introductory comments in Shippey, 1972, 9–16. More fully developed are Overing, 1990, esp. xi–xxvi, 1–32; and Earl, 1994, 1–27.

19. In his first Latin preface (Clemoes, 1997, 174); a second edition of Ælfric's prefaces is Wilcox, 1994.

20. The classic model is Pelikan's magisterial work (1971–89).

21. A quick guide to this enormous field is Matter, 1995. The annual bibliographies published by the *Medieval Feminist Newsletter* are invaluable resources for work on gender and medieval studies in general. The study of medieval masculinities is less well established, but will certainly continue to contribute to our understanding of the relation between gender and belief; see, for example, McNamara, 1994, and Coakley, 1994.

22. Instrumental in prompting much of this recent work are the debates about feudalism and the transition to capitalism; for examples, see the essays in Hilton, 1976, and Aston and Philpin, 1985. See also Hilton, 1985, and, more generally, Anderson, 1974. For literary studies in a similar vein, see Harwood, 1994; Lees, 1994a; and Strohm, 1989.

23. In addition to the studies already mentioned, see, for example, Lomperis and Stanbury, 1993; Kay and Rubin, 1994; Brundage, 1987; Frantzen, 1998; Payer, 1984; Stock, 1983; Gilchrist, 1994; and Overing and Osborn, 1994.

24. That cultural studies cannot be described as a distinctive discipline is almost programmatic in contemporary accounts. In addition to During's introduction (1993, 1–25), see also the introduction to Grossberg, Nelson, and Treichler, 1992, 1–16. During offers a quick history of cultural studies in his introduction (1993, 2–10); for more substantial accounts, see Hall, 1990 and 1992 (a subtle antihistory of these early years).

25. As During notes (1993, 20) and Hall (1992) insists. Such statements do not necessarily mean that cultural studies has lost sight of its overall project of the study of culture, but they do testify to an antiteleological philosophy, which is sometimes at variance with its ostensible political stance.

26. For analogous comments on Wulfstan's treatment of slavery in his *Sermo Lupi*, see Frantzen, 1996c, 331–38.

27. Wilcox (1992, 211–12) suggests plausibly that the general injunction to penance in the face of disaster that opens so many Rogationtide homilies inspired VII Æthelred in the first place.

28. Indeed, this is increasingly the critical perception of Ælfric; see chapter 4 for further discussion.

29. "Cultural Studies is, of course, the study of culture, or, more particularly, the study of *contemporary* culture" (During, 1993, 1; his emphasis).

30. For an outline of historical cultural materialism, see Dollimore and Sinfield, 1985, 2–17. For discussion of cultural materialism and New Historicism, see Greenblatt, 1989, and Montrose, 1989. Dollimore offers further pertinent comments in his revised edition of *Radical Tragedy* (1993, xv–xxix). Stallybrass's "Shakespeare, the Individual, and the Text" is the only essay on the early modern period included in Grossberg, Nelson, and Treichler, 1992; none are included in During, 1993.

31. All three have in fact made use of Williams's work. See Patterson, 1987, esp. 41–74; Frantzen, 1990, 18–22, 106–7; and Aers, 1988, 17. For a discussion of the problems of what might be called actually existing cultural materialism in the early modern period, see Aers, 1992.

32. See especially Williams, 1977. Williams's commitment to the analysis of history is evident throughout his work, whether it be the historical analysis of words, as in *Keywords* (1976), or that of specific cultural formations, as in *The Country and the City* (1973). The distance between cultural studies in the United States and in the United Kingdom may be measured in part by Williams's enormous popularity in the latter and his neglect in the former. Only now is Williams enjoying wider critical attention; see, for example, Prendergast, 1995; for valuable recent critiques, see Pyle, 1993, 1995.

33. Mann's *Sources of Social Power* (1986) is one of the few studies to take up the implications of this relation.

34. Culler, 1994, 5. Culler's position contrasts with that of Gossman in the same issue, who comments on the analogy between literary aesthetic experience and religious experience (1994, 31).

35. Although Bynum's book, in spite of its title, *The Resurrection of the Body in Western Christianity, 200–1336*, unfortunately repeats a familiar paradigm of medieval studies by excluding the Anglo-Saxon period altogether.

36. As Michèle Barrett (1988) argues. Williams, 1977, is devoted in large measure to the theoretical problems that aesthetic form presents for cultural analysis; see also Eagleton, 1990, which addresses the subject of the aesthetic in modern European thought. Jauss

(1982b) examines the historical construction of the aesthetic, although he abandoned his concept of the so-called horizon of expectations in its analysis (1982a); see also the discussion in Holub, 1984, 53–82.

## 1. Tradition, Literature, History

1. Wilcox, 1994, 127.

2. That vernacularity itself is a historical phenomenon, subject to different conditions and contestations, is evident in Watson, 1995.

3. See also Hobsbawm and Ranger, 1983, 1–14, on the invented nature of tradition as opposed to the role of custom in traditional societies. My own feeling is that Anglo-Saxon religious prose is closer to Hobsbawm's sense of an invented tradition than it is a customary practice, although its rules remain, in MacIntyre's sense of the term, presuppositions, rather than inventions.

4. For references to the sources projects, see introduction, note 11.

5. Spencer's important analysis of later medieval preaching (1993) stresses the relation between preaching and other genres in the introduction (3). Although it does not significantly develop Owst's earlier attempts to build a bridge between the literary texts and the practice of preaching for this same period (see 88–90), this book is crucial for its study of later sermon forms as well as its recognition of the interrelation of heresy and orthodoxy.

6. The most influential formulation in this century has been Pidal, 1949. Deyermond, 1980, offers a brief account of the uses of the medieval Castilian sermon, indicating the marginality of this genre from mainstream literary concerns and replicating the emphases of Owst and others by maintaining the distinction between the sermon and other genres that are identified as more formally literary.

7. Most often this characterization is prefatory and perfunctory; few studies have addressed this "astonishing" (Greenfield and Calder, 1986, 38) difference between England and other early medieval cultures in any detail, and none to my knowledge have examined the centrality of the social power of religious prose in its production. Greenfield and Calder speculate that England's isolation from the continent accounts for the early flourishing of the vernacular. By contrast, Wormald (1991) argues that England's political history is central to the early primacy of the vernacular.

8. Recently, analysis of the prose and the verse has drawn closer together, as exemplified by Remley, 1996.

9. There are, however, distinctions in manuscript layout for poetry and prose in the Vercelli Book, briefly discussed in Pasternack, 1995, 149–51. Examples of "homiletic" poetry from the Exeter Book include *Precepts, The Order of the World, Soul and Body II, Judgment Day I, The Descent into Hell, Alms-Giving, The Lord's Prayer I,* and *Homiletic Fragment II* (all in *The Exeter Book,* ed. Krapp and Dobbie, 1936); see also Bliss and Frantzen, 1976. For the theory that the Exeter book displays the influence of both prereform and postreform religious environments in its poetry, see Conner, 1993, esp. 148–63.

10. For Alfred's poetry, see Earl, 1994, 87–89, and O'Brien O'Keeffe, 1990, 77–107. Bede's Latin poetry has been equally neglected; see Lapidge, 1993. Irvine, 1991, 202–8, and O'Brien O'Keeffe, 1990, 108–37, discuss the *Chronicle* poems.

11. In reference to the Vercelli Book homilies, Scragg (1992, xix) points out that "[t]he book is in no sense a homiliary," while the Blickling collection of homilies and saints' lives is at best an incomplete one (Ker 382, ed. Morris, 1874–80). Recensions of Ælfric's Second Series of *Catholic Homilies* (ed. Godden, 1979, xx–lxxviii) reveal how often compilers rearranged his series of homilies for the "temporale" according to other criteria (as he did himself). The one authoritative manuscript witness to his *Lives of Saints,* London, BL, Cotton Julius E. vii (Ker 162), also includes a number of general homilies; see Skeat, vol. 1: I, XII, XIII, XVI, XVII, and XVIII, and vol. 2: XXV.

12. The practice of providing both poetic and prose versions of the same text (by the same author) is more conventional in Latin; for discussion, see Wieland, 1981. The best discussion of Ælfric's style is that in Pope, 1967, 105–36. For Wulfstan, see McIntosh, 1949, 111–44, and Jost, 1950.

13. A good example is Cambridge, Corpus Christi College 41 (Ker 32), a copy of Bede's *Historia Ecclesiastica*, which also includes several anonymous Old English homilies, directions for masses and other liturgical forms, charms in both Latin and Old English, and part of the verse *Solomon and Saturn*, written in blank spaces and in margins.

14. For a related discussion, see chapter 4.

15. These features of anonymous and named collections and their relation to the Benedictine reform are discussed further in chapter 3.

16. For criticism of this methodology, see Chase, 1986, and Waterhouse, 1987, and more generally Lees, 1991, and Frantzen, 1990, 83–95.

17. The foundational work on Ælfric remains Clemoes, 1959, now supplemented by his introduction to the First Series (1997, 1–168); see also the introductions in Godden, 1979, xx–xciv, and Pope, 1967, 6–188. For Wulfstan, see Jost, 1950, and Bethurum, 1957, 24–49, and more recently Cross and Tunberg, 1993.

18. Shils's comments (1981, 7) about the failure of Marxist analyses of society to take account of the traditional are unjustified; see Williams, 1977, 115–20.

19. Studies of this aspect of the homilies are rare, but see Letson, 1979.

20. See Clayton, 1985; Lapidge, 1991; and Ælfric's Latin preface to the First Series of the *Catholic Homilies* (Clemoes, 1997, 173–74).

21. For the Signs of the Last Judgment, ultimately from the Apocalypse of Thomas, see Förster, 1955; Homily 3 in Bazire and Cross, 1982, 40–55; and Ælfric's First Series homily for the Second Sunday in Advent (Clemoes, 1997, 524–30). For Ælfric's knowledge of vernacular prose, see Godden, 1978.

22. For the six ages, see the discussion of Blickling Homily XI in chapter 3 and Ælfric's reworking of the same convention in his Second Series homily for Septuagesima (Godden, 1979, V); for the vices and virtues, see Lees, 1985; and for the groups at the Last Judgment, see Godden, 1973b.

23. By frequently referring to the need for brevity, Ælfric demonstrates that he is alert to the demands of his audience or readers, as Wilcox (1994, 62–63) also notes. This alertness is of course related to his cultivation of a plain prose style.

24. For Ælfric's revision of the *Catholic Homilies,* see the introductions by Pope (1967), Godden (1979), and Clemoes (1997). For the reissuing of the two series of the *Catholic Homilies* as a single set, see also Sisam, 1953. The circulation of Ælfric's prefaces is discussed by Wilcox (1994, 73–85); that of the *Lives of Saints* by Joyce Hill (1996). Wulfstan's use of Ælfric is discussed by Orchard (1992), while the considerable reuse of Wulfstan by anonymous writers is assessed by Wilcox (1992).

25. Ælfric's Latin *Life of Æthelwold* is edited by Lapidge and Winterbottom (1991, 70–80; for discussion, see cxlvi–clv); for Wulfstan's Latin writings, see Cross, 1991, and Cross and Tunberg, 1993.

26. But see Thacker's work (1992) on the pastoral mission of the early English church in the time of Bede, which is an important step forward in the history of preaching in Latin in the early Anglo-Saxon period.

27. This audience was probably much wider than that for the poetry, though I wouldn't argue, as Wilcox does (1994, 21), that this gives the homilies a "democratic stamp." For further discussion of homiletic representations of society, see chapter 4.

28. Classic examples of such debates are Ælfric's discussion of the Eucharist in his Second Series homily for Easter Day and his assessment of the status of the Feast of Saint George. For analysis, see Leinbaugh, 1982; Grundy, 1990; and Hill, 1989. Such examples are instances of the familiar medieval practice of "translatii studii"; they signal both continuity and discontinuity with Latin theological discourses because the vernacular does

not simply substitute for Latin, but implicitly challenges its cultural authority by co-opting and redeploying its forms. For a general discussion, see Copeland, 1991, 103–26.

29. I emphasize this construction of "Englishness" in spite of Charles D. Wright's argument for the influence of the "Irish tradition" on the religious writing of this period (1993, esp. 1–48). Despite the often-rehearsed evidence of the hostility of the English church toward the Irish, the fact that homilies often use Irish or Irish-derived materials testifies to the flexibility of the English in incorporating and appropriating other (religious) cultures.

30. The key works in this debate remain Hilton, 1976, and Aston and Philpin, 1985; cf. Hilton, 1985; Anderson, 1974. Reynolds (1994), whose assessment of the medieval evidence represents a considerable challenge to what conventional history calls feudalism (and what she terms "feudo-vassalic" relations), is comfortable with entertaining the broader Marxist sense of feudalism, while omitting precisely this sense from her study (1–16).

31. Stock, 1974; 1990, 159–71; Patterson, 1990; Aers, 1992. Aers's two explanations (195–97) for the limitations of radical Renaissance critics in taking account of the High Middle Ages also accommodate the reticences of radical critics of the High Middle Ages about earlier periods. Aers is right to stress the importance of Christianity to formulations of the medieval, although this insight needs to be extended to include the many historical changes Christianity undergoes throughout the period. Disciplinary and institutional structures in general account not only for the emphases of Renaissance critics but for those of the critics of the High Middle Ages as well. (Stock, Patterson, and Aers do not explore the early medieval period.)

32. Well exemplified by the use of the word *new* to call attention to these diverse critical practices; see the essays collected in *The New Philology*, ed. Nichols (1990), and *The New Medievalism*, ed. Brownlee, Brownlee, and Nichols (1991).

33. See Nichols's introductory comment on the *Speculum* New Philology volume: "The contributors do not represent a particular school or tendency" (1990, 9). Several of the contributors to the volume are highly aware of the ideological force of labels such as "new" or "old"; see Wenzel and Bloch. Such awareness parallels theoretical reflection on New Historicism, which seems to be initiated by Greenblatt (1989). Patterson (1987, 57–70) offers a lucid critique of New Historicism.

34. Middleton largely addresses the institutionalization of the discipline in the United States, and does so by distinguishing medieval studies from the study of the medieval within the older discipline of philology, with its origins in the nineteenth century. A similar move is made by Cantor (1991), whose account of the origins of medieval studies begins at the turn of the twentieth century.

35. Among the many recent assessments of the impact of contemporary theory on Anglo-Saxon studies, see Overing, 1993; see also the collection of essays in O'Brien O'Keeffe, 1997.

36. The debate about oral-traditional methodologies is still largely conducted with respect to Anglo-Saxon poetry; for a discussion, see Earl, 1994, 79–99. As Earl points out (79–80), recent assessments of the orality of this genre have drawn closer to those derived from literate methodologies, with oral-traditional critics such as Foley (e.g., 1991) relocating the force of traditionality within an aesthetics barely distinguishable from conventional literary aesthetics. Other avenues have been opened up by O'Brien O'Keeffe (1990), who uses manuscript evidence to reconstruct what might be termed the invention of the orality of Anglo-Saxon verse within literacy, and by Pasternack's innovative emphasis on inscribed poetry and its polyphonous aesthetics (1995). Studies of the orality of literate and traditional texts such as sermons have yet to be investigated in detail; Orchard (1992) rests heavily on conventional oral theory (the identification of formulae) as a means of "proving" Wulfstan's traditional oral style.

37. As exemplified by Irvine, 1994. Such studies bypass the question of literariness in favor of a cultural (and frequently all-encompassing) system of signs. The advantages of such an approach are indisputable, since, as is frequently remarked, medieval systems of

sign theory—"grammatica"—are uncannily similar to modern inquiries into signs and their significance. That such studies have concentrated largely on canonical works is perhaps only a symptom of the infancy of this approach.

38. There are, for example, few vernacular rhetorical treatises that would support a close relationship between the Latin system of grammar and the writing of vernacular texts for the Anglo-Saxon period (and the most promising avenue for such research, Ælfric's works, is currently the most neglected). See Irvine's suggestive comments on Ælfric's *Grammar* (1994, 412–14).

39. Notable exceptions are Vance's analysis of Augustinian theories of the word, which forms the basis for his discussion of later medieval poetics (1986), and Colish, 1968, which has important implications for the relation between the study of belief and that of signs (see esp. her discussion of Augustine, 8–81). Historical shifts in reading practices and their impact upon the construction and interpretation of texts are also minimized in studies of textuality; for recent studies, see Saenger, 1982, 1989.

40. Jauss's work has already engaged medievalists; for relevant examples, see Frantzen, 1990, 122–29, and Lees, 1991, 165–68.

41. That the early Jauss was working within post-Romantic notions of literary aesthetics and thus excluding genres such as hagiography and sermons should not be emphasized at the expense of this major advance. His problematic emphasis on the new as a determinative category of aesthetics for the medieval period is evident in his 1979 essay; so too is it in his discussion of "culinary" art in 1982b, 25. For discussion of Jauss's difficulties in combining history with literary aesthetics, see Holub, 1984, 62–63.

42. In some cases, this problem can be approached through concepts like Stock's "textual communities" or via studies of reading practices like Saenger's (1982, 1989), both of which explore the social significance of written texts in relation to specific communities. Stock's definition of such communities focuses on the charismatic individual who so often features in both reform and heretical movements: "What was essential to a textual community was not a written version of a text, although that was sometimes present, but an individual, who, having mastered it, then utilized it for reforming a group's thought and action" (1983, 90). Irvine's definition is looser: "A textual community is formed by the two dimensions of the social function of texts, which are as inseparable as the two sides of a sheet of parchment—a received canon of texts and an interpretive methodology articulated in a body of commentary which accompanied the texts and instituted their authority" (1994, 15). Irvine examines a broad range of such communities across the early Middle Ages, whose specific sociocultural formations need further investigation. It is, for example, quite possible to see in Æthelwold's activities at Winchester a "textual community" in Stock's, rather than Irvine's, sense of the term, although such a case has yet to be made.

43. Patterson comes to a similar conclusion in his discussion of contemporary concepts of the individual: "If the category of the social has faded from view, so too has the category of the historical" (1991, 4). For analysis and critique of the ways in which certain academic formations in the age of postmodernism have in fact returned to history via methods such as anecdote and autobiography, thus revealing postmodernism's connection to modernism, see Simpson, 1995.

## 2. Aesthetics and Belief

1. As Roberta Frank puts it, "Germanic legend matters to us: because it was somehow important to the Anglo-Saxons, who tried harder and harder with each passing century to establish a Germanic identity" (1991, 88); see also Niles's emphasis on ethical and ethnic origins in *Beowulf* (1993).

2. This is not to deny the existence of other systems, most obviously exemplified by traditions of wisdom literature, which have strong affinities with Christian traditions; for a recent study, see Larrington, 1993.

3. As Ælfric puts it in his First Series homily for Shrove Sunday, *Dominica in quin-quagessima:* "... to þisum life. þe is wiðmeten cwearterne" (to this life, which is compared to a prison; Clemoes, 1997, 259/40–1).

4. *The Wanderer,* ed. Dunning and Bliss (1969); *The Seafarer,* ed. Gordon (1960); *The Dream of the Rood,* ed. Swanton (1970). All references are to these editions, in consultation with those in *The Exeter Book,* ed. Krapp and Dobbie (1936), for *The Wanderer* and *The Seafarer;* and for *The Dream of the Rood* in *The Vercelli Book,* ed. Krapp (1932).

5. The source for this homily is Gregory, *PL* 76, 1082–86, in the homiliary of Paulus Diaconus; see Smetana, 1959, 187. For another expression of this homiletic commonplace, see the Blickling Shrove Sunday homily (Morris, 1874–80, 23/3–7): "we synd on þisse worlde ælþeodige, & swa wæron siþþon se æresta ealdor þisses menniscan cynnes Godes bebodu abræc; & forþon gylte we wæron on þysne wræc-siþ sende, & nu eft sceolon oþerne eþel secan, swa wite, swa wuldor, swe we nu geearnian willaþ." (We are strangers in this world, and so have been since the first leader of this human race broke God's commandments; and because of sin we were sent into this exile-path, and now again we must seek another homeland, whether in torment or glory, as we now desire to merit). See also Vercelli Homily XIV, Scragg 1992, lines 17–30.

6. For sources, see Smetana, 1959, 186.

7. The homiletic affinities of *The Wanderer, The Seafarer,* and *The Dream of the Rood* have long been known; see, for example, Dunning and Bliss, 1969, 78–102; Gordon, 1960, 18–27; and Swanton, 1970, 62–78. See also, more generally, Campbell, 1988. The view that implies that transcendence—read mistakenly as closure—is antithetical to polyvocality has surfaced most recently in the work of Pasternack (1995, esp. 8–28, and her comments on *Genesis A* and *Christ II,* 137–46). In assessing the role of the reader in making the meaning of any Anglo-Saxon poem, Pasternack downplays the interrelation between that reader and the cultural system that he or she inhabits. Thus Pasternack locates the aesthetic of Anglo-Saxon poetry in the tension between the traditional truths encoded by the poetry and the inevitable resistance to unitary meaning that the individual reader detects in these same linguistic structures; this aesthetic sounds distinctively modern precisely because of its resistance to structures of transcendence.

8. See esp. Book 4 of Augustine's *De doctrina Christiana,* transl. D. W. Robertson (1958, 117–69); McKitterick (1977, 88–89) summarizes Gregory the Great's emphasis on eloquence in preaching. For the Old English version of Gregory's *Pastoral Care,* see Sweet, 1871–72.

9. There has been little detailed discussion of this feature of the prose style of the Blickling Homilies, for which see the suggestive comments by Clemoes (1995, 43–44 and note 121); see also Vercelli VIII (Scragg, 1992, 149, note to line 1). The formula, "manað us ꝸ myndgað" (reminds us and exhorts), as Vercelli VIII, line 1 puts it, is a good example of such a style, opening not only this homily, but Vercelli IX and Blickling XIV and XVII (for the sake of convenience I refer to Morris's numbering of these texts, but these are inaccurate; cf. Willard, 1960, and Scragg, 1985, note 12). The use of the *Visio Pauli* (better known from the analogous description of the mere in *Beowulf*) in Blickling Homily IV and Homily XVII and the use of rhetorical figures, such as the "Ubi sunt" motif in Blickling V and X, are other salutary reminders of the interrelation of the poetry and the prose. For discussion, see Healey, 1978; Cross, 1956; and McCord, 1981. Vercelli II (Scragg, 1992, 56–57, lines 39–51) offers an example of poetic alliteration, which Scragg suggests (50–51) is probably a feature of the homilist's own style; by contrast, Vercelli XXI (356–57, lines 126–57) appears to incorporate extracts from two poems, one of which is known as the *Exhortation to Christian Living* (347). The poetic versions of the Creed and the Lord's Prayer are rarely studied for their style; for the texts, see Dobbie, 1942, 70, 77–78, 78–80, and *The Exeter Book,* Krapp and Dobbie, 1936, 223–24; for discussion, see Caie, 1994.

10. Pasternack (1995, 147–78) stresses the dynamics of transcendence and conventionality in the Cynewulfian poems, but is less confident about the importance of Christianity in shaping the structure and reception of the poetry generally: "It may even be the case

that poets, scribes and readers can be explicit only about the particulars, omitting translations and resolutions, because they trust in the possibility of a meaning related to but beyond the individual events of the present and past. But while the Christian tenor of inscribed texts suggests that many may have felt this way, we cannot know how widespread such feelings were, or indeed whether anxiety about meaning was not greater than trust in its ultimate force" (146).

11. In a discussion unique within the critical literature, Clemoes (1995, 273–309) traces the interrelation between poet and preacher.

12. My view here differs from that of Schaefer (1991, 122–23), who argues that conventionality (in contrast with traditionality) is an intertextual feature, with little extratextual referentiality.

13. I exclude from discussion here the three so-called Silent Days in Holy Week, during which the laity were also expected to attend church, but for which Ælfric expressly forbids the recital of homilies. That homilies were composed for these three days is important evidence for a counterliturgical tradition, as Hill notes (1985); the surviving texts are, however, largely vernacular paraphrases of the relevant passions from the Gospels assigned for the three days, and provide evidence for a specific kind of repetition of Scripture in English in the liturgical cycle.

14. As Ælfric continues in *De fide catholica:* "we sprecað ymbe god. deadlice be undeadlicum tyddre be ælmihtigum. earmingas be mildheortum. ac hwa mæg wurðfullice sprecan be þam ðe is unasecgendlic" (We speak of God, mortals of the Immortal, the feeble of the Almighty, the wretched of the Merciful; but who may worthily speak of that which is unspeakable? Clemoes, 1997, 340/158–60). For the sources of this homily, see Förster, 1894, 37–38.

15. There is, of course, a mystification at work in the use of the plain metaphor to create the idea of a universal Christian community, since, as I discuss in chapter 4, Ælfric — like the other English homilists — equally insists on maintaining the hierarchies of English society.

16. For further discussion of this homily, including its sources in Alcuin's *De animae ratione* and Alfred's translation of Boethius, see Godden, 1985b, 278–82, and Leinbaugh, 1994.

17. The Creed and the Lord's Prayer are regularly cited as the minimal sacred knowledge for clergy and laity alike; see, briefly, Remley, 1996, 55–58; Bethurum, 1957, 299–300.

18. For discussion, see Greenfield and Calder, 1986, 79–82.

19. Pope (1967, 453–61) has a fine summary of the intertexts of *De Sancta Trinitate, De initio creaturae,* the *Letter to Wulfgeat,* the *Interrogationes,* and their relation to the *Sermo ad populum, In octavis pentecosten dicendus* (Pope, 1967, XI).

20. As Orchard (1992) points out. For Ælfric's use of the so-called Winchester vocabulary, see Gneuss, 1972; for his own distinctive vocabulary, see also Pope, 1967, 99–103.

21. For the other nonhagiographical items in this collection, see chapter 1, note 11.

22. My discussion here is heavily indebted to Pope's own analysis of the tract (Pope, 1968, 667–75, 713–24).

23. See Bethurum, 1957, 335 (note to lines 35–39). For Snorri Sturluson's prologue to the Prose Edda, see Young, 1954, 23–28. The best-known example is in Book 2 of Milton's *Paradise Lost.*

24. Ælfric's independence from even his identified sources is well illustrated in Pope's edition.

25. For relevant manuscripts, see Cambridge, Corpus Christi College 303 (C); Cambridge University Library Ii. I. 33 (L); Cambridge, Corpus Christi College 178 (R); Oxford, Bodley, Hatton 116 (S); and Cotton Julius E. vii (W), all discussed in Pope, 1967, under their respective sigla.

26. For Wulfstan's rewriting of Ælfric's *De septiformi spiritu* (Napier, 1883, VII), see Bethurum, 1957, IX, and Orchard, 1992. See also his rewriting of Ælfric's *In dedicatione ecclesiae* (Godden, 1979, XL) in Bethurum, 1957, XVIII.

27. For verbal echoes of this passage, see Bethurum, 1957, VI, 151–52, lines 138–53. Bethurum comments on Wulfstan's characteristic lack of interest in the Trinity, which drives so much of Ælfric's work, in her discussion of Wulfstan's translation of the Creed (301).

## 3. Conventions of Time in the Old English Homiletic Corpus

1. "...quod iam non est, nisi quia in animo qui illud agit tria sunt? nam et expectat et attendit et meminit, ut id quod expectat per id quod attendit transeat in id quod meminerit...quod non est, sed longum praeteritum longa memoria praeteriti est" (*Augustine: Confessions*, ed. O'Donnell [1992], vols. 1–2, Book 11.28, 162–63; cf. commentary, vol. 3, 294, and the discussion of memory, 174–78). The English translation of the *Confessions* is by Pine-Coffin (1961, 277). Where Augustine and the Old English homilists differ, however, is in the conceptualization of the present: the present, for Augustine, is so transitory that it can barely be conceived; for the homilists, alert to this problem, the Christian present is continually re-presented via articulation and thus insisted upon.

2. For Ælfric's sources for this homily in Boethius and Alcuin's *De animae ratione* and for related discussions, see chapter 2, note 16.

3. "The monastic revival of the tenth century is, I believe, the theological watershed which lies between the work of the earlier, anonymous homilists and that of Ælfric and Wulfstan" (Gatch, 1977, 8). This watershed also informs the structuring of the homiletic corpus, as Scragg (1979) makes plain.

4. For a general discussion, see Jones, 1947.

5. For sources, see Cross, 1969.

6. For the Blickling manuscript, see Ker 382 and Willard, 1960. For detailed analysis, see Scragg, 1985. Although Gatch (e.g., 1989, 101) pushes his argument too far that the Blickling homilies (as opposed to the hagiographical items) are best described as catechetical rather than exegetical, those homilies (e.g., Homilies II, III, VI, XI, and XII in Morris's edition) that do draw on lections use continuous glossing with far greater freedom than we are familiar with from Ælfric's works and his Latin sources. Source analysis, combined with a certain fluency in narrative structure and content across the collection, has contributed to the characterization of the Blickling Homilies as "confused and confusing" (Clayton, 1986, 25; cf. 1990, 232–34). I have made similar observations about Blickling Homily VI (Lees, 1988). As a whole, these works enjoy a reputation for vivid, not to say overenthusiastic, narrative and a taste for apocryphal themes, such as the Descent into Hell (Blickling VII), the "dry bones speak" (Blickling X), the *Visio Pauli* (Blickling IV), and the cluster of nonscriptural stories associated with Mary (Blickling XIII). Such apocryphal themes are by and large avoided by Ælfric and Wulfstan, although they are certainly enjoyed by the Old English poets. Stylistic analysis (in particular the preference for a very loose alliterative noun or verb phrase), in comparison with these known homiletic writers, also contributes to the perception of the collection as, on the whole, less learned and more pastoral in intent, as Clayton (1985, 223–25) argues on the basis of the similarities between the Blickling collection and the conventions of Carolingian homiliaries.

7. Clayton (1985, 222), summarizes the evidence for the Blickling Homilies (cf. Scragg, 1992, xxxvii–xliii, for Vercelli). The firmest evidence for both collections is codicological and paleographical and is confirmed by the text-external evidence of the Benedictine reform, which appears to have had little impact on these collections, even though a number of individual items from both have a considerable afterlife throughout the Anglo-Saxon period: ten of the eighteen items in the Blickling collection occur elsewhere in the corpus (Scragg, 1979, 233); eleven of the twenty-three items in the Vercelli Book are unique (Scragg, 1992, xx); and there is little overlap between the two collections.

8. See, for example, his First Series homily for Ascension Day (Clemoes, 1997, XXI), discussed in Cross, 1968, 67–78; his Second Series homily on the Nativity of Holy Virgins

(Godden, 1979, XXXIX, 330); and his *Sermo de die Iudicii* (Pope, 1968, XVIII, with a useful discussion at 584–89).

9. Godden, 1979, xci–iv, usefully rehearses all the arguments for the dating of the *Catholic Homilies* to the early years of the 990s; see also Clemoes, 1997, 1–168.

10. For a related discussion, which also surveys the poetry, see Trahern, 1991.

11. Only two of the homilies are strictly exegetical (in the sense of expounding a pericope); many are untitled, rubricated for general use or for the catchall season of Rogationtide.

12. As Charles D. Wright's detailed study of Vercelli IX makes plain (1993, esp. 215–71).

13. Vercelli Homilies XIX–XXI, all Rogationtide homilies, form an extended set in the collection and all draw on the homiliary of St. Père de Chartres, whose earliest complete witness is the Pembroke homiliary. For discussion, see Scragg, 1992, 310–14, and Cross, 1987, 96–173.

14. Alfred's letter is conveniently edited in Mitchell and Robinson, 1992, 204–7.

15. In 991 and 994; for discussion, see Keynes, 1980, 190, and Brooks, 1984, 281–85.

16. For Æthelweard, see Campbell, 1962, xii–xvi. Æthelweard dedicated his Latin Chronicle to his relative, Matilda, abbess of Essen, granddaughter of Otto I and Otto's English wife, Edith. For the family's prominence at Æthelred's court, where Byrhtnoth was also a major figure, see Keynes, 1980, 186–92. Some of the lands with which Eynsham was endowed in 1005 appear to have belonged to Byrhtnoth's family at one time, suggestive of the relation between the two families (discussed by Stafford, 1989, 38).

17. Ælfric acknowledges Ælfheah's role in his career in his First Series English preface to the *Catholic Homilies* (Clemoes, 1997, 174). Ælfheah of Winchester, who succeeded Æthelwold in 984, became in 1005/6 archbishop of Canterbury, where he was martyred by the Danes in 1011; see Brooks, 1984, 283–85; James W. Earl, "Violence and Non-violence in Anglo-Saxon England: Ælfric's Passion of St. Edmund" (forthcoming); and McDougall, 1993. For Æthelwold, see Yorke, 1988.

18. For the Letter to Sigeweard, see Crawford, 1922, 15–18. The Latin prefaces to these letters are edited by Wilcox (1994, as 8a, c, and d).

19. The homiletic version of Assmann I, the Letter to Wulfgeat, is in Oxford, Bodleian Library, Junius 121 (Ker 338, item 28); that of the Letter to Sigefryth is edited as Assmann III.

20. Useful summaries of this period are Lapidge and Winterbottom, 1991, li–lx; Stafford, 1978, and 1989, 180–94; Wormald, 1988; and John, 1966, 154–80.

21. The classic work on the *Concordia* is that by Dom Thomas Symons (1941, 1953, 1975), who became progressively more convinced of the independence of the English reform from its continental counterparts. For another edition of the *Concordia*, see Symons et al., 1984.

22. Gatch, 1977, 41–47. Clayton comments, "It is evident that priests did preach to the people, therefore, but what is less certain is whether the collections of vernacular homilies which survive represent this preaching or whether there was differentiation within the vernacular texts comparable to that which can be seen in the Carolingian Latin texts" (1985, 221). For Ælfric's regularization of the monastic night offices later in the period in the Eynsham customary, see Gatch, 1985.

23. The extent to which our understanding of the reform has been skewed by our attentiveness to its ideologues is discussed by Gransden, 1989. Another area of weakness or strength, depending on point of view, is the absence of firm support for female religious in spite of the *Concordia*'s address to both monks and nuns. For a brief discussion, see Stafford, 1989, 192–93, and more generally chapter 5.

24. The standardization of Late West Saxon is largely a Winchester phenomenon, as Gneuss (1972) argues, and as Scragg demonstrates in the case of Vercelli Homilies XIX–XXI (1992, xl–xlii; cf. lxx–lxxi).

25. For Lantfred's Latin *Life of Swithun*, Wulfstan's metrical version of this life, and his own Latin *Life of Æthelwold*, see Lapidge and Winterbottom, 1991, xciv–xcvii, 2–69.

For extracts from the *Life of Dunstan* by writer "B" and from Byrhtferth's *Life of Oswald*, see Whitelock, 1955, 826–31, 839–43.

26. For the sources for Ælfric's *Life of Cuthbert*, see Bede's *Vita S. Cuthberti*, probably in a version similar to that assembled in Paris, BN lat. 5362 (Lapidge and Winterbottom, 1991, cxlviii–cxlix). For Gregory and Benedict, see Godden, 1968, and 1978, 107. For Ælfric's experimentation with hagiography in the cases of both Cuthbert and Gregory, see also Godden, 1996.

27. Again most probably in a form similar to that in Paris, BN lat. 5362 (Lapidge and Winterbottom, 1991, cxlviii–cxlix). For Oswald, see also Stancliffe and Cambridge, 1995.

28. But see Lantfred's Latin *Life of Swithun*, which may have been known to Ælfric (Lapidge and Winterbottom, 1991, cxlviii–cxlix). For the important identification of the Cotton-Corpus legendary as a source for the *Lives of Saints*, see Zettel, 1982, and Jackson and Lapidge, 1996.

29. That this minor element may be intentional on Ælfric's part is suggested by the gathering and excerpting of the relevant Latin sources in BN lat. 5362. On the anomalous nature of Ælfric's *Lives of Saints* in comparison with other English liturgical traditions, see Lapidge, 1996.

30. As argued by Earl, "Violence and Non-Violence in Anglo-Saxon England."

31. For discussion, see Clayton, 1996. For the importance of the cult of Cuthbert in the tenth century as an aspect of reform and royal politics, from which Ælfric may have derived his own later interest, see Rollason, 1989b.

32. The best discussion of this passage is by Godden (1994, 134–36), who argues that Ælfric is indeed referring to the contemporary events of his own time. I differ from Godden only in emphasizing the rhetorical nature of the passage and its exemplary force.

33. The *ordo* probably used for Edgar's coronation in 973 stresses the importance of the royal duty to establish peace (cf. Janet Nelson, 1986), and Ælfric's emphasis here, as elsewhere, is probably an acknowledgment of that duty.

34. For discussion, see Powell, 1994; Earl, "Violence and Non-Violence"; and Lawson, 1994, 148–49.

35. See Whitelock, 1976, 1–5; Cross and Brown, 1989; and Godden's fine study of the *Sermo*'s place in the tradition of apocalypticism (1994, 142–62), to which my more general remarks are heavily indebted.

36. The contrast with Ælfric's use of negation in *De falsis diis* could not be plainer; see chapter 2.

37. Hollis, 1977, is characteristic, but see also Cross and Brown, 1989, and Godden, 1994.

38. Although Godden points out Ælfric's degree of political engagement in his writing (1994, 131–42).

39. By, for example, issuing in his own authority Ælfric's Pastoral Letters; for general discussion, see Hill, 1992b.

40. For Wulfstan's awkward integration of the theme of apocalypse in the *Sermo*, see Godden, 1994, 155–56 (a view not shared by Hollis, 1977).

## 4. Didacticism and the Christian Community

1. This is especially characteristic of art-historical studies of the period; see, for example, Backhouse, Turner, and Webster, 1984.

2. Moore (1987) argues in broad strokes, largely to counter a historiographical emphasis that views persecution as "natural" to this period without inquiring into its processes. While his arguments need testing against the individual instance, they have yet to be substantially challenged.

3. The critical literature is long and complex. Foucault's *History of Sexuality* (1980, esp. 3–73) has been instrumental in furthering the debate, as have recent studies on gender and the troubadours (esp. Kay, 1990, 1996). This debate is contested from a variety of

perspectives on the terrain of the fourteenth century as a direct response to a widespread postmedieval assumption that the "subject" was invented in the early modern period. For a useful introduction, see Aers, 1992; see also Aers, 1988; Aers and Staley (1996); and Patterson's essays on the Wife of Bath and the Pardoner (1991, 280–321, 367–421).

4. Proscription and regulation of sexual behavior has attracted more attention than idolatry (a capital sin) or heresy, both of which are regularly proscribed in the pentitentials. For discussion of sexuality, see Frantzen, 1983, and more explicitly, 1996a. Sexual behavior and heresy are the subjects of Ælfric's Letter to Wulfsige (ed. Fehr, 1914, 1–34). The subjects of heathenism, heresy, and idolatry in ecclesiastical and civil law merit further analysis, though it is clear that these are regular concerns of the monarchy and the church throughout the period, with proscriptions against heathenism resurfacing in the late Anglo-Saxon period, largely as a result of the presence of the Vikings in England. *Wulfstan's Canons of Edgar* (ed. Fowler, 1972) is a good witness to the kinds of proscriptions made throughout the later period, because of its inclusion of earlier clauses (as is habitual for the laws); see, for example, paragraphs 16 and 18. See also V Æthelred and II Cnut (trans. Whitelock, 1955, 405.1, 420.5)

5. While annual confession is mandated by the Fourth Lateran Council, both private and public confession and penance are already assumed in practice by the homiletic literature of the late Anglo-Saxon period; see Frantzen, 1983, 122–74.

6. Although this chapter begins this process of refining our historical understanding of the late Anglo-Saxon period by using the homilies, its evidence needs to be assessed in relation to the laws and the penitentials of this period in particular. Few have yet challenged the glow of the "golden age," although John (1983) offers some unsentimental perceptions about Ælfric's theology.

7. Bede recounts the massacre of the monks at Bangor at the hands of Æthelfrith in fulfillment of Augustine's prophecies that unless they accept English custom for religious practices (including the dating of Easter), they would suffer death at their hands (Colgrave and Mynors, 1969, II, 2). The ideological contest between the Irish and the English (Roman) Christians, which largely took the form of the controversy over the dating of Easter, is well known.

8. Keynes, for example, argues that "there might be good cause if not to applaud then at least to condone rather than to deplore the making of payments to the Vikings and the massacre of St. Brice's Day" (1980, 208). For the disputes between the regular and monastic clergy, see the Old English account of Edgar's establishment of monasteries (generally agreed to be by Æthelwold), excerpts from which are conveniently translated in Whitelock, 1955, 846–49.

9. A full study of the regulation of heresy in the canons and religious literature of the period is a desideratum for future research. Ælfric is still warning of the dangers of Arianism in the late tenth century; his First Series *De fide catholica* spells out the death of Arius in ways intended to recall that of Judas (Clemoes, 1997, 342–43).

10. Hermann's study of *Elene, Andreas,* and *Judith* (1989) is one of the few to foreground the ideological importance of Judaism in Anglo-Saxon literature.

11. Where community is concerned, the only study of any detail has concentrated on the poetry, not the prose; see Magennis, 1996.

12. Miller (1996) similarly points out that the role of the agent in later medieval penitential discourse has been underestimated by historians of subjectivity.

13. The most recent survey of the evidence is Irvine, 1994, 272–460. Ælfric's *Grammar* (ed. Zupitza, 1880), the Pastoral Letters (ed. Fehr, 1914), and the *Colloquy* (ed. Garmonsway, 1939) all bear witness to the late-tenth, early-eleventh-century emphasis on the need to educate regular and monastic clerics. The evidence of standard Late West Saxon is also a measure of the reach of standardized vernacular education among the clergy; see Gneuss, 1972.

14. For an introduction, see Murphy, 1971, xvii–xx. For a fuller discussion, see Spencer, 1993, 78–133 (on medieval views of preaching) and 228–68 (on sermon form).

15. For Ælfric's Latin source (Gregory), see Smetana, 1959, 198.

16. These readings are often invisible in the critical editions, especially in Thorpe's 1844 edition of the *Catholic Homilies*; cf. Clemoes, 1997. For full citations, see Cook, 1898, 1903, and Napier, 1898, 1899, 1901. Godden supplies all pericopes to the Second Series in his 1979 edition. For discussion of the vernacular homiletic translations of the Old Testament, see Marsden, 1995, 395–443.

17. For discussion of this homily, see Godden, 1990, 56–59. The source—a Latin legend for the martyrdom of Saints Peter and Paul—was identified by Cross, 1972, 26–28, 33–36.

18. For Ælfric's source (Gregory's homily for the same day in the homiliary of Paulus Diaconus), see Smetana, 1959, 187–88. For other examples of this common analogy, see the First Series homilies on the Lord's Prayer, *De Dominica oratione* (Clemoes, 1997, 329), and for mid-Lent Sunday (275–80), an exegesis of the miracle of the five loaves.

19. I differ from Jolly by emphasizing the importance of truth as a law in the homilies rather than as an exemplification of right or wrong practices (see her comments, 1996, 87).

20. Jolly, 1996, 18–24. Jolly's emphasis on crossing binary divisions needs to be complemented by an analysis of how those divisions actually operate in the homilies and of the social forces at work in them.

21. Jolly, 1996, 87–88. For a more nuanced reading of this homily, see Wilcox, 1994, 26–27.

22. Jolly, for example, describes Ælfric as going "off on a tangent" in the second part of the homily (1996, 87), while most commentators see the homily as divided into two parts (Wilcox, 1994, 26–27; Smetana, 1959, 185).

23. The word *rihtlicost* (most correct) is repeated almost as often as *gescead* (reason) in this homily.

24. Althusser's concept of interpellation (1971, 127–86), the process whereby the individual is "hailed" or subjected by an ideological discourse, or an ideological state apparatus, as Althusser puts it, although often rightly critiqued for its idealism and ahistoricist impulses (e.g., Larrain, 1979, 154–64), is nevertheless a useful way of approaching the relation of the individual to the group in Christianity (Althusser's own examples include the church).

25. For the sources to this homily (Gregory and Bede in the homiliary of Paulus Diaconus), see Smetana, 1959, 190–91.

26. For Ælfric's use of Augustine in this homily, see Förster, 1894, 33.

27. Ælfric names his source as Haymo; for discussion, see Smetana, 1959, 186.

28. As is evident throughout his writing, but see especially his First Series English preface (Clemoes, 1997, 174–77).

29. But see Godden, 1979, 195–96. Ælfric's attitude toward the *Visio Pauli* is discussed in Godden, 1978, 100–101. The fullest discussion of the *Visio* is that by Charles D. Wright (1993, 106–74).

30. In even the most explicit homilies, tithing remains a general obligation, as in Blickling IV, and is implemented in law only in the tenth century (Willard, 1949); see also Ælfric's First Series homily for the First Sunday in Lent (Clemoes, 1997, 272–74). The relation of tithing to chastity is discussed in chapter 5.

31. Clayton (1990, 260–65) comes to a similar conclusion on the basis of her analysis of the Marian homilies.

32. Ælfric's prefaces in fact offer useful precursors to the concepts of authorship explored by Minnis (1984).

33. This preface was reissued to form an addition to the First Series homily for the First Sunday in Advent in Cambridge, Corpus Christi College 188 (Ker 43, art. 43), and as a short homily in Cambridge, Corpus Christi College 178, Bodleian Library, Junius 121, and Bodleian Library, Hatton 115 (Ker 41, art. 12; 338, art. 34; and 332, art. 28, respectively). For a brief discussion, see Wilcox, 1994, 68.

34. For an important critique of postmodernist theories of the subject, the political power of authenticity, and the importance of historical analysis, see Dollimore, 1991, 39–73.

35. As explained by Ælfric in his First Series homily for Lent, for example (Clemoes, 1997, 273–74), and discussed further in chapter 5.

36. Other homilies await detailed analysis of their use of ritual and include Ælfric's First Series homily for Lent (Clemoes, 1997, 273–74), the Feast of the Purification of Mary (256–57), and Palm Sunday (296–98). For general discussion of Ælfric's use of the liturgy, see Jones, 1998.

37. My comments on ritual and its relation to the individual follow Asad's critique (1993, 126–35). Addressing monastic discipline in particular, Asad argues that rites did "not simply evoke or release universal emotions, they aimed to construct and reorganize distinctive emotions," which are "the product not of mere readings of symbols but of processes of power" (134).

38. Butler, 1993, 1–23. For a related critique of Butler's use of performativity in a reading of *Elene*, see Lees, 1997a, 159–67.

39. As Aers and Staley (1996) brilliantly point out, using the examples of Chaucer, Langland, and Julian of Norwich.

## 5. Chastity and Charity

Parts of this chapter are revised from Lees, 1997b, esp. 20–22, 31–36.

1. For discussion, see Lees and Overing, 1994, and Hollis, 1992, 1–14. For a more general introduction to the study of gender in Anglo-Saxon England, see Lees, 1997a, and the bibliography therein; see also Frantzen, 1998.

2. It is not entirely beside the point that Æthelwold is widely held to be the author of the *Regularis concordia*.

3. The formulaic language of this comment, which, in other contexts, is symptomatic of Ælfric's well-known taste for brevity, should not obscure its particular force here. It is characteristic of Ælfric, as well as of the Anglo-Saxon homilists in general, that the most pointed comments are couched in conventional topoi. For a discussion of Ælfric's use of brevity and analogous passages, see Wilcox, 1994, 62–63.

4. For related analyses of the manly woman, see Frantzen, 1993, and Roy, 1992.

5. Bede's version of the *Libellus* does not explicitly mention the act of ejaculation as a consequence of impure dreams, but regards the problem that such "illusions" present for defining sin and chastity. For similar discussions of what is more often known as nocturnal pollution, see Brundage, 1987, 80–81, 109–10, 214, 400–401, and Elliott, 1997.

6. Beckwith (1994) makes a similar point in her discussion of the later medieval *Ancrene Wisse*.

7. See the related discussions by Frantzen, 1996a, and more generally, 1983.

8. Although the gender continuum for men is much broader in the pentitential literature, as Frantzen (1996a, 273–80) points out.

9. For discussion of the legal body, see O'Brien O'Keeffe, 1998. Analysis of exchange systems has been revived recently in criticism of Old English poetry, following similar analysis in the Norse and Spanish literatures of the period (see, for example, Hill, 1995; Miller, 1990, esp. 85–140; and Harney, 1993). To the best of my knowledge, few have explored the analogous phenomenon of the sacrifice-as-offering or gift within Anglo-Saxon religious literature.

10. For discussion and sources, see Clayton, 1990, 220–22.

11. Thomas D. Hill (1996) discusses the importance of the icon in understanding hagiographical discourse. For analysis of the relation between the iconic and the feminine, see Lees, 1997a.

12. Hill (1992a, 225–28) surveys the sources for this homily.

13. Hill (1992a, 228) notes that the source for this section of the homily is as yet unidentified; I would suggest that Ælfric is here recalling and modifying his earlier First Series homily on the Purification.

14. Most of the discussion centers on the meanings of *bicgan* (to buy or pay for) and *agan* (to own) and the morning gift. For a preliminary discussion that repeats the ideology of marriage as free choice, see Fell, 1984, 15–17, 56–59. For a related analysis of marriage, see Lees, 1994a.

15. The relevant *Lives* are Skeat, 1, II (Eugenia), VII (Agnes), VIII (Agatha), IX (Lucy), and XX (Æthelthryth), and Skeat, 2, XXIIIB (Mary of Egypt), XXXIII (Euphrosyne), and XXXIV (Cecilia). Skeat, 2, XXIIIB (Mary of Egypt) and XXXIII (Euphrosyne) are assumed to be anonymous works on stylistic grounds, although they are included in the main manuscript witness to the collection, London, BL, Cotton Julius E. vii (Ker 162). For critical discussion, see Magennis 1985, 1986; Szarmach, 1990, 1996a; Frantzen, 1993; and Roy, 1992. These lives, like Anglo-Saxon vernacular lives in general, are rarely considered in general studies of medieval sanctity, as is illustrated by the classic study by Weinstein and Bell (1982); they are also often neglected by Anglo-Saxon literary historians (see Lees, 1994b).

16. Gaunt (1995) emphasizes the sexuality of sanctity in his analysis of Old French hagiography. Anglo-Saxon female lives, however, do not so much scrutinize the saint's sexuality, as Gaunt suggests of the French material, as radically defend it from scrutiny.

17. For discussion of homoeroticism in Euphrosyne and Eugenia, see Gaunt, 1995, and Frantzen, 1993, 457–67. For a different emphasis, see Roy, 1992.

18. For a related discussion, see Lees, 1994b, 110–12.

19. In addition to the lives of Julian and Basilissa (Skeat, 1, IV) and Chrysanthus and Daria (Skeat, 2, XXXV), Ælfric praises Basil's chastity, for example, and comments favorably on the cohabitation of Anastasius, a priest, with a chaste virgin (Skeat, 1, III); he also insists on clerical chastity in his account of Peter (Skeat, 1, X) and on chastity and lawful marriage in his sermon on the memory of saints (Skeat, 1, XVI).

20. For further discussion of this life, see Fell, 1994; Griffiths, 1992; and Waterhouse, 1996.

21. Hollis, 1992, amply demonstrates the inadequacy of this position for the early centuries of Anglo-Saxon culture.

# Works Cited

## Primary

Assmann, Bruno, ed. 1889. *Angelsächsische Homilien und Heiligenleben.* Kassel: G. H. Wigland. Reprint with introduction by Peter Clemoes, Darmstadt: Wissenschaftliche Buchgesellschaft, 1964.

Baker, Peter S. and Michael Lapidge, eds. 1995. *Byrhtferth's Enchiridion.* Oxford: EETS ss 15.

Bately, Janet, ed. 1980. *The Old English Orosius.* Oxford: EETS ss 6.

Bazire, Joyce, and James E. Cross, eds. 1982. *Eleven Old English Rogationtide Homilies.* Toronto: University of Toronto Press.

Bethurum, Dorothy, ed. 1957. *The Homilies of Wulfstan.* Oxford: Clarendon.

Campbell, A., ed. 1962. *The Chronicle of Æthelweard.* London: Nelson.

Clemoes, Peter, ed. 1997. *Ælfric's Catholic Homilies: The First Series Text.* Oxford: EETS ss 17.

Colgrave, Bertram, and R. A. B. Mynors, eds. 1969. *Bede's Ecclesiastical History of the English People.* Oxford: Clarendon.

Crawford, S. J., ed. 1921. *Ælfric's Exameron Anglice; or, The Old English Hexameron.* Hamburg: Bibliothek der angelsächsischen Prosa 10.

———, ed. 1922. *The Old English Version of the Heptateuch.* London: EETS 160.

Cross, James E., ed. 1987. *Cambridge Pembroke College MS. 25: A Carolingian Sermonary Used by Anglo-Saxon Preachers.* London: King's College London Medieval Studies 1.

———, ed., with Dennis Brearley, Julia Crick, Thomas N. Hall, and Andy Orchard. 1996. *Two Old English Aprocrypha and Their Manuscript Source: "The Gospel of Nichodemus" and "The Avenging of the Saviour."* Cambridge: Cambridge University Press.

Cross, James E., and Jennifer Morrish Tunberg, eds. 1993. *The Copenhagen Wulfstan Collection: Copenhagen Kongelige Bibliothek Gl. kgl. sam. 1595.* Copenhagen: EEMF 25.

Dobbie, Elliott Van Kirk, ed. 1942. *The Anglo-Saxon Minor Poems.* ASPR 6. New York: Columbia University Press.

Dunning, T. P., and A. J. Bliss, eds. 1969. *The Wanderer.* London: Methuen.

Fehr, B., ed. 1914. *Die Hirtenbriefe Ælfrics.* Hamburg: Bibliothek der angelsächsischen Prosa 9. Reprint, with introduction by Peter Clemoes, Darmstadt: Wissenschaftliche Buchgesellschaft, 1964.

Fowler, Roger, ed. 1972. *Wulfstan's Canons of Edgar.* London: EETS 266.

Garmonsway, G. N., ed. 1939. *Ælfric's Colloquy.* London: Methuen.

Godden, Malcolm, ed. 1979. *Ælfric's Catholic Homilies: The Second Series Text.* London: EETS ss 5.

Gordon, I. L., ed. 1960. *The Seafarer.* London: Methuen.

Henel, Heinrich, ed. 1942. *Ælfric's De Temporibus Anni.* London: EETS 213. Reprint, 1970.

Jost, Karl, ed. 1950. *Die "Institutes of Polity, Civil and Ecclesiastical," ein Werk Erzbischof Wulfstans von York.* Bern: A. Francke.

Ker, N. R. 1957. *Catalogue of Manuscripts Containing Anglo-Saxon.* Oxford: Clarendon.

Krapp, George Philip, ed. 1932. *The Vercelli Book.* ASPR 2. New York: Columbia University Press.

Krapp, George Philip, and Elliott Van Kirk Dobbie, eds. 1936. *The Exeter Book*. ASPR 3. New York: Columbia University Press.

Lapidge, Michael, and Michael Winterbottom, eds. 1991. *Wulfstan of Winchester: The Life of St Æthelwold*. Oxford: Clarendon.

Liebermann, Felix, ed. 1903. *Die Gesetze der Angelsachsen*. vol. 1. Halle: M. Niemayer. Reprint, Aalen: Scientia, 1966.

Liuzza, R. M., ed. 1994. *The Old English Version of the Gospels*. Vol. 1. Oxford: EETS 304.

MacLean, George E., ed. 1883–84. "Ælfric's Version of Alcuini Interrogationes Sigeuulfi in Genesin." *Anglia* 6:425–73, 7:1–59.

Mitchell, Bruce, and Fred C. Robinson, eds. 1992. *A Guide to Old English*. 5th ed. Oxford: Blackwell.

Morris, R., ed. 1874–80. *The Blickling Homilies*. London: EETS 58, 63, 73. Reprint, 1 vol., 1967.

Murphy, James J., ed. 1971. *Three Medieval Rhetorical Arts*. Berkeley: University of California Press.

Napier, Arthur, ed. 1883. *Wulfstan: Sammlung der ihm zugeschriebenen Homilien nebst Untersuchungen über ihre Echtheit* Berlin: Weidmann.

O'Donnell, James J., ed. 1992. *Augustine: Confessions*. 3 vols. Oxford: Clarendon.

Pine-Coffin, R. S., trans. 1961. *Saint Augustine: Confessions*. Harmondsworth: Penguin.

Pope, John C., ed. 1967–68. *Homilies of Ælfric: A Supplementary Collection*. 2 vols. London: EETS 259, 260.

Roberts, Jane, ed. 1979. *The Guthlac Poems of the Exeter Book*. Oxford: Clarendon.

Robertson, D. W., Jr., trans. 1958. *On Christian Doctrine*, by Augustine. Indianapolis, Ind.: Liberal Arts Press.

Scragg, D. G., ed. 1981. *The Battle of Maldon*. Manchester: Manchester University Press.

———, ed. 1992. *The Vercelli Homilies and Related Texts*. Oxford: EETS 300.

Sisam, Celia, ed. 1976. *The Vercelli Book*. Copenhagen: EEMF 19.

Skeat, Walter W., ed. 1881–1900. *Ælfric's Lives of Saints*. London: EETS 76, 82, 94, 114. Reprint, 2 vols. 1966.

Swanton, Michael, ed. 1970. *The Dream of the Rood*. Manchester: Manchester University Press.

Sweet, Henry, ed. 1871–72. *King Alfred's West-Saxon Version of Gregory's Pastoral Care*. London: EETS 45, 50.

Symons, Dom Thomas, ed. and trans. 1953. *Regularis concordia Anglicae nationis monachorum sanctimonialiumque*. New York: Oxford University Press.

Symons, Dom Thomas, S. Spath, M. Wegener, and K. Hallinger, eds. 1984. "Regularis concordia Anglicae nationis." In *Consuetudinum saeculi X/XI/XII monumenta non-Cluniacensia*, ed. K. Hallinger. Corpus Consuetudinum Monasticarum 7.3. Siegburg: F. Schmitt.

Thorpe, Benjamin, ed. 1844–46. *The Homilies of the Anglo-Saxon Church. The First Part, Containing The Sermones Catholici or Homilies of Ælfric*. 2 vols. London: Ælfric Society. Reprint, Hildesheim: Georg Olms, 1983.

Whitelock, Dorothy, ed. and trans. 1955. *English Historical Documents c. 500–1042*. Vol. 1. London: Eyre & Spottiswoode.

———, ed. 1976. *Sermo Lupi ad Anglos*. 3rd ed. Exeter: University of Exeter.

Whitelock, Dorothy, M. Brett, and C. N. L. Brooke, eds. and trans. 1981. *Councils and Synods, with Other Documents Relating to the English Church*. Vol. 1: *AD 871–1204*. Oxford: Clarendon.

Wilcox, Jonathan, ed. 1994. *Ælfric's Prefaces*. Durham: Durham Medieval Texts.

Willard, Rudolph, ed. 1960. *The Blickling Homilies*. Copenhagen: EEMF 10.

Young, Jean I., trans. 1954. *The Prose Edda*, by Snorri Sturluson. Berkeley: University of California Press.

Zupitza, Julius, ed. 1880. *Ælfrics Grammatik und Glossar*. Sammlung englischer Denkmäler in kritischen Ausgaben 1. Berlin: Weidmann. Reprint, 1966.

## Secondary

Abulafia, Anna. 1994. "Bodies in the Jewish-Christian Debate." In *Framing Medieval Bodies*, ed. Kay and Rubin, 123–37.

Aers, David. 1988. *Community, Gender, and Individual Identity: English Writing, 1360–1430*. London and New York: Routledge.

———. 1992. "A Whisper in the Ear of Early Modernists; or, Reflections on Literary Critics Writing the 'History of the Subject.'" In *Culture and History, 1350–1660: Essays on English Communities, Identities, and Writing*, ed. Aers, 177–202. Detroit, Mich.: Wayne State University Press.

———. 1994a. "Altars of Power: Reflections on Eamon Duffy's *The Stripping of the Altars*." *Literature and History* 3:90–105.

———. 1994b. "Class, Gender, Medieval Criticism, and *Piers Plowman*." In *Class and Gender in Early English Literature*, ed. Harwood and Overing, 59–75.

———. 1995. Review of Margherita, 1994. *Speculum* 70:933–36.

———. 1996. "Preface." *Historical Inquiries/Psychoanalytic Criticism/ Gender Studies*. *JMEMS* 26:200–208.

Aers, David, and Lynn Staley. 1996. *The Powers of the Holy: Religion, Politics, and Gender in Late Medieval English Culture*. University Park: Pennsylvania State University Press.

Althusser, Louis. 1971. *Lenin and Philosophy and Other Essays*. Trans. Ben Brewster. New York: Monthly Review Press.

Anderson, Perry. 1974. *Passages from Antiquity to Feudalism*. London: Verso.

Asad, Talal. 1993. *Genealogies of Religion: Discipline and Reasons of Power in Christianity and Islam*. Baltimore, Md.: Johns Hopkins University Press.

Aston, T. H., and C. H. E. Philpin, eds. 1985. *The Brenner Debate: Agrarian Class Structure and Economic Development in Pre-Industrial Europe*. Cambridge: Cambridge University Press.

Backhouse, Janet, D. H. Turner, and Leslie Webster, eds. 1984. *The Golden Age of Anglo-Saxon Art, 966–1066*. London: British Museum Publications.

Barrett, Michèle. 1988. "The Place of Aesthetics in Marxist Criticism." In *Marxism and the Interpretation of Culture*, ed. Nelson and Grossberg, 697–713.

Bately, Janet. 1991. "The Nature of Old English Prose." In *The Cambridge Companion to Old English Literature*, ed. Godden and Lapidge, 71–87.

Beckwith, Sarah. 1993. *Christ's Body: Identity, Culture, and Society in Late Medieval Writings*. London: Routledge.

———. 1994. "Passionate Regulation: Enclosure, Ascesis, and the Feminist Imaginary." *SAQ* 93(4): 803–24.

Bennett, Judith M. 1987. *Women in the Medieval English Countryside: Gender and Household in Brigstock before the Plague*. Oxford: Oxford University Press.

———. 1996. *Ale, Beer, and Brewsters in England: Women's Work in a Changing World, 1300–1600*. Oxford: Oxford University Press.

Bennett, Tony. 1992. "Putting Policy into Cultural Studies." In *Cultural Studies*, ed. Grossberg, 23–37.

Bethurum, Dorothy. 1942. "Archbishop Wulfstan's Commonplace Book." *PMLA* 57:916–29.

Biggs, Frederick M. 1986. *The Sources of Christ III: A Revision of Cook's Notes*. Old English Newsletter Subsidia 12.

Biggs, Frederick M., Thomas D. Hill, and Paul E. Szarmach, eds. 1990. *Sources of Anglo-Saxon Literary Culture: A Trial Version*. Binghamton, N.Y.: Center for Medieval and Early Renaissance Studies.

Biller, Peter, and Anne Hudson, eds. 1994. *Heresy and Literature, 1000–1530*. Cambridge: Cambridge University Press.

Blair, Peter Hunter. 1977. *An Introduction to Anglo-Saxon England*. 2nd ed. Cambridge: Cambridge University Press.

Bliss, Alan, and Allen J. Frantzen. 1976. "The Integrity of *Resignation." Review of English Studies* 27:385–402.

Bloch, R. Howard. 1990. "New Philology and Old French." In *The New Philology*, ed. Nichols, 38–58.

Bragg, Lois. 1991. *The Lyric Speakers of Old English Poetry.* Rutherford, N.J.: Fairleigh Dickinson University Press.

Brennan, Teresa. 1993. *History after Lacan.* London: Routledge.

Brooks, Nicholas. 1984. *The Early History of the Church at Canterbury.* Leicester: Leicester University Press.

Brownlee, Marina S., Kevin Brownlee, and Stephen G. Nichols, eds. 1991. *The New Medievalism.* Baltimore, Md.: Johns Hopkins University Press.

Brundage, James A. 1987. *Law, Sex, and Christian Society in Medieval Europe.* Chicago: University of Chicago Press.

Butler, Judith. 1993. *Bodies That Matter: On the Discursive Limits of "Sex."* New York: Routledge.

Bynum, Caroline Walker. 1987. *Holy Feast and Holy Fast: The Religious Significance of Food to Medieval Women.* Berkeley: University of California Press.

———. 1992. *Fragmentation: Essays on Gender and the Human Body in Medieval Religion.* New York: Zone Books.

———. 1995. *The Resurrection of the Body in Western Christianity, 200–1336.* New York: Columbia University Press.

Caie, Graham D. 1994. "Text and Context in Editing Old English: The Case of the Poetry in Cambridge, Corpus Christi College 201." In *The Editing of Old English*, ed. Scragg and Szarmach, 155–62.

Campbell, Jackson J. 1988. "Ends and Meanings: Modes of Closure in Old English Poetry." *Medievalia et Humanistica* 16:1–49.

Cantor, Norman F. 1991. *Inventing the Middle Ages.* New York: William Morrow.

Chase, Colin. 1986. "Source Study as a Trick with Mirrors: Annihilation of Meaning in the Old English 'Mary of Eygpt.'" In *Sources of Anglo-Saxon Culture*, ed. Szarmach, 23–33.

Clayton, Mary. 1985. "Homiliaries and Preaching in Anglo-Saxon England." *Peritia* 4:207–42.

———. 1986. "Blickling Homily XIII Reconsidered." *Leeds Studies in English* 17:25–40.

———. 1990. *The Cult of the Virgin Mary in Anglo-Saxon England.* Cambridge: Cambridge University Press.

———. 1993. "Of Mice and Men: Ælfric's Second Homily for the Feast of a Confessor." *Leeds Studies in English* 24:1–26.

———. 1996. "Hermits and the Contemplative Life in Anglo-Saxon England." In *Holy Men and Holy Women*, ed. Szarmach, 147–75.

Clemoes, Peter. 1959. "The Chronology of Ælfric's Work." In *The Anglo-Saxons: Studies in Some Aspects of Their History and Culture Presented to Bruce Dickens*, ed. Peter Clemoes, 212–47. London: Bowes & Bowes.

———. 1966. "Ælfric." In *Continuations and Beginnings*, ed. Stanley, 176–209.

———. 1975. "Late Old English Literature." In *Tenth-Century Studies*, ed. Parsons, 103–14.

———. 1986. "'Symbolic' Language in Old English Poetry." In *Modes of Interpretation in Old English Literature: Essays in Honor of Stanley B. Greenfield*, ed. Phyllis Rugg Brown, Georgia Ronan Crampton, and Fred C. Robinson, 3–14. Toronto: University of Toronto Press.

———. 1995. *Interactions of Thought and Language in Old English Poetry.* Cambridge: Cambridge University Press.

Clover, Carol J. 1993. "Regardless of Sex: Men, Women, and Power in Early Northern Europe." In *Studying Medieval Women*, ed. Partner, 363–87.

Coakley, John. 1994. "Friars, Sanctity, and Gender: Mendicant Encounters with Saints, 1250–1325." In *Medieval Masculinities*, ed. Lees, 91–110.

Cohen, Jeremy. 1982. *The Friars and the Jews: The Evolution of Medieval Anti-Judaism.* Ithaca, N.Y.: Cornell University Press.

Coleman, Julie. 1992. "Sexual Euphemism in Old English." *Neuphilologische Mitteilungen* 93:93–98.

Colish, Marcia L. 1968. *The Mirror of Language: A Study in the Medieval Theory of Knowledge.* New Haven, Conn.: Yale University Press.

Collins, Marie, Jocelyn Price, and Andrew Hamer, eds. 1985. *Sources and Relations: Studies in Honour of J. E. Cross. Leeds Studies in English* 16.

Conner, Patrick W. 1993. *Anglo-Saxon Exeter: A Tenth-Century Cultural History.* Woodbridge: Boydell.

Cook, A. S. 1898. *Biblical Quotations in Old English Prose Writers.* London: Macmillan.

———. 1903. *Biblical Quotations in Old English Prose Writers: Second Series.* London: Edward Arnold.

Copeland, Rita. 1991. *Rhetoric, Hermeneutics, and Translation in the Middle Ages.* Cambridge: Cambridge University Press.

Coward, Harold, and Toby Foshay, eds., with a conclusion by Jacques Derrida. 1992. *Derrida and Negative Theology.* Albany: SUNY Press.

Cross, James E. 1956. "'Ubi Sunt' Passages in Old English: Sources and Relationships." *Vetenskaps-societetens i Lund, Årsbok,* 25–44.

———. 1964. "The 'Coeternal Beam' in the O.E. Advent Poem (*Christ I*), ll. 104–29." *Neophilologus* 48:72–81.

———. 1965. "Oswald and Byrhtnoth: A Christian Saint and a Hero Who Is Christian." *ES* 46:93–109.

———. 1968. "More Sources for Two of Ælfric's *Catholic Homilies.*" *Anglia* 86:59–78.

———. 1969. "On the Blickling Homily for Ascension Day (No. XI)." *Neuphilologische Mitteilungen* 70:228–40.

———. 1972. "The Literate Anglo-Saxon: On Sources and Disseminations." *Proceedings of the British Academy* 58:67–100.

———. 1991. "Wulfstan's *De Antichristo* in a Twelfth-Century Worcester Manuscript." *ASE* 20:203–20.

———. 1992. "A Newly Identified Manuscript of Wulfstan's 'Commonplace Book,' Rouen, Bibliothèque Municipale 1382 (U. 109), fols. 173r-198v." *Journal of Medieval Latin* 2:63–83.

Cross, James E., and Alan Brown. 1989. "Literary Impetus for Wulfstan's *Sermo Lupi.*" *Leeds Studies in English* 20:270–91.

Culler, Jonathan. 1994. "Lace, Lance, and Pair." *Profession 94,* 5–10.

Curtius, Ernst Robert. 1953. *European Literature and the Latin Middle Ages.* Trans. Willard R. Trask. London: Routledge and Kegan Paul.

Dalbey, Marcia A. 1973. "Patterns of Preaching in the Blickling Easter Homily." *American Benedictine Review* 24:478–92.

———. 1978. "Themes and Techniques in the Blickling Lenten Homilies." In *The Old English Homily and Its Backgrounds,* ed. Szarmach and Huppé, 221–39.

———. 1980. "'Soul's Medicine': Religious Psychology in the Blickling Rogation Homilies." *Neophilologus* 64:470–77.

Damico, Helen, and Alexandra Hennessey Olsen, eds. 1990. *New Readings on Women in Old English Literature.* Bloomington: Indiana University Press.

Davis, Craig R. 1992. "Cultural Assimilation in the Anglo-Saxon Royal Genealogies." *ASE* 21:23–36.

Day, Virginia. 1974. "The Influence of the Catechical *Narratio* on Old English and Some Other Medieval Literature." *ASE* 3:51–61.

Deyermond, Alan. 1980. "The Sermon and Its Uses in Medieval Castilian Literature." *La Coronica* 8(2): 127–45.

Dollimore, Jonathan. 1991. *Sexual Dissidence: Augustine to Wilde, Freud to Foucault.* Oxford: Clarendon.

# Works Cited

———. 1993. *Radical Tragedy: Religion, Ideology, and Power in the Drama of Shakespeare and His Contemporaries.* 2nd ed. Durham, N.C.: Duke University Press.

Dollimore, Jonathan, and Alan Sinfield. 1985. *Political Shakespeare: New Essays in Cultural Materialism.* Manchester: Manchester University Press.

Duffy, Eamon. 1992. *The Stripping of the Altars: Traditional Religion in England c. 1400–c. 1580.* New Haven, Conn.: Yale University Press.

Dumville, David N. 1992. *Liturgy and the Ecclesiastical History of Late Anglo-Saxon England.* Woodbridge: Boydell.

During, Simon, ed. 1993. *The Cultural Studies Reader.* London: Routledge.

Eagleton, Terry. 1990. *The Ideology of the Aesthetic.* Oxford: Blackwell.

Earl, James W. 1994. *Thinking about "Beowulf."* Stanford, Calif.: Stanford University Press.

———, ed. 1986. *Psychoanalysis and Religion: Postmodern Perspectives. Thought* 61 (March).

Edwards, John. 1988. *The Jews in Christian Europe, 1400–1700.* London: Routledge.

Elad, Amikam. 1995. *Medieval Jerusalem and Islamic Worship: Holy Places, Ceremonies, Worship.* Leiden: E. J. Brill.

Eliot, T. S. [1917] 1932. "Tradition and the Individual Talent." In *Selected Essays,* 3–11. New York: Harcourt, Brace. Rev. ed., 1950.

Elliott, Dyan. 1993. *Spiritual Marriage: Sexual Abstinence in Medieval Wedlock.* Princeton, N.J.: Princeton University Press.

———. 1997. "Pollution, Illusion, and Masculine Disarray: Nocturnal Emissions and the Sexuality of the Clergy." In *Constructing Medieval Sexuality,* ed. Karma Lochrie, Peggy McCracken, and James A. Schultz, 1–23. Minneapolis: University of Minnesota Press.

Fell, Christine E. 1994. "Saint Æðelþryð: A Historical-Hagiographical Dichotomy Revisited." *Nottingham Medieval Studies* 38:18–34.

Fell, Christine E., with Cecily Clark and Elizabeth Williams. 1984. *Women in Anglo-Saxon England.* Oxford: Blackwell.

Fischer, Andreas. 1986. *Engagement, Wedding, and Marriage in Old English.* Anglistische Forschungen 176. Heidelberg: Carl Winter Universitätsverlag.

Fisher, D. J. V. 1950–52. "The Anti-Monastic Reaction in the Reign of Edward the Martyr." *Cambridge Historical Journal* 10:254–70.

Foley, John Miles. 1991. "Texts That Speak to Readers Who Hear: Old English Poetry and the Languages of Oral Tradition." In *Speaking Two Languages,* ed. Franzten, 141–56.

Förster, Max. 1894. "Über die Quellen von Ælfrics exegetischen Homiliae Catholicae." *Anglia* 16:1–61.

———. 1955. "A New Version of the *Apocalypse of Thomas* in Old English." *Anglia* 73:6–36.

Foucault, Michel. 1980. *The History of Sexuality.* Vol. 1. Transl. Robert Hurley. New York: Vintage Books.

Fradenburg, Louise O. 1990. " 'Voice Memorial': Loss and Reparation in Chaucer's Poetry." *Exemplaria* 2:169–202.

Frank, Roberta. 1991. "Germanic Legend in Old English Literature." In *The Cambridge Companion to Old English Literature,* ed. Godden and Lapidge, 88–106.

———. 1992. "*Beowulf* and Sutton Hoo: The Odd Couple." In *Voyage to the Other World: The Legacy of Sutton Hoo,* ed. Calvin B. Kendall and Peter S. Wells, 47–64. Minneapolis: University of Minnesota Press.

———. 1994. "Poetic Words in Late Old English Prose." In *From Anglo-Saxon to Early Middle English,* ed. Godden, Gray, and Hoad, 87–107.

Frantzen, Allen J. 1983. *The Literature of Penance in Anglo-Saxon England.* New Brunswick, N.J.: Rutgers University Press.

———. 1990. *Desire for Origins: New Language, Old English, and Teaching the Tradition.* New Brunswick, N.J.: Rutgers University Press.

———. 1993. "When Women Aren't Enough." In *Studying Medieval Women,* ed. Partner, 445–71.

———. 1994. *"The Pardoner's Tale,* the Pervert, and the Price of Order in Chaucer's World." In *Class and Gender in Early English Literature,* ed. Harwood and Overing, 131–47.

———. 1996a. "Between the Lines: Queer Theory, the History of Homosexuality, and Anglo-Saxon Penitentials." *JMEMS* 26:255–96.

———. 1996b. "The Disclosure of Sodomy in *Cleanness.*" *PMLA* 111:451–64.

———. 1996c. "The Fragmentation of Cultural Studies and the Fragments of Anglo-Saxon England." *Anglia* 114:310–39.

———. 1998. *Before the Closet: Same-Sex Love from "Beowulf" to "Angels in America."* Chicago: University of Chicago Press.

———, ed. 1991. *Speaking Two Languages: Traditional Disciplines and Contemporary Theory.* Albany: SUNY Press.

Gaites, Judith. 1982. "Ælfric's Longer *Life of St Martin* and Its Latin Sources: A Study in Narrative Technique." *Leeds Studies in English* 13:23–41.

Gatch, Milton McC. 1965. "Eschatology in the Anonymous Old English Homilies." *Traditio* 21:117–65.

———. 1977. *Preaching and Theology in Anglo-Saxon England: Ælfric and Wulfstan.* Toronto: University of Toronto Press.

———. 1985. "The Office in Late Anglo-Saxon Monasticism." In *Learning and Literature in Anglo-Saxon England,* ed. Lapidge and Gneuss, 341–62.

———. 1989. "The Unknowable Audience of the Blickling Homilies." *ASE* 18:99–115.

Gaunt, Simon. 1995. "Straight Minds/'Queer' Wishes in Old French Hagiography: La Vie de Sainte Euphrosyne." *GLQ: A Journal of Lesbian and Gay Studies* 1:439–57.

Gilchrist, Roberta. 1994. *Gender and Material Culture: The Archaeology of Religious Women.* London: Routledge.

Gneuss, Helmut. 1972. "The Origin of Standard Old English and Æthelwold's School at Winchester." *ASE* 1:63–83.

———. 1985. "Liturgical Books in Anglo-Saxon England and Their Old English Terminology." In *Learning and Literature in Anglo-Saxon England,* ed. Lapidge and Gneuss, 91–142.

Godden, Malcolm. 1968. "The Sources for Ælfric's Homily on St Gregory." *Anglia* 86:79–88.

———. 1973a. "The Development of Ælfric's Second Series of *Catholic Homilies.*" *ES* 54:209–16.

———. 1973b. "An Old English Penitential Motif." *ASE* 2:221–39.

———. 1975. "Old English Composite Homilies from Winchester." *ASE* 4:57–65.

———. 1978. "Ælfric and the Vernacular Prose Tradition." In *The Old English Homily and Its Backgrounds,* ed. Szarmach and Huppé, 99–117.

———. 1985a. "Ælfric's Saints' Lives and the Problem of Miracles." In *Sources and Relations,* ed. Collins, Price, and Hamer, 83–100.

———. 1985b. "Anglo-Saxons on the Mind." In *Learning and Literature in Anglo-Saxon England,* ed. Lapidge and Gneuss, 271–98.

———. 1990. "Money, Power, and Morality in Late Anglo-Saxon England." *ASE* 19:41–65.

———. 1991. "Biblical Literature: The Old Testament." In *The Cambridge Companion to Old English Literature,* ed. Godden and Lapidge, 206–26.

———. 1994. "Apocalypse and Invasion in Late Anglo-Saxon England." In *From Anglo-Saxon to Early Middle English,* ed. Godden, Gray, and Hoad, 130–62.

———. 1996. "Experiments in Genre: The Saints' Lives in Ælfric's *Catholic Homilies.*" In *Holy Men and Holy Women,* ed. Szarmach, 261–87.

Godden, Malcolm, Douglas Gray, and Terry Hoad, eds. 1994. *From Anglo-Saxon to Early Middle English: Studies Presented to E. G. Stanley.* Oxford: Clarendon Press.

Godden, Malcom, and Michael Lapidge, eds. 1991. *The Cambridge Companion to Old English Literature.* Cambridge: Cambridge University Press.

Gossman, Lionel. 1994. "History and the Study of Literature." *Profession 94*, 26–33.

Graff, Gerald. 1987. *Professing Literature: An Institutional History.* Chicago: University of Chicago Press.

Gransden, Antonia. 1989. "Traditionalism and Continuity during the Last Century of Anglo-Saxon Monasticism." *Journal of Ecclesiastical History* 40:159–207.

Greenblatt, Stephen. 1988. *Shakespearean Negotiations: The Circulation of Social Energy in Renaissance England.* Berkeley: University of California Press.

———. 1989. "Toward a Poetics of Culture." In *The New Historicism*, ed. Veeser, 1–14.

Greenblatt, Stephen, and Giles Gunn, eds. 1992. *Redrawing the Boundaries: The Transformation of English and American Literary Studies.* New York: Modern Language Association.

Greenfield, Stanley B. 1955. "The Formulaic Expression of the Theme of 'Exile' in Anglo-Saxon Poetry." *Speculum* 30:200–206.

Greenfield, Stanley B., and Daniel G. Calder. 1986. *A New Critical History of Old English Literature.* New York: New York University Press.

Griffiths, Gwen. 1992. "Reading Ælfric's Saint Æthelthryth as a Woman." *Parergon* 10:35–49.

Grossberg, Lawrence, Cary Nelson, and Paula A. Treichler, eds. 1992. *Cultural Studies.* London: Routledge.

Grundy, Lynne. 1990. "Ælfric's *Sermo de Sacrificio in Die Pascæ: Figura* and *Veritas.*" *Notes and Queries* 235:265–69.

———. 1991. *Books and Grace: Ælfric's Theology.* London: King's College London Medieval Studies 6.

Guillory, John. 1993. *Cultural Capital: The Problem of Literary Canon Formation.* Chicago: University of Chicago Press.

Gurevitch, Aron. 1988. *Medieval Popular Culture: Problems of Belief and Perception.* Trans. János M. Bak and Paul A. Hollingsworth. Cambridge: Cambridge University Press.

Hall, Stuart. 1990. "The Emergence of Cultural Studies and the Crisis of the Humanities." *October* 53:11–23.

———. 1992. "Cultural Studies and Its Theoretical Legacies." In *Cultural Studies*, ed. Grossberg, Nelson, and Treichler, 277–94.

Hanning, Robert W. 1966. *The Vision of History in Early Britain.* New York: Columbia University Press.

Harney, Michael. 1993. *Kinship and Polity in the "Poema de Mio Cid."* West Lafayette, Ind.: Purdue University Press.

Harvey, L. P. 1990. *Islamic Spain, 1250–1500.* Chicago: University of Chicago Press.

Harwood, Britton J. 1991. "The Plot of *Piers Plowman* and the Contradictions of Feudalism." In *Speaking Two Languages*, ed. Frantzen, 91–114.

———. 1994. "Building Class and Gender into Chaucer's *Hous.*" In *Class and Gender in Early English Literature,* ed. Harwood and Overing, 95–111.

Harwood, Britton J., and Gillian R. Overing, eds. 1994. *Class and Gender in Early English Literature: Intersections.* Bloomington: Indiana University Press.

Healey, Antonnette diPaolo. 1978. *The Old English Vision of St. Paul.* Speculum Anniversary Monographs 2. Cambridge, Mass.: Medieval Academy.

Hermann, John P. 1989. *Allegories of War: Language and Violence in Old English Poetry.* Ann Arbor: University of Michigan Press.

Heslop, T. A. 1990. "The Production of *de luxe* Manuscripts and the Patronage of King Cnut and Queen Emma." *ASE* 19:151–95.

Hicks, Carola, ed. 1992. *England in the Eleventh Century.* Stamford, Lincolnshire: Paul Watkins.

Hill, John M. 1995. *The Cultural World in "Beowulf."* Toronto: University of Toronto Press.

Hill, Joyce. 1985. "Ælfric's 'Silent Days'." In *Sources and Relations*, ed. Collins, Price, and Hamer, 118–31.

———. 1989. "Ælfric, Gelasius, and St. George." *Mediaevalia* 11:1–17.

———. 1991. "The 'Regularis Concordia' and Its Latin and Old English Reflexes." *Revue Bénédictine* 101:299–315.

———. 1992a. "Ælfric and Smaragdus." *ASE* 21:203–37.

———. 1992b. "Monastic Reform and the Secular Church: Ælfric's Pastoral Letters in Context." In *England in the Eleventh Century*, ed. Hicks, 103–17.

———. 1994. "Ælfric, Authorial Identity and the Changing Text." In *The Editing of Old English*, ed. Scragg and Szarmach, 177–89.

———. 1996. "The Dissemination of Ælfric's *Lives of Saints*: A Preliminary Survey." In *Holy Men and Holy Women*, ed. Szarmach, 235–59.

Hill, Thomas D. 1986. "Literary History and Old English Poetry: The Case of *Christ I, II, III*." In *Sources of Anglo-Saxon Culture*, ed. Szarmach, 3–22.

———. 1996. "'Imago Dei': Genre, Symbolism, and Anglo-Saxon Hagiography." In *Holy Men and Holy Women*, ed. Szarmach, 35–50.

Hilton, Rodney. 1985. *Class Conflict and the Crisis of Feudalism*. London: Verso.

———, ed. 1976. *The Transition from Feudalism to Capitalism*. London: Verso.

Hobsbawm, Eric, and Terence Ranger, eds. 1983. *The Invention of Tradition*. Cambridge: Cambridge University Press.

Hodge, Robert, and Gunther Kress. 1988. *Social Semiotics*. Ithaca, N.Y.: Cornell University Press.

Hoggart, Richard. 1957. *The Uses of Literacy*. Harmondsworth: Penguin.

Hollis, Stephanie. 1977. "The Thematic Structure of the *Sermo Lupi*." *ASE* 6:175–95.

———. 1992. *Anglo-Saxon Women and the Church: Sharing a Common Fate*. Woodbridge: Boydell.

Holub, Robert C. 1984. *Reception Theory: A Critical Introduction*. London: Methuen.

Howe, Nicholas. 1989. *Migration and Mythmaking in Anglo-Saxon England*. New Haven, Conn.: Yale University Press.

Howell, Martha. 1986. *Women, Production, and Patriarchy in Late Medieval Cities*. Chicago: University of Chicago Press.

Huizinga, Johan. 1924. *The Waning of the Middle Ages*. Trans. F. Hopman. Harmondsworth: Penguin. New ed., *The Autumn of the Middle Ages*. Trans. Rodney J. Payton and Ulrich Mammitzch. Chicago: University of Chicago Press, 1996.

Hurt, James. 1972. *Ælfric*. New York: Twayne.

Irvine, Martin. 1991. "Medieval Textuality and the Archaeology of Textual Culture." In *Speaking Two Languages*, ed. Frantzen, 181–210.

———. 1994. *The Making of Textual Culture: "Grammatica" and Literary Theory, 350–1100*. Cambridge: Cambridge University Press.

Jackson, Peter, and Michael Lapidge. 1996. "The Contents of the Cotton-Corpus Legendary." In *Holy Men and Holy Women*, ed. Szarmach, 131–46.

Jauss, Hans Robert. 1979. "The Alterity and Modernity of Medieval Literature." *New Literary History* 10:181–229.

———. 1982a. *Aesthetic Experience and Literary Hermeneutics*. Trans. Michael Shaw. Minneapolis: University of Minnesota Press.

———. 1982b. *Toward an Aesthetic of Reception*. Trans. Timothy Bahti. Minneapolis: University of Minnesota Press.

John, Eric. 1966. *Orbis Britanniae and Other Studies*. Leicester: Leicester University Press.

———. 1983. "The World of Abbot Ælfric." In *Ideal and Reality in Frankish and Anglo-Saxon Society*, ed. Patrick Wormald, Donald Bullough, and Roger Collins, 300–16. Oxford: Blackwell.

Jolly, Karen Louise. 1996. *Popular Religion in Late Saxon England: Elf Charms in Context*. Chapel Hill: University of North Carolina Press.

Jones, Charles W. 1947. *Saints' Lives and Chronicles in Early England*. Ithaca, N.Y.: Cornell University Press.

Jones, Christopher A. 1998. "The Book of the Liturgy in Anglo-Saxon England." *Speculum* 73:659–702.

Jost, Karl. 1923. "Wulfstan und die angelsächsische Chronik." *Anglia* 47:105–23.

———. 1959. *Wulfstanstudien.* Schweizer anglistische Arbeiten 23. Bern: A. Francke.

Kay, Sarah. 1990. *Subjectivity in Troubadour Poetry.* Cambridge: Cambridge University Press.

———. 1996. "The Contradictions of Courtly Love and the Origins of Courtly Poetry." *JMEMS* 26:209–53.

Kay, Sarah, and Miri Rubin, eds. 1994. *Framing Medieval Bodies.* Manchester: Manchester University Press.

Keynes, Simon. 1980. *The Diplomas of King Æthelred "The Unready," 978–1016.* Cambridge: Cambridge University Press.

Kiernan, Kevin. 1981. *Beowulf and the Beowulf Manuscript.* New Brunswick, N.J.: Rutgers University Press.

Kintz, Linda. 1997. *Between Jesus and the Market: The Emotions That Matter in Right-Wing America.* Durham, N.C.: Duke University Press.

Lapidge, Michael. 1975. "The Hermeneutic Style in Tenth-Century Anglo-Latin Literature." *ASE* 4:67–111.

———. 1988. "Æthelwold as Scholar and Teacher." In *Bishop Æthelwold: His Career and Influence,* ed. Yorke, 89–117.

———. 1991. "The Saintly Life in Anglo-Saxon England." In *The Cambridge Companion to Old English Literature,* ed. Godden and Lapidge, 243–63.

———. 1993. *Bede the Poet.* Newcastle upon Tyne: Jarrow Lecture.

———. 1996. "Ælfric's *Sanctorale.*" In *Holy Men and Holy Women,* ed. Szarmach, 115–29.

Lapidge, Michael, and Helmut Gneuss, eds. 1985. *Learning and Literature in Anglo-Saxon England.* Cambridge: Cambridge University Press.

Larrain, Jorge. 1979. *The Concept of Ideology.* Athens: University of Georgia Press.

Larrington, Carolyne. 1993. *A Store of Common Sense: Gnomic Theme and Style in Old Icelandic and Old English Wisdom Poetry.* Oxford: Clarendon Press.

Lawson, M. K. 1993. *Cnut: The Danes in England in the Early Eleventh Century.* London: Longman.

———. 1994. "Archbishop Wulfstan and the Homiletic Element in the Laws of Æthelred II and Cnut." In *The Reign of Cnut: King of England, Denmark, and Norway,* ed. Alexander R. Rumble, 141–64. Leicester: Leicester University Press.

Leclercq, Jean. 1982. *The Love of Learning and the Desire for God.* Trans. C. Misrahi. 3rd. ed. New York: Fordham University Press.

Lees, Clare A. 1985. "The Dissemination of Alcuin's *De Virtutibus et Vitiis Liber* in Old English: A Preliminary Survey." In *Sources and Relations,* ed. Collins, Price, and Hamer, 174–89.

———. 1986. "Theme and Echo in an Anonymous Old English Homily for Easter." *Traditio* 42:116–42.

———. 1988. "The Blickling Palm Sunday Homily and Its Revised Version." *Leeds Studies in English* 19:1–30.

———. 1991. "Working with Patristic Sources: Language and Context in Old English Homilies." In *Speaking Two Languages,* ed. Frantzen, 157–80.

———. 1994a. "Gender and Exchange in *Piers Plowman.*" In *Class and Gender in Early English Literature,* ed. Harwood and Overing, 112–30.

———. 1994b. "Whose Text Is It Anyway? Contexts for Editing Old English Prose." In *The Editing of Old English,* ed. Scragg and Szarmach, 97–114.

———. 1997a. "At a Crossroads: Old English and Feminist Criticism." In *Reading Old English Texts,* ed. O'Brien O'Keeffe, 146–69.

———. 1997b. "Engendering Religious Desire: Sex, Knowledge, and Christian Identity in Anglo-Saxon England." *JMEMS* 27:17–45.

———, ed. 1994c. *Medieval Masculinities: Regarding Men in the Middle Ages.* Minneapolis: University of Minnesota Press.

Lees, Clare A., and Gillian R. Overing. 1994. "Birthing Bishops and Fathering Poets: Bede, Hild, and the Relations of Cultural Production." *Exemplaria* 6:35–65.

Leinbaugh, Theodore H. 1982. "Ælfric's *Sermo de Sacrificio in Die Pascae:* Anglican Polemic in the Sixteenth and Seventeenth Centuries." In *Anglo-Saxon Scholarship: The First Three Centuries,* ed. Carl T. Berkhout and Milton McC. Gatch, 51–68. Boston: Hall.

———. 1994. "Ælfric's *Lives of Saints* I and the Boulogne Sermon: Editorial, Authorial, and Textual Problems." In *The Editing of Old English,* ed. Scragg and Szarmach, 191–211.

Lerer, Seth. 1991. *Literacy and Power in Anglo-Saxon Literature.* Lincoln: University of Nebraska Press.

Letson, D. R. 1979. "The Form of the Old English Homily." *American Benedictine Review* 30:399–431.

Lewis, C. S. 1964. *The Discarded Image.* Cambridge: Cambridge University Press.

Lochrie, Karma. 1991. *Margery Kempe and Translations of the Flesh.* Philadelphia: University of Pennsylvania Press.

Lomperis, Linda, and Sarah Stanbury, eds. 1993. *Feminist Approaches to the Body in Medieval Literature.* Philadelphia: University of Pennsylvania Press.

Lucas, Peter J. 1990. "The Place of *Judith* in the *Beowulf*-Manuscript." *Review of English Studies* 41:463–78.

MacIntyre, Alasdair. 1988. *Whose Justice? Which Rationality?* Notre Dame, Ind.: University of Notre Dame Press.

MacKay, Angus. 1977. *Spain in the Middle Ages: From Frontier to Empire, 1000–1500.* New York: St. Martin's Press.

Magennis, Hugh. 1985. "On the Sources of Non-Ælfrician Lives in the Old English *Lives of Saints,* with Reference to the Cotton-Corpus Legendary." *Notes and Queries,* n.s., 32:292–9.

———. 1986. "Contrasting Features in the Non-Ælfrician Lives in the Old English *Lives of Saints.*" *Anglia* 104:316–48.

———. 1995. "'No Sex Please, We're Anglo-Saxons'? Attitudes to Sexuality in Old English Prose and Poetry." *Leeds Studies in English* 26:1–27.

———. 1996. *Images of Community in Old English Poetry.* Cambridge: Cambridge University Press.

Mann, Michael. 1986. *The Sources of Social Power.* Vol. 1. Cambridge: Cambridge University Press.

Margherita, Gayle. 1994. *The Romance of Origins: Language and Sexual Difference in Middle English Literature.* Philadelphia: University of Pennsylvania Press.

Marsden, Richard. 1995. *The Text of the Old Testament in Anglo-Saxon England.* Cambridge: Cambridge University Press.

Matter, E. Ann. 1995. "Women and the Study of Medieval Christianity." *Medieval Feminist Newsletter* 19:16–17.

McCord, Laura R. 1981. "A Probable Source for the *Ubi Sunt* passage in Blickling Homily V." *Neuphilologische Mitteilungen* 82:360–1.

McDougall, Ian. 1993. "Serious Entertainments: An Examination of a Peculiar Type of Viking Atrocity." *ASE* 22:201–25.

McIntosh, Angus. 1949. "Wulfstan's Prose." Gollancz Lecture. Reprinted in *British Academy Papers on Anglo-Saxon England,* ed. E. G. Stanley. British Academy: Oxford University Press, 1990.

McKitterick, Rosamond. 1977. *The Frankish Church and the Carolingian Reforms, 789–895.* London: Royal Historical Society.

McNamara, Jo Ann. 1994. "The *Herrenfrage:* The Restructuring of the Gender System, 1050–1150." In *Medieval Masculinities,* ed. Lees, 3–29.

Meaney, Audrey L. 1985. "Ælfric's Use of His Sources in His Homily on Auguries." *ES* 66: 477–95.

Middleton, Anne. 1992. "Medieval Studies." In *Redrawing the Boundaries*, ed. Greenblatt and Gunn, 12–40.

Miller, Mark. 1996. "Displaced Souls, Idle Talk, Spectacular Scenes: *Handlyng Synne* and the Perspective of Agency." *Speculum* 71:607–32.

Miller, William Ian. 1990. *Bloodtaking and Peacemaking: Feud, Law, and Society in Saga Iceland.* Chicago: University of Chicago Press.

Milner, Andrew. 1993. *Cultural Materialism.* Melbourne: Melbourne University Press.

Minnis, A. J. 1984. *Medieval Theory of Authorship: Scholastic Literary Attitudes in the later Middle Ages.* London: Scolar Press.

Mirrer, Louise. 1994. "Representing 'Other' Men: Muslims, Jews, and Masculine Ideals in Medieval Castilian Epic and Ballad." In *Medieval Masculinities*, ed. Lees, 169–86.

Montrose, Louis A. 1989. "Professing the Renaissance: The Poetics and Politics of Culture." In *The New Historicism*, ed. Veeser, 15–36.

Moore, R. I. 1987. *The Formation of a Persecuting Society: Power and Deviance in Western Europe, 950–1250.* Oxford: Blackwell.

Morris, Colin. 1972. *The Discovery of the Individual, 1050–1200.* Toronto: University of Toronto Press. Reprint, 1987.

Morrison, Karl F. 1992. *Understanding Conversion.* Charlottesville: University of Virginia Press.

Napier, A. S. 1898, 1899, 1901. "Nächtrage zu Cook's *Biblical Quotations in Old English Prose Writers I, II, III." Archiv für das Studium der neueren Sprachen und Literaturen* 101:309–24; 102:29–42; 107:105–6.

Nelson, Cary, and Lawrence Grossberg, eds. 1988. *Marxism and the Interpretation of Culture.* Urbana: University of Illinois Press.

Nelson, Janet L. 1977. "Inauguration Rituals." In *Early Medieval Kingship*, ed. P. H. Sawyer and I. N. Wood, 50–71. Leeds: School of History, University of Leeds.

———. 1986. "The Second English *Ordo." In Politics and Ritual in Early Medieval Europe*, 361–74. London: Hambledon.

Newman, Barbara. 1995. *From Virile Woman to WomanChrist: Studies in Medieval Religion and Literature.* Philadelphia: University of Pennsylvania Press.

Nichols, Stephen G., ed. 1990. *The New Philology. Speculum* 65.

Niles, John D. 1993. "Locating *Beowulf* in Literary History." *Exemplaria* 5:79–109.

O'Brien O'Keeffe, Katherine. 1990. *Visible Song: Transitional Literacy in Old English Verse.* Cambridge: Cambridge University Press.

———. 1994. "Source, Method, Theory, Practice: On Reading Two Old English Verse Texts." *Bulletin of the John Rylands Library* 76:51–73.

———. 1998. "Body and Law in Late Anglo-Saxon England." *ASE* 27:209–32.

———, ed. 1997. *Reading Old English Texts.* Cambridge: Cambridge University Press.

Orchard, A. P. McD. 1992. "Crying Wolf: Oral Style and the *Sermones Lupi." ASE* 21:239–64.

Overing, Gillian R. 1990. *Language, Sign, and Gender in "Beowulf."* Carbondale: Southern Illinois University Press.

———. 1993. "Recent Writing on Old English: A Response." *Æstel* 1:135–49.

Overing, Gillian, and Marijane Osborn. 1994. *Landscape of Desire: Partial Stories of the Medieval Scandinavian World.* Minneapolis: University of Minnesota Press.

Owst, G. R. 1926. *Preaching in Medieval England: An Introduction to Sermon Manuscripts of the Period c. 1350–1450.* Cambridge: Cambridge University Press.

———. 1933. *Literature and Pulpit in Medieval England.* Cambridge: Cambridge University Press. 2nd ed., Oxford: Blackwell, 1961.

Parsons, David, ed. 1975. *Tenth-Century Studies: Essays in Commemoration of the Millennium of the Council of Winchester and "Regularis Concordia."* Chichester: Phillimore.

Partner, Nancy F., ed. 1993. *Studying Medieval Women: Sex, Gender, Feminism. Speculum* 68 (2).

Pasternack, Carol Braun. 1995. *The Textuality of Old English Poetry.* Cambridge: Cambridge University Press.

Patterson, Lee. 1987. *Negotiating the Past: The Historical Understanding of Medieval Literature.* Madison: University of Wisconsin Press.
———. 1990. "On the Margin: Postmodernism, Ironic History, and Medieval Studies." In *The New Philology,* ed. Nichols, 87–108.
———. 1991. *Chaucer and the Subject of History.* Madison: University of Wisconsin Press.
Payer, Pierre J. 1984. *Sex and the Penitentials: The Development of a Sexual Code.* Toronto: University of Toronto Press.
Pelikan, Jaroslav. 1971–89. *The Christian Tradition: A History of the Development of Doctrine.* 5 vols. Chicago: University of Chicago Press.
Pidal, Ramón Menéndez. 1949. *Historia general de las literaturas hispánicas,* ed. G. Díaz-Plaja. Vol. 1. Barcelona: Barna.
Powell, Timothy E. 1994. "The 'Three Orders' of Society in Anglo-Saxon England." *ASE* 23:103–32.
Prendergast, Christopher, ed. 1995. *Cultural Materialism: On Raymond Williams.* Minneapolis: University of Minnesota Press.
Pyle, Forest. 1993. "Raymond Williams and the Inhuman Limits of Culture." In *Views beyond the Border Country: Raymond Williams and Cultural Politics,* ed. Dennis D. Dworkin and Leslie G. Roman, 260–74. London: Routledge.
———. 1995. "Demands of History: Narrative Crisis in *Jude the Obscure.*" *New Literary History* 26:359–78.
Reilly, Bernard F. 1993. *The Medieval Spains.* Cambridge: Cambridge University Press.
Remley, Paul G. 1996. *Old English Biblical Verse: Studies in "Genesis," "Exodus," and "Daniel."* Cambridge: Cambridge University Press.
Reynolds, Susan. 1994. *Fiefs and Vassals: The Medieval Evidence Reinterpreted.* Oxford: Oxford University Press.
Richards, Mary P., and B. Jane Stanfield. 1990. "Concepts of Anglo-Saxon Women in the Laws." In *New Readings on Women in Old English Literature,* ed. Damico and Olsen, 89–99.
Ridyard, Susan. J. 1988. *The Royal Saints of Anglo-Saxon England.* Cambridge: Cambridge University Press.
Robertson, D. W., Jr. 1962. *A Preface to Chaucer: Studies in Medieval Perspective.* Princeton, N.J.: Princeton University Press.
Rollason, David. 1989a. *Saints and Relics in Anglo-Saxon England.* Oxford: Blackwell.
———. 1989b. "St Cuthbert and Wessex: The Evidence of Cambridge Corpus Christi College MS 183." In *St Cuthbert, His Cult, and His Community to AD 1200,* ed. Gerald Bonner, David Rollason, and Clare Stancliffe, 413–24. Woodbridge: Boydell.
Ross, Margaret Clunies. 1985. "Concubinage in Anglo-Saxon England." *Past and Present* 108:3–34.
Roy, Gopa. 1992. "A Virgin Acts Manfully: Ælfric's *Life of St Eugenia* and the Latin Versions." *Leeds Studies in English* 23:1–27.
Rubin, Miri. 1991. *Corpus Christi: The Eucharist in Late Medieval Culture.* Cambridge: Cambridge University Press.
Russell, James C. 1994. *The Germanization of Early Medieval Christianity: A Sociohistorical Approach to Religious Transformation.* Oxford: Oxford University Press.
Saenger, Paul. 1982. "Silent Reading: Its Impact on Late Medieval Script and Society." *Viator* 13:367–414.
———. 1989. "Books of Hours and the Reading Habits of the Latter Middle Ages." In *The Culture of Print: Power and the Uses of Print in Early Modern Europe,* ed. Roger Chartier, trans Lydia G. Cochrane, 141–73. Princeton, N.J.: Princeton University Press.
Said, Edward W. 1975. *Beginnings: Intention and Method.* New York: Basic Books.
Schaefer, Ursula. 1991. "Hearing from Books: The Rise of Fictionality in Old English Poetry." In *Vox Intexta: Orality and Textuality in the Middle Ages,* ed. A. N. Doane and Carol Braun Pasternack, 117–36. Madison: University of Wisconsin Press.

Schulenburg, Jane Tibbetts. 1989. "Women's Monastic Communities, 500–1100: Patterns of Expansion and Decline." *Signs* 14(2): 261–92.

Schwartz, Regina M. 1995. "Monotheism and the Violence of Identities." *Raritan* 14(3): 119–40.

Scragg, D. G. 1977. "Napier's 'Wulfstan' Homily XXX: Its Sources, Its Relationship to the Vercelli Book and Its Style." *ASE* 6:197–211.

———. 1979. "The Corpus of Vernacular Homilies and Prose Saints' Lives before Ælfric." *ASE* 8:223–77.

———. 1985. "The Homilies of the Blickling Manuscript." In *Learning and Literature in Anglo-Saxon England*, ed. Lapidge and Gneuss, 299–316.

———. 1996. "The Corpus of Anonymous Lives and Their Manuscript Context." In *Holy Men and Holy Women*, ed. Szarmach, 209–30.

———. 1997. "Source Study." In *Reading Old English Texts*, ed. O'Brien O'Keeffe, 39–58.

Scragg, D. G., and Paul E. Szarmach, eds. 1994. *The Editing of Old English.* Cambridge: Brewer.

Shils, Edward. 1981. *Tradition.* Chicago: University of Chicago Press.

Shippey, T. A. 1972. *Old English Verse.* London: Hutchinson.

Simpson, David. 1995. *The Academic Postmodern and the Rule of Literature.* Chicago: University of Chicago Press.

Sims-Williams, Patrick. 1990. *Religion and Literature in Western England, 600–800.* Cambridge: Cambridge University Press.

Sisam, Kenneth. 1953. "MSS. Bodley 340 and 342: Ælfric's *Catholic Homilies.*" In *Studies in the History of Old English Literature*, ed. Kenneth Sisam, 148–98. Oxford: Clarendon.

Smetana, Cyril L. 1959. "Ælfric and the Early Medieval Homiliary." *Traditio* 15:163–204.

———. 1961. "Ælfric and the Homiliary of Haymo of Halberstadt." *Traditio* 17:457–69.

Spearing, A. C. 1985. *Medieval to Renaissance in English Poetry.* Cambridge: Cambridge University Press.

Spencer, H. Leith. 1993. *English Preaching in the Late Middle Ages.* Oxford: Clarendon.

Stafford, Pauline. 1978. "Church and Society in the Age of Aelfric." In *The Old English Homily and Its Backgrounds*, ed. Szarmach and Huppé, 11–42.

———. 1989. *Unification and Conquest: A Political and Social History of England in the Tenth and Eleventh Centuries.* London: Edward Arnold.

———. 1990. "The King's Wife in Wessex, 800–1066." In *New Readings on Women in Old English Literature*, ed. Damico and Olsen, 56–78.

———. 1994. "Women and the Norman Conquest." *Transactions of the Royal Historical Society*, 6th series, 4:221–49.

———. 1997. *Queen Emma and Queen Edith: Queenship and Women's Power in Eleventh-Century England.* Oxford: Blackwell.

Staley, Lynn. 1994. *Margery Kempe's Dissenting Fictions.* University Park: Pennsylvania State University Press.

Stallybrass, Peter. 1992. "Shakespeare, the Individual, and the Text." In *Cultural Studies*, ed. Grossberg, Nelson, and Treichler, 593–612.

Stancliffe, Clare, and Eric Cambridge, eds. 1995. *Oswald: Northumbrian King to European Saint.* Stamford, Lincolnshire: Paul Watkins.

Stanley, Eric Gerald. 1975. *The Search for Anglo-Saxon Paganism.* Cambridge: Brewer.

———, ed. 1966. *Continuations and Beginnings: Studies in Old English Literature.* London: Nelson.

Stock, Brian. 1974. "The Middle Ages as Subject and Object: Romantic Attitudes and Academic Medievalism." *New Literary History* 5:527–47.

———. 1983. *The Implications of Literacy: Written Language and Models of Interpretation in the Eleventh and Twelfth Centuries.* Princeton, N.J.: Princeton University Press.

———. 1990. *Listening for the Text: On the Uses of the Past.* Baltimore, Md.: Johns Hopkins University Press.

Stow, Kenneth R. 1992. *Alienated Minority: The Jews of Medieval Latin Europe*. Cambridge, Mass.: Harvard University Press.

Strohm, Paul. 1989. *Social Chaucer*. Cambridge, Mass.: Harvard University Press.

Symons, Dom Thomas. 1941. "The Sources of the *Regularis Concordia*." *Downside Review* 59:14–36, 143–70, 264–89.

———. 1975. "*Regularis Concordia:* History and Derivation." In *Tenth-Century Studies*, ed. Parsons, 37–59.

Szarmach, Paul E. 1990. "Ælfric's Women Saints: Eugenia." In *New Readings on Women in Old English Literature*, ed. Damico and Olsen, 146–57.

———. 1996a. "St. Euphrosyne: Holy Transvestite." In *Holy Men and Holy Women*, ed. Szarmach, 353–65.

———, ed. 1986a. *Sources of Anglo-Saxon Culture*. Kalamazoo, Mich.: Medieval Institute.

———, ed. 1986b. *Studies in Earlier Old English Prose*. Albany: SUNY Press.

———, ed. 1996b. *Holy Men and Holy Women: Old English Prose Saints' Lives and Their Contexts*. Albany: SUNY Press.

Szarmach, Paul E., and Bernard F. Huppé, eds. 1978. *The Old English Homily and Its Backgrounds*. Albany: SUNY Press.

Taylor, Mark C. 1984. *Erring: A Postmodern A/Theology*. Chicago: University of Chicago Press.

Thacker, Alan. 1992. "Monks, Preaching, and Pastoral Care in Early Anglo-Saxon England." *Pastoral Care before the Parish*, ed. John Blair and Richard Sharpe, 137–70. Leicester: Leicester University Press.

Thompson, E. P. 1963. *The Making of the English Working Class*. New York: Vintage.

———. 1993. *Customs in Common: Studies in Traditional Popular Culture*. New York: New Press.

Trahern, Joseph B., Jr. 1991. "Fatalism and the Millennium." In *The Cambridge Companion to Old English Literature*, ed. Godden and Lapidge, 160–71.

Vance, Eugene. 1986. *Mervelous Signals: Poetics and Sign Theory in the Middle Ages*. Lincoln: University of Nebraska Press.

Veeser, H. Aram, ed. 1989. *The New Historicism*. New York: Routledge.

Waterhouse, Ruth. 1987. " 'Wæter æddre asprang': How Cuthbert's Miracle Pours Cold Water on Source Study." *Parergon* 5:1–27.

———. 1989. "Ælfric's 'Usitatus': Use of Language in *Lives of Saints*." *Parergon* 7:1–45.

———. 1996. "Discourse and Hypersignification in Two of Ælfric's Saints' Lives." In *Holy Men and Holy Women*, ed. Szarmach, 333–52.

Watson, Nicholas. 1995. "Censorship and Cultural Change in Late-Medieval England: Vernacular Theology, the Oxford Translation Debate, and Arundel's Constitutions of 1409." *Speculum* 70:822–64.

Weinstein, Donald, and Rudolph M. Bell. 1982. *Saints and Society: The Two Worlds of Western Christianity, 1000–1700*. Chicago: University of Chicago Press.

Wenzel, Siegfried. 1978. *Verses in Sermons: "Fasciculus Morum" and Its Middle English Poems*. Cambridge, Mass.: Medieval Academy of America.

———. 1986. *Preachers, Poets, and the Early English Lyric*. Princeton, N.J.: Princeton University Press.

———. 1990. "Reflections on (New) Philology." In *The New Philology*, ed. Nichols, 11–18.

Whitelock, Dorothy. 1937. "A Note on the Career of Wulfstan the Homilist." *EHR* 52:460–5.

———. 1948. "Wulfstan and the Laws of Cnut." *EHR* 63:433–52.

Wieland, Gernot. 1981. "*Geminus Stilus:* Studies in Anglo-Latin Hagiography." In *Insular Latin Studies: Papers on Latin Texts and Manuscripts of the British Isles, 550–1066*, ed. Michael W. Herren, 113–33. Toronto: Pontifical Institute.

Wilcox, Jonathan. 1991. "Napier's 'Wulfstan' Homilies XL and XLII: Two Anonymous Works from Winchester?" *JEGP* 90:1–19.

———. 1992. "The Dissemination of Wulfstan's Homilies: The Wulfstan Tradition in Eleventh-Century Preaching." In *England in the Eleventh Century*, ed. Hicks, 199–217.

Willard, Rudolph. 1945. "Vercelli Homily XI and Its Sources." *Speculum* 24:76–87.

———. 1949. "The Blickling-Junius Tithing Homily and Caesarius of Arles." In *Philologica: The Malone Anniversary Studies*, ed. Thomas A. Kirby and Henry Bosley Woolf, 65–78. Baltimore, Md.: Johns Hopkins University Press.

Williams, Raymond. 1958. *Culture and Society, 1780–1950.* Harmondsworth: Penguin.

———. 1961. *The Long Revolution.* Harmondsworth: Penguin.

———. 1973. *The Country and the City.* Oxford: Oxford University Press.

———. 1976. *Keywords: A Vocabulary of Culture and Society.* Oxford: Oxford University Press.

———. 1977. *Marxism and Literature.* Oxford: Oxford University Press.

———. 1980. *Problems in Materialism and Culture.* London: Verso.

———. 1981. *Culture.* London: Fontana.

Winquist, Charles E. 1995. *Desiring Theology.* Chicago: University of Chicago Press.

Wood, Graham. 1995. *Barthes, Derrida, and the Language of Theology.* Cambridge: Cambridge University Press.

Woolf, Rosemary. 1966. "Saints' Lives." In *Continuations and Beginnings*, ed. Stanley, 37–66.

———. 1968. *The English Religious Lyric in the Middle Ages.* Oxford: Clarendon.

Wormald, Patrick. 1988. "Æthelwold and His Continental Counterparts: Contact, Comparison, Contrast." In *Bishop Æthelwold*, ed. Yorke, 13–42.

———. 1991. "Anglo-Saxon Society and Its Literature." In *The Cambridge Companion to Old English Literature*, ed. Godden and Lapidge, 1–22.

Wright, Charles D. 1993. *The Irish Tradition in Old English Literature.* Cambridge: Cambridge University Press.

Wright, Roger. 1982. *Late Latin and Early Romance in Spain and Carolingian France.* Liverpool: Cairns.

Yorke, Barbara, ed. 1988. *Bishop Æthelwold: His Career and Influence.* Woodbridge: Boydell.

Zettel, Patrick H. 1982. "Saints' Lives in Old English: Latin Manuscripts and Vernacular Accounts: Ælfric." *Peritia* 1:17–37.

Zumthor, Paul. 1972. *Essai de poetique medievale.* Paris: Editions de Seuil. Trans. Philip Bennett under the title *Toward a Medieval Poetics* (Minneapolis: University of Minnesota Press, 1992).

# Index

# Index

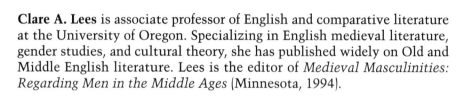

**Clare A. Lees** is associate professor of English and comparative literature at the University of Oregon. Specializing in English medieval literature, gender studies, and cultural theory, she has published widely on Old and Middle English literature. Lees is the editor of *Medieval Masculinities: Regarding Men in the Middle Ages* (Minnesota, 1994).